Escape
Bound

D1246319

How losing a home helped
me find my heart

Christy Rounds

ISBN: 979-8-9873148-0-7 (pb)
ISBN: 979-8-9873148-1-4 (Kindle)

Library of Congress Control Number: 2022922045

First edition, November 23, 2022

Cover Image: Calista Rounds
Back Cover Photo: Liberty at MN Department of Motor Vehicles
Proofreading by Linnea Bader

Published by Christy Rounds, Two Harbors, MN 55616

For information, please visit:
www.EscapeBound.com

For Gracie, Callie, and Christopher:

My escape bound partners in crime

Author's Note

Where are you from?

The place we live is one of the first pieces of information we exchange when meeting a person for the first time.

Over the past three and a half decades, I've moved fifteen times and lived in six states. I've visited thirty-five countries and spent a month or more in eleven of them. Needless to say, my sense of "home," my identity, had more to do with my family than the places we lived.

Then, in 2020, my marriage of twenty-three years ended. Not only did I lose my physical home, but my family was scattered across the country as well. They say home is where the heart is. So for the first time in my life, instead of looking for a physical place to live or relying on other people to shape my identity, I went out in search of my own heart.

After four months exploring the western United States in a pop-up trailer, followed by several months living in youth hostels in Mexico and Costa Rica, I discovered that validation is an inward journey, and life is the playground where that journey finds expression.

These adventures inspired me to write a book and create expeditionary retreats to allow other people to engage in immersive, physically rigorous, spiritual and cultural experiences, designed to challenge, inspire, and transform.

Escape Bound is an invitation to play, to explore, to ask life's deepest questions in the context of travel. Welcome to the adventure!

Warmly,

Christy

INTRODUCTION

In my wildest dreams, I never imagined that divorce was something that could happen to me. The very thought of divorce was preposterous. We had the perfect family, which included three teenagers. We had lived in a million dollar home. We took spectacular trips. We were enjoying the perfect life. I had Facebook to prove it!

Much to my shock and dismay, after twenty-three mostly happy years with John, our marriage indeed ended. A picture-perfect family, financial success, social standing—all pillars that had provided decades of validation—crumbled in a heap of rubble.

Validation. Prior to divorce, I'd never given that word much thought. For most of my life, validation was something you got for free parking. Where validation comes from—how and where we get it—never really crossed my mind. After my divorce, it suddenly seemed like a very important topic.

Through my late teens and twenties, validation came from being a high achiever. Accomplishments as a classical pianist, strong academic performer, writer and international traveler provided early fodder for validation.

Much of my identity shifted from "I" to "we" as I married the man of my dreams. In our thirties, athletic pursuits like mountain biking, cross country skiing, and bagging high-altitude peaks played a role in our identity as a couple.

In time, we brought three delightful human beings into the world. Family was the centrifugal force that held each of us in orbit, and travel became a recurring theme in our family's little universe.

In the months following the divorce, I decided to re-invent myself by embarking on a self-designed pilgrimage of the spirit. I wanted to surrender my mind and body to the whims of a wild and free soul with heart forward, head back, and arms flung wide. I wanted to allow this world to mark my heart and allow my heart to mark this world. I made the decision to live with bold, unapologetic, unmitigated passion.

That sounded so cool when I wrote it. But the sad reality is that for a year and a half, I felt almost nothing. My first months of itinerancy, a pilgrimage dedicated to reclaiming my lost emotions, yielded only the faintest stirrings of empathy, love, and happiness: characters that had played a vibrant role in most of my colorful life's story. So I hit the road again. And again. And again.

Just when I'd swear my heart was indeed being reborn, the emotions would die. Like a phoenix who repeatedly traverses the valley of death, I became intimate with the taste of ashes.

After a year living borderline homeless, first in a pop-up trailer, then in Latin American youth hostel dormitories, my soul was marked alright; battered and bruised, hair matted and snarled. I also recall the distinctly pungent smell of an unwashed body...namely mine. I barely recognized this shape and form my new soul had taken. Like a butterfly freshly emerged from a chrysalis, wings still wet and utterly useless, it took time to remember I was made to fly.

My three teens seemed to have fared better than me, though they too spent most of the year sharing in my wanderings; embarking on their own unique journeys through love, loss, and redemption. Whenever the kids used the word "homeless," I would say, "We're not homeless. We're nomadic! There's a difference!"

Whether you call it homeless, nomadic, or some kind of massive walk-about, for one solid year we had no longitudinal nor latitudinal point on the map, no spot on the globe's x-y axis, no place on this planet that we considered home. All my worldly possessions were contained inside my 2012 Honda Odyssey, packed in the pop-up trailer, or socked away in a very messy ten by twenty storage unit, which offered the faint, cloying odor of mental illness upon opening.

Never knowing where we would sleep from one night to the next was like jumping from an airplane over and over without a parachute. But every single time we jumped, the Universe caught us. And each time we were caught, we developed just…a little…more…trust.

I told the kids, "I know things look pretty bleak right now. But I promise you, this next chapter will be truly amazing!"

How could I look my kids in the eye and say those words with full conviction?

Because I was full of crap.

To be fair, on a cellular level, I believed that time-worn adage, "Everything happens for a reason." However, that didn't keep me from going into a full DEFCON 1 panic every time a new challenge appeared on the horizon. And the prospect of being financially hung out to dry scared the living bejeezus out of me. The pendulum of trust swung wildly from full acceptance to paralyzing anxiety and back again. I just knew enough to keep my mouth shut when I was scared shitless.

Eventually, after much weeping and gnashing of teeth, love became my lifeline. Not the love I received from others—though there was plenty of love and support from family and friends—but the love I finally received from myself.

At some point along the way, I realized that life isn't about convincing someone else to fall in love with me for who I'm not. It's about falling in love with myself, over and over, for who I am. And that, my friend, was my lifeline.

The way I came to receive that lifeline, allowing safe passage through one of the most tumultuous times of my life, is interwoven into the fabric of the story I'm about to tell. In the pages that follow you will discover the secret that allowed me to transcend divorce.

Through the first six months of the Covid pandemic, I created a small student travel business that allowed my kids and I to escape to Costa Rica and Mexico when winter weather prevented us from continuing our exploration of the American West in the pop-up trailer.

My eighteen-year-old daughter overcame anger issues and became a scholarship recipient in environmental studies at the University of Vermont. My sixteen-year-old daughter, who partied heavily in high school, graduated at sixteen and traveled the world as a paid model, photographer, and drone pilot. My overweight fifteen-year-old son lost one hundred pounds!

For my part, after twenty-two fabulous years (and one not-so-fabulous year) of marriage, I was no longer a supporting actor in our family's larger-than-life movie. Testing the waters as star of my own show, I was grateful beyond tears to discover that I have my own unique, quiet, precious kind of glow.

The dissolution of my marriage was never my choice. Still, I had the unwavering conviction that divorce was something happening *for* me, not *to* me. Though I have no spiritual pedigree and have absolutely no claim to divine grace, I was on the receiving end of miracle upon miracle.

The fact that I managed to survive divorce, not only with my soul intact but significantly more alive and vibrant than it had been within the context of marriage, is indeed evidence of divine grace. But my authentic soul came at a price. That price was paid through a spiritual treasure hunt. I had to listen to my intuition and follow the clues.

There is more magic, more mystery, more glory, more light and more love in this world than I ever could have

4

imagined. Though my story contains grace, it also includes a lot of needless suffering. If there is even the tiniest chance this book can help someone avoid that angst, it will have been worth the writing,

We are all in the midst of a bold, daring social experiment. Some people would just call it "life." But with each day that passes, I'm less and less convinced that life is something that can be passed off as ordinary or mundane.

Behind each human being is a story. These stories are as varied as the stars in the night sky, each one a tiny pinprick of light that represents a journey across mind-bending distances. All those human stories share common characteristics, a common point of origin. We are made from the same stuff, you and I. In this regard, my story is one we share.

The fact that you are reading this story is evidence that your own life may be on the brink of something marvelous and transformative. Of all the books you could be reading, you chose this one, which is something akin to the miracle required to witness the light of a distant star.

Think about it: in the light years it takes for a star's light to reach the earth, a single revolution of a planet, a moon, an asteroid or even space dust could have blocked its light. To see the star, all the planets had to align. The starlight needed to travel unimpeded. More importantly, the viewer needed to be looking. This book is in your hands because you are looking for it.

Our meeting is destiny; both yours and mine. I share these stories with great love. In sharing them, they become your stories. Many will even sound strangely familiar, like music from a favorite song whose words you've forgotten. We are connected. I am yours and you are mine.

Thank you for sharing this profoundly transformative journey with me.

CHAPTER 1

January 30, 2020. It was a drizzly grey afternoon, unseasonably warm for a mid-winter day in the little Western New York ski town of Ellicottville. Clouds hung low over the ski hills, shrouding tree-filled gaps between the slopes in a gauzy haze of fog. Skiers in their bright jackets cascaded down the slopes, like bits of confetti dumped from the steel-grey sky.

I sat in the passenger seat of my husband's truck in the parking lot at the base of the hill. My husband, John, sat in the driver's seat beside me.

"We need to talk," he said.

After three months of veiled hostility and thinly concealed contempt, I knew this was the day of reckoning. *Finally!* I thought with relief. *We are going to clear the air and figure out what the hell is going on.* This talk was long overdue. In twenty-three years of marriage, we'd rarely fought. The past three months had been a living hell. I desperately wanted my best friend back.

Just three hours earlier, I'd dropped our sixteen-year old-daughter, Callie, at the airport in Toronto, where she was taking an Ethiopian Air flight to Tanzania, Africa. Callie would spend five weeks volunteering at a school and children's hospital in Arusha, traveling to an elephant sanctuary in Kenya, and exploring the tropical island of Zanzibar. Looking at the clock on the truck's dashboard, I realized Callie's flight would be taking off.

"We're getting a divorce," John announced, snapping me out of my reverie.

He didn't say "I want a divorce" or "I'm thinking we should consider a divorce." John was a stickler for precise communication. I knew he'd carefully chosen the words, which were blowing like so many bits of dryer lint in the vent that was my head.

Divorce we're getting…A getting divorce…Getting we're a divorce… The words reordered themselves. I looked at them curiously, dispassionately. They didn't make any sense.

I peered through the front window of the truck with a vacant stare.

What did he just say?

To my surprise the words fell back into the correct order in my mind. *We're getting a divorce.*

They didn't make any more sense that way than they did before.

My brain was in a state of suspended animation. Like a person who just had a bucket of ice water dumped over her head, I sat frozen for an indeterminate period of time.

Then something inside me relaxed. *He's bluffing. He's just looking for attention.*

Of course divorce couldn't actually happen to us. It was a scientific impossibility. There was some law of physics that prevented it, a law that would come to our rescue and save our marriage. After all, we were soulmates, for heaven's sake. Soulmates! That means something, doesn't it? Tearing soul mates apart was like trying to rip a phone book. It simply couldn't be done.

After twenty-three years of marriage, we'd spent more of our adult lives together than apart. I'd never doubted the fact that I'd found my soulmate. As John yammered on about how we were philosophically misaligned, faded images from those twenty-three years spun through my mind like chairs on a ferris wheel.

7

Look! There's the one where Gracie was born. Look at her sweet little rosebud lips. Oh, and there's the pool at the villa in Riva del Garda, Italy, where the kids swam naked with their pool floaties when they were little.

The mental ferris wheel spun faster, images flying by with dizzying speed. A month stand up paddle boarding on the shores of Lake Atitlan, Guatemala, with volcanoes rising in the distance. A month in San Juan del Sur, Nicaragua, amid civil unrest and political revolts. Six months in the Sacred Valley of Peru. A month in Chiang Mai and Phuket, Thailand. A sweltering month in the penthouse apartment with a rooftop pool in Cartagena, Columbia. Ski vacations every year in Vail and Beaver Creek. Languid summer days boating on Lake Charlevoix, Michigan, when the kids were little. Mountain biking in Colorado. Climbing Aconcogua, the highest mountain in the western hemisphere.

I allowed each travel memory to surface, mentally polishing each one until it shined. Those memories were made of steel, the same stuff as an anchor. I clung to my memories as a storm of words buffeted the air inside the truck, threatening to blast our happy existence to smithereens. My memories were solid and real. They were firmly rooted in truth, in stark contrast to the preposterous wind blowing from John's mouth. It seemed safest to just check out.

I thought about the time when John and I met at the Outdoor Retailer trade show in Salt Lake City, Utah. I was the product manager for a water filtration company and John was one of our sales guys, working for his dad as an independent outdoor rep.

My coworkers and friends thought John and I would make a great couple. But as my career at the water filtration company was following a meteoric trajectory, I told them I wasn't interested. Just two years earlier, I'd been a temp, filling in for the president's secretary. Weeks later, I was hired as a sales and marketing analyst and was promoted to co-op advertising brand manager, then product manager in ensuing months. In the span of a year and half, my salary quadrupled.

I bought a duplex, rented the larger downstairs unit to a friend, and shared my small two bedroom upstairs apartment with a roommate. I was living free and raking in the dough.

An outdoor club called the Minnesota Rovers provided a great network of friends. Weekends were spent rock climbing, mountain biking, white water canoeing, hiking, cross country skiing, and even winter camping.

My work friends and I enjoyed back yard barbecues, as well as darts and pool at trendy brew-pubs near the University of Minnesota campus. I was young and cute, accustomed to catching rides on OPBs (other people's boats) on Lake Minnetonka, and getting invited to events my co-workers sarcastically called, "parties for the pretty people."

A rails-to-trails bike system in Minneapolis provided bike paths for the twenty mile commute between home and work. In the winter, the proximity of a cross country ski center made it possible to catch a quick skate ski session after work before I headed home for an evening of spaghetti and Star Trek reruns.

In short, I loved my life. I loved my routines. I felt strong, independent, and capable.

That carefree single life came to a screeching halt after a January Outdoor Retailer trade show in Salt Lake City. While doing my presentation to the sales force, I couldn't keep my eyes from wandering to John. The men I'd typically dated were attractive, but not striking. John was striking. Adonis-god-like striking. He was six feet two inches with curly blonde hair, high cheekbones, mesmerizing sea-glass green eyes, an aquiline nose and a warm, engaging smile. The intensity of his stare was unnerving and I stumbled over my words whenever I looked in his direction.

Later that afternoon, he came to my trade show booth to ask a product-related question. As I replied, I felt as if I was drowning in those sea-green eyes. Despite the fact that we were standing in the middle of a crowded trade show floor, my heart fluttered as if I was anticipating the final seconds before a first kiss.

Words came out in a jumble and I doubt they made any sense. I could feel the eyes of my co-workers burning a hole in the back of my head and even heard someone snicker. My breath was coming in gasps and I felt like I was going to choke. "Let's go for a walk," I muttered to John.

My panic subsided, heartbeat mercifully slowed and breathing resumed to normal once we were clear of the trade show booth. Regaining my composure, I asked, "You guys represent Moonstone, don't you?" as John and I wound our way through the crowded trade show aisles. Moonstone was a trendy little outdoor clothing company. I'd been drooling over one of their new three-layer Gore-tex jackets.

"Yeah," John replied. "We also represent Osprey and Yakima. If you want deals on any of those products, I can hook you up. They have pro-deals for industry employees. I can get you anything you need."

Hmm...It almost seemed like John was a little breathless too. Arriving at the Moonstone booth, I found my stunning aquamarine jacket. Having perused every aisle at Outdoor Retailer, I hadn't seen anything like it. "This one!" I exclaimed. "I absolutely love it!"

"Done," said John. "You can have our sales sample. I'll need it for a few weeks for retail presentations. After that, it's yours. I'm pretty sure it's your size."

Was it my imagination, or did he blush? A self-satisfied smirk crossed my face. He did. He blushed. I desperately wanted to see it again. Though normally pretty reticent around men, it felt like I could say anything at all to John. We'd only shared a few words. But somehow, I knew in my heart of hearts that there was no such thing as saying the "wrong" thing to him. The freedom of this knowledge was intoxicating. I could just be myself. No games. No posturing. Most importantly, I could mess with him mercilessly and not have to worry about scaring him away.

One of my co-workers had done some reconnaissance after the morning presentations. She'd learned that John had a girlfriend, but it had been an on-again, off-again relationship that was reputedly doomed to failure.

As John and I resumed our stroll through the trade show isles, I said coyly, "I have to tell you. I was absolutely devastated to hear you have a girlfriend." *OMG. Did those words just come out of my mouth?* I was mortified and elated. Much to my delight, the now-familiar shade of pink colored his cheeks.

"Um..." He stammered, "Yeah...well...ah...yeah."

Just then, we arrived back at my booth. Giddy with power, I said, "I'll be looking forward to getting that jacket. Here's my phone number."

That afternoon as the trade show was ending, I was responsible for dismantling our trade show booth. I'd been in charge of the team designing the new booth. Over the previous several months, I'd interviewed trade show booth design companies, researched flow patterns, worked with a team of color consultants, and collaborated with professional photographers from our marketing agency, to design a space that was roughly the size of a loft apartment.

I was suddenly exhausted. In addition to the booth, I'd been responsible for procuring mock-ups of the new products from engineering, working with our ad agency on ad design and print ad placement in outdoor publications, laying waste to vast stretches of forests to produce a solid ton of catalogs and marketing materials, preparing the agenda for the sales meeting, working with sales reps to schedule appointments with key customers, and forecasting the massive increase in sales that would surely be the end result of all this effort.

The trade show, which had been the culmination of countless hours of labor, was over. It had been a great success. Despite the fact we had strong competition, early indicators showed our company would capture sixty percent of the market share in our category. I was relieved and proud, but just a little deflated coming off the trade show high.

John and his dad came to my booth to help me pack up. My heart skipped a beat when I saw John, not only because I was finding him to be increasingly magnetic, but because I sincerely needed the help. Our company's sales manager and most of my other co-workers had caught flights from Salt Lake City back to Minneapolis earlier that day. The prospect of dismantling the massive trade show booth was daunting.

John's dad left when he realized the booth's packing crates had yet to arrive. From years of trade show experience, he knew crates could take hours for delivery as vendors from virtually every manufacturer in the outdoor industry attended this biannual event.

"Come on," I said to John casually. "It might be a while before the crates show up. I'll take you to dinner. By the time we're done, hopefully the crates will be here."

That evening's dinner conversation was scintillating. Sitting across the table from each other was like sitting in our own biosphere, actively participating in our own little genesis story. We weren't just "meant for each other," we were the only individuals of our kind, a species which I'd previously thought was comprised of only me. More than soulmates, we were species-mates, each uniquely and exclusively designed for the other.

In a crowded restaurant, we cultivated the soil in our biosphere, preparing it for the birth of a new terrestrial entity. Again, I had the sensation that I was falling into the pool of John's hypnotically green eyes. And again, I didn't feel the need to hold anything back. I could be fully and completely transparent with John. I had this strange sensation of possession or ownership. It didn't matter if he had a girlfriend now, or even if he had another girlfriend after this one. On a deeper level, he was mine, I was his, and it had always been this way.

John wasn't one to talk about himself. The consummate fisherman, John dropped hints about his life, teased me with small bits of information, and delighted in the fact that I begged to hear more. He had been an avid ski racer as a kid and missed a medal in the Junior Olympics by a couple hundredths of a second. He'd gone on to become a top level ski instructor in Vail and Beaver Creek and had even competed in pro ski races in the United States, Chile, and Japan.

John's extensive travels in Latin America mirrored mine in Eastern Europe. He was fluent in Spanish. While working for a friend's tool company, he'd spent a year living in Guadalajara, Mexico and another year living in Santiago, Chile.

"Let's tell each other our deepest, darkest secrets," I enthused. "I'll go first. I'm deathly afraid of boredom. The image of white picket fences terrifies me. I literally can't imagine staying at the same job, or living in the same place, all my life. I guess I was born without roots."

John stared at me for a minute, then said, "With me, I guarantee you'd never be bored."

My heart skipped a beat as I realized John shared my rootlessness. "Your turn. What's your deepest, darkest secret?"

John hesitated, then looked me in the eye. "I have high expectations for myself and others. People never live up to my expectations. I'm constantly disappointed."

A knowing smile tugged at the corner of my lip. Exceeding expectations was my specialty.

In eighth grade, after less than four years of piano lessons, I was playing the 3rd Movement of Beethoven's Moonlight Sonata, a famously challenging classical music composition. My piano teacher was firmly convinced I would be attending Juilliard.

With ridiculously little effort, I finished high school in three years and college in another three years, earning a 3.8 GPA and a degree in International Relations with an Eastern European focus.

I spoke French and Russian, had traveled to twenty-one countries, and had worked as a programs coordinator and tour guide for a non-profit organization called Friendship Ambassadors to promoted cultural exchange between Eastern Europe and the United States.

My work with Friendship Ambassadors yielded relationships that I'd hoped to someday leverage into a position with the U.S. embassy in Russia. For nearly a decade, I'd secretly (or sometimes not-so-secretly) been planning to run for president of the United States in the 2012 presidential election.

High expectations were my forte. My ambitions verged on maniacal. The thought that John could ever be disappointed in me was simply comical.

Our genesis story continued to unfold. Rather than being bound to this earth, we were creating our own planet. I could almost feel tectonic plates shifting beneath our feet.

"Tell me the thing you're most proud of. What is your greatest accomplishment?" I asked. John shared his proudest moments, his hopes and dreams, his highest aspirations. They felt so philosophically aligned with my own goals.

Life forms developed on our new planet. It was a veritable garden of Eden, saturated with vegetation unfurling before our eyes, flowers of every shape and color shooting up straight out of the earth, trees soaring skyward.

The synergy between John and I was like tasting oxygen for the first time. It was destiny, fate, kismet, love.

Finally, unable to control my excitement, I blurted out, "Tell me there's hope!"

John froze, staring back at me, startled. His eyes widened and the now-familiar blush rose to his cheeks.

"I'm dating someone. But she and I both know we aren't heading toward marriage. Still…I don't feel comfortable talking about starting something with you while I'm still in a relationship with someone else."

Wow. Character with a capital "C." I was proud of him. After all, he was mine, and I loved the fact that he had deep integrity and honored his commitments.

Unabashed, I replied, "I get it. Feel free to date her as long as you want, and anyone else you want to date for that matter. But when you're done dating other women, tell me there is hope. For me."

He knew what I was asking. We were both surprised by my forwardness and we were both a little startled by his response. "Yes," he replied. "There's hope."

On some level, it felt like he'd just accepted a marriage proposal. And on some level, I suppose he had.

We spent several hours packing my trade show booth into crates at the convention center. Near midnight, we hailed a cab and he escorted me back to my hotel, where he hopped out and gave me a quick goodbye hug.

The next morning, my heart leapt when we ran into each other at the airport. Words poured out in gushes as we savored our last few moments together. He made me promise to call him later that night to let him know I got home safely.

As my plane taxied down the runway, my throat was choked with emotion, and I was slightly abashed when tears of gratitude streamed down my face. My heart was full. I'd met the man I was going to marry, and I was so humbled and in awe of his specialness. He was just so different from anyone I'd ever met.

That night, John called me before I'd gotten the chance to call him. "I've broken up with my girlfriend," he announced. "Sorry to make you wait twenty-four hours. But I needed to be respectful. When can we see each other again?"

We made a plan to fly to Chicago two weeks later for Valentine's Day weekend. John and I talked every night on the phone, excitedly planning our impending reunion. Our relationship was fun, easy, and playful. He would send me emails in Spanish, which I promptly translated back to him in Spanglish. He sent a huge bouquet of flowers to my office. My coworkers swooned.

One night, as I was sitting in the bathtub, talking on the phone, John said, "If I asked you to marry me tomorrow, what would you say?"

My heart started racing. "Is that a proposal?" I asked.

"Not yet," he replied. "When I propose to you, I'm going to do it right."

I was hyperventilating. A crazy thought went through my head. *What if I have a heart attack and drown right here on the phone?* My voice was shockingly steady, belying the panic that had a death-grip on my heart.

"I would say yes, but we would need a long engagement. At least a year and a half. It takes at least a year and a half to really get to know a person, am I right?"

Oh my gosh! Did I just agree to marry a guy I met less than two weeks ago? We haven't even held hands! Even though I knew I'd found the man I was going to marry, it somehow came as a shock that he felt the same way!

Valentines Day weekend arrived and my nervousness and excitement could barely be contained. Then in a wash of panic, I realized I couldn't picture John's face. A Facebook profile would have been *so* handy. But in 1997, the internet was in its infancy and Mark Zuckerberg was only thirteen years old. I ran to my best friend Candace's office and grabbed her by the shoulders.

"I can't remember his face! I agreed to marry John and I have no idea what he looks like!" Candace, a fellow product manager for a much larger division of our company, was like an older sister to me. More importantly, since she'd attended the trade show in Salt Lake City, she was my only friend who'd met John.

"Wow. Okay. Let's breathe, lady," she said reassuringly. Candace knew I had a problem remembering faces. We jokingly referred to it as "the glitch in my facial recognition software."

I took a few deep breaths. Candace had me run through every detail I could remember of John's physical description. "Do you think you might be rushing this a little, kiddo?" she asked in a motherly tone.

"I know it looks that way," I said, somewhat disconcerted. "But it's like he's another species; one that was made just for me." The words sounded less convincing than they had two weeks earlier when I first told Candace how John and I had met.

After the short flight from Minneapolis to Chicago, my nerves were all bunched up and tingling, like a frayed electrical cord tied in knots. I peered around the arrival area, nonchalantly examining each face.

Is it him? No…I don't think so…but maybe that one. He's tall, blonde…nope. Too old. Oh my gosh. Where the heck is he? What if he didn't come? After a couple minutes that I swear to god were six hours, John poked his head out from behind a pillar.

"Having trouble with that facial recognition software?" he teased.

"Oh. My. Gosh. Candace told you!" I exclaimed, mortified.

"Don't worry. You'll have plenty of time to get to know my face," he replied and pulled me into our first kiss.

We were married in Sea Island, Georgia exactly four months later on June 14 in a very private, very exclusive wedding ceremony. No, we weren't pregnant. It was just too much work to see each other every two weeks when we lived over ten hours apart.

The criteria for invitation to our wedding was that the guest had to have contributed a sperm or an egg to our conception…or needed to be the guest of someone who contributed a sperm or an egg to our conception. For this reason, the only people in attendance were my parents, John's parents, and their partners. John and I spent our wedding day collecting shells on the beach with our six wedding guests. We also took a decadent two hour nap before the ceremony itself.

Continuing to write the script for our unique marriage journey, we took not one, but two honeymoons. The first was a brief stop at Epcot before a two week trek to Peru to visit Machu Picchu and hike the Inca Trail. The second was an all-expense paid trip to San Salvador Island in the Bahamas, compliments of our friends, Bill and Lori Northrup, whose small island off the coast of San Salvador was thought to be Christopher Columbus's first sighting of the New World.

Our first year of married life wasn't perfect. Our attitudes towards money were dramatically different. We enjoyed a pre-Christmas stroll in the affluent community of Petoskey, Michigan, where we window shopped high-end boutiques and jewelry shops. I awoke Christmas morning to find every single item in which I'd expressed the slightest interest, carefully wrapped under the tree. I knew one amber necklace alone was over three hundred dollars. My single gift to John was less than fifty dollars. I was mortified, to say the least.

As a lifelong athlete, John was committed to a daily exercise routine. In one chapter of his life, he'd even co-owned a fitness center and worked as a personal trainer. He insisted that I create a daily habit of personal development that included physical fitness and reading inspirational or motivational books.

At times, I willingly complied. At other times, it just pissed me off. *Why can't he just accept me as I am? Why is he always trying to change me?* I felt like a petulant child.

Last, but certainly not least, were our different perspectives on the role of extended family. John's parents were divorced and he'd been a boarding student at Vail Mountain School from the time he was thirteen. My parents were my best friends. I wanted to see my parents monthly. He was good with once or twice a year. We fought to the point of exhaustion over how much family time was reasonable.

With the exception of those momentary meltdowns, marital bliss was truly blissful. Most nights, I laid curled around John's back feeling his chest rise and fall as he slept. In the cool darkness, tears of gratitude welled up in my eyes. The poignant beauty of this love was simply too deep to fathom. I was overwhelmed by the shape and complexity of it. How did I get so lucky?

Still…twice I had a dream that I never shared with anyone. In my dream, I saw the face of another man—a stranger—staring back at me, and realized with horror I'd married the wrong person. Both times I woke up, choking back a heaving sob in my chest.

CHAPTER 2

There's nothing like climbing a 22,837 foot peak to provide context for a relationship. When we climbed Aconcogua, the highest mountain in the western hemisphere, we'd been married for two and a half years and had already summited some pretty high Latin American peaks. Our work as independent manufacturer's reps in the outdoor industry provided the flexibility to travel extensively, inspiring us to dream up increasingly outrageous adventures.

Prior to Aconcogua, I was passionately in love with John. But it was on the Aconcogua expedition that I felt like I truly melded with him on a deeply spiritual level. As it turns out, being trapped at eighteen thousand feet in a blizzard for thirty-six hours really gives you time to get to know a person. And having your spouse rescue you from an Incan mummy's tomb is one of those once-in-a-lifetime experiences that tends to make a lasting impression.

The idea to climb Aconcogua was a collaborative endeavor, shared by our buddy, Ty, who we'd met on the Inca Trail during our honeymoon in Peru. Ty was a German citizen who grew up outside Chicago and spent most of his adult life in Pisac, Peru, helping his German mother run a restaurant called Ulrike's. Ty played an integral role in our lives, sharing his domain with us in South America as we later shared ours with him in western New York. Ty showed up—and continues to show up—in nearly every chapter in our lives.

Since neither John, Ty, nor I were in possession of the kind of knowledge required to climb a twenty-two thousand foot peak, we contracted the services of Carlos Zarate. Carlos was a renowned Peruvian guide, who had been part of the party that discovered the famous mummy, Juanita, a five-hundred-year-old Incan child, sacrificed on Ampato mountain, outside Arequipa, Peru. We had used Carlos's guide service on a prior climb to summit El Misti, in Arequipa. Carlos, Ty, John, and I met in Santiago, Chile in December, 1999, which was the start of the summer climbing season in the lower part of the southern hemisphere.

After an active mountain biking season and several weeks of weight training, I was in the best shape of my life. John and Ty were also in peak physical condition. Though Aconcogua is not considered a technical climb, many mountaineers rank the climb as significantly harder than others at a similar altitude in the Himalayas, due to its distance from the equator.

As December is early summer in Argentina, the very first climbing parties of the season had summited Aconcogua mere days before we arrived. We would need crampons to cross steep ice fields, still thick with snow from the previous winter.

Upon arrival in Santiago, we began making preparations for an acclimatization climb of El Plomo, a 17,783 ft. peak in the Chilean Andeas. El Plomo would give our bodies the chance to become accustomed to the high altitude we would encounter on Aconcogua.

El Plomo, which can be seen from Santiago, is an easy day's drive from the city. On a clear day, you can see El Plomo's peak rising above the Valle Nevado ski area. Valle Nevado would be the launching point for our acclimatization climb. Carlos had arranged for us to stay at the resort's employee housing the night before beginning our ascent.

Carlos instructed Ty, John, and me to do the grocery shopping while he made other preparations for the trip. Scanning Carlos's grocery list, we noticed it included a lot of canned goods. We scoffed at the idea of carrying cans up a mountain.

"Hah. This is so old-school!" Ty exclaimed. "The guides in Peru do this all the time. On early Everest climbing expeditions, the guides used porters to carry their gear. So they didn't care about weight. They had horses and mules to carry their shit. Then they left cans and garbage all over the mountain. We are *not* going to do that."

"Yeah, Carlos probably doesn't know that there are dehydrated soup options. We don't need to haul a bunch of cans around," I agreed. It was settled. We replaced all of the canned items with dehydrated soups.

The next evening, we arrived at Valle Nevado, which was closed for the summer. It was eerily quiet. Chairlift towers rose like skeletons from the earth, arms supporting their daisy chains of vacant chairs.

Unlike ski resorts in the United States that offer offseason activities, Valle Nevado received no tourists outside ski season. We spent half an hour searching for a security guard who could direct us to the now-vacant employee housing where we'd be spending the night.

Safe and snug in our dorm room, sheltered from the biting alpine wind, Carlos instructed us to make a pile of supplies, which would be divided among us for the next day's climb. Carlos was dismayed to see we replaced the cans with dehydrated food.

Fluent in Spanish, John translated for Carlos. "There is no water on El Plomo," he informed us. "Only ice and snow. If I'd known you were going to bring dehydrated food, I would have brought more fuel canisters to melt snow for water." Silence. We all stared at each other. Oops. Well, there was nothing to do about it now.

Carlos went out in search of the security guard, hoping to miraculously find fuel canisters or even canned soup. But he was unable to find the guard. Santiago was a half day's drive away. Delaying our departure would delay our trip to Aconcogua. We made the decision to leave the next day in spite of our limited fuel.

The next morning, sun was just illuminating the top of the mountain, when we began our climb to Federacion, El Plomo's base camp. My pack felt impossibly heavy on my hips, though I knew each of the men's packs were significantly heavier. I couldn't imagine having to carry cans!

For most of the day, we wound our way up a long sweeping valley that stretched on for miles. I distracted myself from my blistered feet and badly bruised hips by counting to one hundred, then counting back down to zero. I switched to counting in Spanish until the altitude addled my brain, forcing me to resume the count in English. As the day wore on, the effects of dry air, sun, and altitude continued to take their toll.

Water, which was our first line of defense against altitude sickness, was consumed sparingly, in light of our dire fuel situation. By mid-afternoon, we all suffered from headaches. John's headache was so bad, he could barely open his eyes.

Upon reaching Federacion, John sat on a rock while we made camp, eagerly retiring to the tent as soon as it was set up. Carlos gave him aspirin, powdered for quicker absorption, to put under his tongue. John shuddered at the bitterness of the powder, with nothing more than a few drops of water to wash away the residual taste.

Carlos had just finished preparing dinner when the stove spluttered out, its fuel canister spent. In the final light of the setting sun, Ty and I scanned barren patches of brown grass and scattered boulders, dotting fields of ice and snow, trying to find a little rivulet of melt water. There was none. Exhausted and thirsty, with heads throbbing from altitude and dehydration, we retired for the few hours of sleep we hoped to get before waking at one in the morning for our summit bid.

Carlos and I were the only ones who got a couple hours of rest, as Ty and John spent the evening battling headaches. At one in the morning, I woke feeling like I'd been in a car accident. Every muscle ached. My hips were horribly bruised, unaccustomed to the weight of the pack. My feet were swollen so badly, I couldn't imagine they would fit into my boots. John's fourth toe and pinky toe were melded together into one bloody pulp of flesh and raw skin.

Each of us had packed our Camelback reservoirs with snow, hoping they would melt if we slept with them inside our sleeping bags. I pulled mine out, eager to see the full bag of water I was sure would be my reward for sleeping next to an ice baby. I was dismayed to discover a few meager ounces of freezing cold liquid and an icy chunk of semi-solid snow. There would be no water to make oatmeal.

A howling wind shook the tent. Though the tent was well-staked, I had no doubt it would have blown off the mountain if John and I were not inside it. Our breath formed a thick verglas on the inside of the tent walls and tiny ice crystals rained down on us when particularly strong gusts blasted down the mountainside.

By the light of our headlamps, John and I donned every piece of clothing we owned and gave each other a reassuring hug. Packing our sleeping mats and sleeping bags at that attitude felt like a monumental task. We paused frequently to catch our breath.

Previous expeditions had revealed my body's unique altitude-induced coping mechanism, an undesirable response to over-exertion at altitude. Stress, due to oxygen-deprivation, created an immediate and intense urge to pee. It wasn't the same as simply having a full bladder. The pee-muscles spasmed involuntarily, like a sneeze. It took focus and great force of will to counteract the contraction. As a result, I moved at a snails pace, expending as little energy as possible, to prevent oxygen deprivation and spastic urination.

Unzipping the tent, my headlamp cast a beam of light that cut through the night, revealing a cold barren landscape, silent and still, completely devoid of life. As alien lifeforms on this desolate planet, we were the only source of movement, along with our tents, which were wildly flapping in the howling wind. Exposed skin was immediately frozen.

Despite acute dehydration, my eyes teared in the icy wind and snot blew sideways before I had the chance to wipe my runny nose.

We huddled together in the light of our headlamps, miserably gagging on dry oatmeal. Without saliva to moisten it, the oatmeal presented a choking hazard, and we finally opted to make our summit bid without food. After all, at one in the morning, it was more of a midnight snack than breakfast anyway. Ty handed out frozen Powerbars that he'd purchased for a deeply discounted price on Ebay because they had passed their expiration date. They were so hard, it took several minutes and significant effort to gnaw off a corner.

Carlos's headlamp showed the way as we departed for the summit. The rest of us turned off our headlamps to conserve precious batteries. Consumed by darkness, the world seemed gentler in contrast to the harsh light from the headlamp, and somewhat warmer despite the howling wind. As my eyes slowly adjusted, it seemed as if the dimmest light emanated not from the moon, but from the mountain itself. Boulders had the faintest iridescent glow, like bioluminescent fish, emerging out of the blackness of the ocean's depths.

The mountain's energy felt stronger at night. Or maybe the energy was the same, but I wasn't distracted by the visual beauty that overwhelmed my senses by day. In darkness, the mountain's voice was nearly audible. I was sure that if one listened hard enough, they'd perceive the story it was telling: one continuous tale that stretched back to the very beginning of time itself, a story of ice and snow, wind and relentless sun. A story that told of Incans traveling this very path, somber and reverent, braving the cold icy wind, with nothing but leather sandals and ceremonial garb.

The Incan people believed each mountain was a spirit called an Apus. Their holy men made spiritual pilgrimages to the mountain's summit to commune with the gods. On rare occasions, they brought a child to sacrifice in the culmination of a ceremony called capacocha. Carlos informed us that our trail passed the very site where the body of an Incan child had been discovered.

As darkness softened, a nearly imperceptible light formed in the east. At first, it seemed a trick of the mind. Then slowly, the edges of rocks became sharper and I could see their shapes more clearly. The force of the wind, which had torn at us relentlessly through the night, seemed to subside a bit. It was still over an hour before the sun's first rays would appear on the horizon. But I felt a sense of excitement, an inexplicable joy and awe at the prospect of the coming dawn.

Filled with wonder, I marveled at this place I was traveling: a land more remote and desolate than I ever could have imagined. I was humbled to be blessed with a life partner who was courageous and adventurous, physically and mentally strong enough to embark on a trek of this magnitude. And he was fluent in Spanish!

The sun rose, and those first beams of virgin light felt pure and raw, like the first rays of light touching a brand new earth. Surrounded by this stark, lifeless landscape, it wasn't hard to imagine a planet newly formed by the big bang, exposed to light for the very first time.

Then, in a miracle known as a "brocken spectre," the sun cast our shadows over the low-lying mist in the valley below, illuminating our shapes in giant form like a scene cast from a mountain-sized movie projector. The sun ignited tiny droplets in the mist, creating rainbows of light surrounding our colossal shadows. The majesty of the moment surmounted pain, exhaustion, dehydration, and headaches.

Resuming our climb, I made fake chewing motions in an attempt to trick my body into making enough saliva to moisten my parched mouth. It didn't work. By mid-morning, I was well beyond the point of exhaustion. My mind was playing tricks on me.

Is that a rock or a cat? I'm sure I just saw it move. Poor thing. It must be hungry. On one level, I knew I was hallucinating. Still, I had to resist the urge to bend down and pet the rock. When I saw a beach chair in the middle of the trail, and actually shimmied along the cliff to get past the chair, I knew I was in trouble.

As it turned out, John was hallucinating too. He told me he'd been watching two soccer teams playing on the field below…then asked if I could see them too. Carlos told us we were very near the summit. It was less than forty minutes away. The wind, which had died for a short bit at daybreak, resumed after the sun rose, stronger than ever.

Carlos shepherded us off the trail to take shelter in the empty tomb where the body of a sacrificed Incan child had been discovered. Sitting in a circle on the bare earth, sheltered from the wind, I was alarmed (or would have been alarmed if I'd had the energy to register alarm) at the exhaustion in Ty and John's faces. Carlos was unfazed. A seasoned guide, he was accustomed to the rigors of summiting major peaks.

I was vaguely aware of the fact that I was only catching snippets of the conversation as we sat in the Incan tomb. It seemed like people were talking without finishing their sentences. Or they would start talking mid-sentence. Then I realized I wasn't able to follow the conversation because I was slipping in and out of consciousness.

When my breathing slowed, my oxygen levels would drop and I would pass out. After a few seconds, some kind of redundancy system kicked in, and I would regain consciousness, gasping for air. A minute later, the cycle would repeat. I had no energy to move a single muscle. My body temperature dropped as damp clothing stole precious heat. Dehydration prevented us from creating as much sweat as this level of exertion normally generated, a fact that likely saved our lives. Still, our clothing was slightly wet and we were all dangerously close to hypothermia.

I slipped into hallucination. Unlike previous delusions where I knew the images weren't real, I fully believed I was seeing the dead Incan child sitting next to me. She stared at me, mildly inquisitive and fully self-assured. This was her tomb. What right did I have to be here? Then, I realized she was me as a child, and I was staring into my own eyes.

Oh yes, I thought. *It's me! I'm the Incan child. This is my tomb. I belong here.* I was bone-weary. The faces of the men around me were the faces of strangers. *They don't belong here. They are intruders. This is my home. My tomb.*

I was aware of the fact that the men had stopped talking and were looking at me. John must have asked a question. I hadn't responded. Carlos made a motion to get up. It was time to leave. I stared at him as if he was insane. *Get up? I was dead! How could he expect me to get up? I've been here for hundreds of years! I belonged to the mountain. My soul had merged with the apus, the mountain spirit who inhabited this place.*

With vacant eyes, I perceived the effort it took for John and Ty to rise and was overcome with dread knowing they would expect me to do the same. But I couldn't. I wasn't strong enough. The very act of standing seemed as difficult as the entire climb all together, culminating in this one movement. And I couldn't do it. It was entirely impossible.

The men stood waiting for me. I was paralyzed. I couldn't move a muscle. By some kind of miracle, my eye managed to produce a single tear, which promptly leaked from the corner of my eyelid.

"Hey, you guys can just leave me," I said in a vain attempt to fein nonchalance. "I'll wait for you here. You can pick me up on the way down." Even as I formed the words, I knew with certainty that I would die if they left me.

John shook his head, having neither the strength nor the saliva to form the word "no." I knew tears would be streaming down my face if I'd had the water to form them. Instead, my face contorted into a tearless sob as John extended his hand. If I took that hand, I knew there would be a life-giving transfer of energy, but I wasn't at all convinced it would be enough.

It was like an angel from heaven was bidding me to rise, but I wasn't sure even the angel was strong enough to pull me up. That image, of John extending his hand, harrowingly weary, yet offering what little strength he had to pull me to my feet, imprinted itself on my heart.

We made it to the top of El Plomo. More impressively, we made it back to Valle Nevado, where we drank enough water to fill your average camel.

On Aconcogua, it took nearly a week to reach the mountain's 22,837 foot summit. At Nido de Condores, a camp at eighteen thousand feet, we spent thirty-six hours confined to our tents, socked in by a late-season blizzard. Our intended shelter at nineteen and a half thousand feet, Refugio Berlin, was full. So we (mostly Ty) had to dig out another smaller shelter that was packed with snow.

Ty's exertion digging out the small cabin left him calorie-deprived and dehydrated, which affected his summit bid the next day. He barely made it to the top and Carlos needed to tie a harness around his waist to short-rope him down, arresting Ty's falls when he passed out. John carried both his own pack and Ty's on the way down.

For all our trials and tribulations on Aconcogua, none was as poignant as the experience in the mummy's tomb, during the acclimatization climb on El Plomo. Throughout two decades of marriage, my thoughts returned to John's hand, extended, beaconing me to rise from the tomb. I felt like I owed John my life and had been happy to give it to him. The image of John as protector, guardian, even savior, made up for a multitude of perceived shortcomings.

Still, I couldn't shake the feeling that some part of me was left behind in that tomb.

CHAPTER 3

Our early years of marriage were dedicated to covering as much horizontal and vertical distance possible. Exploration was central to our ethos.

For our first seven years together, home base was the little town of Boyne City, Michigan. Nestled on the eastern shore of Lake Charlevoix, Boyne City provided endless trails for running, mountain biking, cross country and downhill skiing. In the summer we raced our J-22 sailboat, *Habanero*, on Lake Charlevoix.

We had a fabulous group of friends who shared our love of outdoor activities and long dinners at exclusive restaurants with great food and lots of wine. Life was outstandingly good.

Ty told me that on the summit of Aconcogua, I'd said, "I'm going to have babies so I don't have to climb mountains anymore." Though I have no recollection of anything I said at over twenty-two thousand feet, a year later and after five years of marital bliss, I was pregnant with our first child.

Our first baby, Gracie Madison Rounds, was born in the spring of 2002. She was perfect. I remember the ride home from the hospital. John was driving well below the speed limit, trying to avoid every bump in the road. We both marveled at the fact that we'd been entrusted to care for something so precious as this newborn baby girl.

We were so in love. Our whole world centered around this precious little being whose every smile elicited a flutter of joy. Her laughter made everyone in the room laugh right along with her. Gracie's laugh was like the world's most powerful magical spell, one Gracie could use at will to create sheer joy. Perfect strangers unwittingly fell under her power, captivated by the mischievous grin on her rosebud lips and the expansive intelligence in her bright blue eyes. There was nothing we wouldn't do for her.

My parents traveled with us to trade shows and sales meetings, at their own expense, to babysit Gracie, as they were nearly as enamored with her as we were.

We also took trips alone with our new little family.

Once, Gracie and I traveled to England with John while he attended a sales meeting in Scotland.

Late one night in London, Gracie and I weren't able to sleep as we were both befuddled by the time change. John was in Edinburgh. So we hopped a double-decker bus and spent two hours marveling at the city lights of London. People waved up at us as they saw Gracie watching in wonder from her snug little Baby Bjorn carrier on my chest. It started to drizzle, and the sidewalk and pavement exploded into a carpet of diamonds, illuminated by London's brilliant city lights. Seeing the world through my baby's eyes was a magical, deeply bonding experience. Gracie helped me rediscover the beauty I'd forgotten to notice in everyday scenes.

When Gracie was a year old, I started working on a book called *Baby Travel Made Easy*. At a book expo in Chicago, I handed a single copy of the book proposal to a single prospective publisher. Several months later, I received a call saying that but for a single vote, *Baby Travel Made Easy* would have been published by the Insider's Guide series.

Though the news was discouraging, I realized the project had potential. I registered domain names and developed baby and toddler travel websites. I also worked with an app developer to create a BabyTravel iPhone app that included a packing list and soothing background sounds to help babies sleep in unfamiliar environments.

A mere eighteen months after Gracie was born, we were blessed with the arrival of Calista "Callie" Christine Rounds on November 14, 2003. In the womb, Callie was a spectacularly active baby. With all the roughhousing taking place in my stomach, I was fully convinced she was a highly energetic boy.

From the day Callie was born, she hit the ground running. She laughed easily and was continually moving, legs kicking, arms flailing, jumping in the bouncer until I was sure we were going to need to replace the springs. Callie was pure light in motion.

When Callie was just two months old, John took a temporary position as CamelBak Hydration's national sales manager. We moved from Boyne City to Sonoma, California, then Petaluma, California.

Half of *Baby Travel Made Easy* had to be simplified and re-written after Callie was born, because I'd outrageously overpacked when traveling with one child.

Both Gracie and Callie hated their car seats with every fiber of their being. Callie protested loudly at being confined for more than a few minutes at a time. I tried every kind of music to soothe her misery. But there were only two things that would quell the caterwauling. The first was high energy electronic dance music with ultra heavy bass. The other was Uncle Remus's Disney song, "Zip-A-Dee-Doo-Dah"…as long as everyone in the car sang along.

In California, I got pregnant for the third time in three years and officially threw the *Baby Travel Made Easy* project out the window. Because let's face it: there is *nothing* easy about traveling with three young children!

Having set a precedent of moving every time I got pregnant or had a new baby, we continued that winning streak with a move to Denver when John took a job as global sales manager for Cloudveil outdoor clothing.

"Are you bored yet?" John asked, referencing the conversation from our first dinner together, where I'd revealed "fear of boredom" as my deepest darkest secret. "I told you that you'd never be bored living with me. How am I doing so far?"

Though most people strive to settle down after having kids, we seemed to be just as itinerant as ever. Denver was our sixth move in eight years. Much as I truly abhorred packing and unpacking boxes, the excitement of moving still thrilled me. More importantly, it seemed like some kind of life extension hack.

Each new location created a new file in my mental filing cabinet. This concept applied to extended vacations as well. By creating a new backdrop for memories, I was able to anchor more scenes in my mind. The more locations where we lived or visited for a month or longer, the more files were added to the cabinet, until the cabinet itself was forced to expand. Travel and movement yielded a rich life, filled with bountiful memories.

It was in Denver that we met our baby boy for the first time. As energetic as Callie had been during pregnancy, Christopher was the exact opposite. He was completely and totally chill, often nearly motionless for days at a time. For this reason, I guessed the gender of my baby incorrectly for the third time. I'd been so convinced Christopher would be a girl, we hadn't even chosen a boy's name. So much for stereotypes!

John had been named after his father. He wasn't keen on the idea of having yet another John Christopher Rounds on the planet, as two had seemed confusing enough. However, staring into his son's eyes, John had to agree with my assessment that naming our boy John Christopher Rounds III was a choice-less decision.

As a baby, Christopher proved to be as tranquil as Callie was rambunctious. Whenever Christopher considered a display of disapproval, he generally thought better of it, and quietly self-soothed with his pacifier or entertained himself with whatever toy was nearest at hand. Nothing amused him more than watching his older sisters. And nothing amused his older sisters more than entertaining their baby brother.

Giving birth to three babies in just over four years was almost more than my body could physically handle. When Christopher was born, Gracie had just turned three. I went straight from nursing Callie to nursing Christopher. The physical depletion showed up as stress and bone-weary exhaustion. Naps were an integral part of my survival, and I longed for them like a desert nomad longs for water.

Three year old Gracie, however, decided that she was done with her afternoon naps. A battle of wills ensued. Afraid to allow my three year old to wander the house unsupervised while I slept, I insisted she take her nap. Gracie protested fiercely.

To anyone who has never been a parent, this exchange might seem hardly worth mentioning. However, our knock-down drag-out battle over naps occurred daily, with threats, promises, tears, punishments, shouts, consequences, shame, and ultimately my utter defeat. My ship of sanity was nearly destroyed, battered upon the solid rock of Gracie's will. I'd spent what little emotional resources I had left, fighting for my precious nap. It nearly broke me. That's when we found Denise.

Denise was in her early twenties when she moved from Mexico to Denver to learn English, which she practiced with the girls whilst cooing to Christopher in her native tongue. I adored Denise, not only because she provided respite from the soul-numbing exhaustion of raising three kids under four years of age, but because she truly loved the kids. With Denise's support, I was even able to help John launch a network marketing business that paid most of our living expenses, a feat that seems herculean in retrospect, especially considering the fact we were out of the country for six weeks that fall.

John was truly gifted at crafting flexible working arrangements, which proved to be a boon for our travel-minded family. A master negotiator in the interview process, John opted to negotiate an at-distance work agreement, rather than lobbying for a higher salary. His agreement with Cloudveil allowed our family to escape a dreary November and December in Denver to spend several weeks living in San Miguel de Allende, Mexico.

We fell in love with San Miguel's stunning mountains, high-desert sunshine, vibrant art, active culture scene, and warm, friendly people. John spent his days working remotely for Cloudviel while the kids and I enrolled in Spanish immersion classes and explored the city. I'd spent quite a bit of time at Mexican beach destinations like Cancun, Cabo, and Puerto Vallarta. But none of those trips remotely resembled this deep dive into Mexican culture.

The Mexican celebration of Dia de los Muertos was one of the most profoundly impactful travel experiences of my life. One of my Spanish instructors had lost her teenage son in a motorcycle accident the prior year. My natural emotional response was one of horror and despair for her loss.

Through Dia de los Muertos, I witnessed how the Mexican culture infuses grief with beauty. Death is not pushed away as something abhorrent or unnatural. I was humbled and in awe of this woman's ability to laugh through her tears, telling funny stories about her son, as the other language school teachers built an altar of marigolds, candles, sugar skulls, candy, and favorite personal belongings to honor her son's life.

The night of the Dia de los Muertos parade, the kids and I walked through the streets, viewing the beautiful altars constructed to honor loved ones who had died. Tears streamed down my face, as I gratefully received this new reframing of the cycle of life and death as something natural, beautiful, and precious.

We returned to Denver the week before Christmas. Denise, her mother, and her sister had purchased and decorated a Christmas tree for us, underscoring the generous, open-hearted spirit of that beautiful culture.

As much as I enjoyed living in new places, after spending two years in California and Denver with three babies, I longed to be nearer to family. My parents flew to visit us every few months. But I missed being closer to extended family and friends. Our tight-knit friend group in Michigan now had kids the same age as ours. And I really, really missed being near the water.

One scorching hot summer day in Denver, I was playing inside with Gracie and Callie, aching for Lake Charlevoix with a visceral longing. The Denver sun, so benevolent in the winter, assaulted the back patio with a fervor akin to vengeance. Ribbons of heat radiated in waves from the patio bricks.

With shades drawn to save electricity, the artificial, semi-coolness of air conditioning transformed the living room to a tepid, gloomy prison. Summer days in Minnesota and Michigan were incalculably precious, each warm day something to treasure. To a midwesterner, seeking shelter from summer's heat was a foreign concept. I just wanted to be outside.

I called Bridget, my friend from Boyne City, Michigan.

"Hey, Christy! It's so good to hear your voice," Bridget exclaimed. "We were just talking about you!"

I felt a pang of longing for my friend who had two boys the same age as Callie and Christopher.

"We just got back from Glenwood Beach. The Kuhns and Glasses were there too."

The pang became a sharp knife of envy. Chris and Tammie Kuhn had two kids who were the same age as Gracie and Callie. Josh and Jenny Glass's son was also Callie's age.

"We had a picnic at Glenwood Beach. Everyone was saying how much they missed you guys. Your family needs to move back to Michigan." The knife twisted.

In that moment, I could almost physically smell the blue-green water of Lake Charlevoix, feel its coolness caressing my body like a soft liquid blanket, see the sun dancing on the tips of its gently rippling waves.

In Denver, our only kid-friendly access to water was the heavily chlorinated, grossly overcrowded outdoor waterpark at a nearby community center. On a hot day like this, the relentless ferocity of Denver's high-altitude sun would make even the water park inhospitable for our two toddlers and a baby. Lake Charlevoix's sandy shores and warm, knee-deep water were ideal for children to spend endless hours frolicking while adults lounged nearby, enjoying beer or a glass of wine.

"Oh, Bridget," I replied. "You just made me *so* homesick!"

"I'm sorry! Just remember, Boyne City is a small town. It's nothing like Denver, where there's always something happening!" She exclaimed hurriedly, attempting to assuage my homesickness. "There's very little intellectual stimulation here. Most people don't even know the basics of quantum physics!"

I burst out laughing at the randomness of that statement and exclaimed, "Oh yeah. Here in Denver, we have a quantum physicist on every corner!" Bridget's quirky comment made me miss her even more. She was a physical therapist who loved discussing alternative medicine, spiritual healing, and metaphysics.

Late spring the following year, John and I took the kids to Boyne City to visit John's dad and reconnect with friends. Not willing to miss a chance to see the grandbabies, my parents drove from Minnesota to meet us in Boyne City.

Mom and Dad volunteered to babysit not only our kids, but our friends' children as well, providing the opportunity for four couples to have an adult dinner together. As my mom and dad stood in the yard, looking just a bit overwhelmed, our friends waved their goodbyes and blew kisses to eight children under five years of age, a couple of whom were loudly protesting their parents' departure.

That night's dinner was one of celebration, raucous laughter, and revelry. Gazing around the table at the faces so dear to me, my chest swelled with emotion. Suddenly, my friend, Tammie, turned to John and me and declared, "You're not leaving. You're not going back to Colorado. You guys are coming home."

One by one, other friends around the table reaffirmed that statement. "You guys have to come back. This is where you belong."

Their words felt like an incantation, a magical spell we were powerless to resist. The more they spoke, the more the spell became a solid thing, a truth, an unshakable reality. John and I looked at each other, silently affirming their words.

Despite having spent the previous two years in California and Colorado, we still owned the farmhouse and guest house where we'd lived when Gracie and Callie were born. We'd opted to rent out the main house, rather than putting the property up for sale, when we left for California. Some part of us must have known we'd return some day.

"No way!" Josh exclaimed as he caught the intention behind our gaze. "Are you guys seriously thinking about it?" Without having said a word, we knew it was true.

"I guess so!" John declared enthusiastically. A great cheer rose up from the table and champagne was ordered.

John stayed in Michigan with the kids, while my mom and I flew to Denver to spend five days packing the house. Mom and I returned to Michigan in my minivan to watch the kids while Ty joined John in Denver to drive the moving van back home.

Our network marketing business would pay our basic expenses while John sorted out his next career move. We were excited to begin this new chapter in northern Michigan.

CHAPTER 4

Sitting in the parking lot of the ski resort on that grey morning in January, 2020, I half-heartedly listened as John rambled on about how we had always been philosophically misaligned. Mentally scanning the first ten years of married life for signs of fracture, some evidence that the bedrock upon which our marriage was built had been unsound from the start, I came up empty handed. It's true that we had differing opinions and perspectives. But our core values were largely in sync.

At the start of our second decade together, we'd had five years without kids and five years with them. When John and I started our married life as sales reps in the outdoor industry, the seasonality of that venture provided a lot of free time for travel. John's flexible work arrangements and lucrative pay with CamelBak and Cloudviel provided time and money to continue traveling when kids were added to the equation.

Shortly after moving back to Michigan, our closest friends from Camelbak introduced John to a company called V.I.O. Years before GoPro took the helmet-camera world by storm, Michigan-based V.I.O. was vying for lucrative government contracts selling helmet cameras to the military.

Always the visionary, John saw the opportunity to introduce V.I.O.'s helmet cameras to the outdoor consumer market. Just months after John was hired, GoPro came out with its first digital helmet camera, the GoPro Hero, and the helmet camera business exploded. John found himself front and center in one of the fastest growing categories in the consumer electronics industry.

Though I wasn't working outside the home, John gave me the unofficial title "Spreadsheet Queen." During my time as a sales and marketing analyst for PUR, I'd become pretty adept at creating spreadsheets. This skill proved useful when John needed to do sales projections, reporting, and analysis. He also called on me when technical writing skills were required. It felt good to be working together, side-by-side, like we had in the manufacturer's rep business.

John's travel requirements with V.I.O. were brutal. One year after he was hired, John's Marriott statement showed he'd spent over one hundred nights in Marriott hotels. And V.I.O.'s headquarters in Marquette didn't even have a Marriott! John had been gone over a third of the year, and achieved the dubious honor of being inducted into United Airline's million mile club.

The kids cried unconsolably when John left and celebrated in jubilant elation when he returned. I told myself that the travel was harder on him than it was on me, but that probably wasn't the case.

When we moved back to the farm in Michigan, we spent the first year living in the two bedroom guest house, since we had leased out the main house. Christopher, who was one year old, had his own room. The girls slept on an inflatable queen-sized mattress that fit perfectly into our closet.

The cosiness made the house feel less empty when John was away. It also left no option to escape when the kids were fighting. It bears mentioning that this newly renovated guest house didn't have television or internet. That first winter, I struggled to maintain my sanity.

We settled into a double life: the life with Dad and the life without Dad.

Having Dad home meant more dinners out in restaurants, as I rarely braved a restaurant dinner with three kids in tow. Dinners at home when John was around were more healthy, thoughtful, and planned, as opposed to the pizza and sandwiches that dominated our diet when he was gone.

Having John home meant I could exercise without getting a babysitter. I could go outside to feed the chickens in the winter without having to bundle all three kids. I could go grocery shopping without a cart half-filled with children, schedule my teeth cleaning appointments, and take care of other personal hygiene that didn't happen in the kid-centric chaos. When John was out of town, I barely found time to take a shower or clip my toenails, much less shave legs, blow dry hair, or put on makeup.

Best of all…having Dad home meant singing "Let's Get It Started" by the Black Eyed Peas every day before preschool.

Finally, our tenant moved out and the family spilled into the sprawling main house. The farm in Michigan was an ideal place to raise three young kids, where summer days were predominantly centered around agriculture, nudity, boating, and time with friends. If our family's life trajectory was previously characterized as a fast-moving river, the Michigan farm provided eddies, where we had the opportunity to pause and catch our breath.

Our Michigan farmhouse was certainly nothing special. We often said we purchased the land and they threw in the house for free. The original structure, perched on its fieldstone foundation, was built in the late 1800s and suffered from two poorly planned additions. Consequently, it was unevenly heated.

In the winter, snow collected inside the window sill, when old wooden casings in the kitchen and dining room failed to keep the elements at bay. Exterior living room walls were insulated with shredded up newspapers, circa 1920s.

We dug up a rusted gasoline drum, buried at the edge of the driveway, because it was located dangerously close to the well that provided our drinking water. After decades of fueling tractors and farm implements, a former gas pump mounted over nothing but dirt had almost certainly contaminated the well already.

Speaking of dirt…the basement under the original 1800s section of the house was dirt, providing a happy home for a prolific little family of eastern milk snakes. The kids captured one of the babies trying to escape up the stairs. We stuck her in an aquarium and named her Lucy.

One day, the kids went to feed Lucy and discovered her cage was empty. Apparently, snakes are strong enough to push the top off their cages! Who knew?

The whole "snake-on-the-loose" situation proved problematic, as John has a fairly significant fear of snakes. At first, I didn't bother telling him about Lucy's escape. After all, why worry him? But near day's end, I began fretting that he might step on Lucy if he went to the bathroom at night, an occurrence that would threaten not only Lucy's life, but John's as well.

John took the news as well as could be expected, and expressed in no uncertain terms his desire that Lucy be found first thing the next morning. Unfortunately, I spent hours snake hunting over the next two days with no success. Then, on day three, I was channeling my inner snake, trying to divine where Lucy might be hiding, when I received a flash of inspiration.

She would go somewhere warm! I started pulling grates from the forced air ducts around the house. Lo and behold, Lucy was in the hot air duct in our bedroom! John wasn't nearly as pleased to hear this news as you'd think, since the heebie jeebies outweighed his sense of relief from Lucy's capture.

Lucy was indeed returned to her aquarium, and was all well and good, until Lucy bit Gracie on the hand, at which point she (Lucy, not Gracie!) was donated to the Raven Hill Discovery Center.

Indoor snow flurries, gas-tainted water, and snakes aside, life at the farmhouse was idyllic. The view from the house was heaven on earth. An old wooden porch spanned the entire front of the home, casting expansive views over miles of uninhabited wetlands.

When we first acquired the property, we dug a pond just below the house in a spot where a natural spring was surrounded by apple trees. A massive barn with three horse stalls also held a chicken coop, which would soon become the scene for ill-begotten forays into animal husbandry. The newly remodeled guest house, where we lived the first year, was perched atop a massive fieldstone foundation, constructed nearly a hundred years ago to house tractors and farm equipment.

John bought a brand new Kubota tractor and cleared space for a garden. I spent countless hours and dollars, running miles of irrigation tubing in an attempt to create a home-grown irrigation system, the complexity of which would have baffled the most worthy irrigation engineer.

My irrigation system was successful in one regard. It cultivated the most prolific crop of weeds any farmer in that region had ever seen. A few exceedingly hardy vegetables managed to grow, in spite of my weed-producing endeavors. Our family enjoyed snap peas and fresh spinach from the garden, as well as fancy little fingerling potatoes in every shade and color.

By my calculations, our vegetables cost around $2,586 a pound, when factoring the tractor into the equation, a computation that improved significantly when John recouped some of that capital by selling the tractor some years later.

Our second summer in Michigan, our dear friends the Kuhns called dibs on two golden retriever puppies from a local breeder. "There's only one puppy left! He's so sweet. You guys should come see him!" they exclaimed.

"You don't just 'go see' a golden retriever puppy when you have three little kids," John remarked, laughing. Truer words have ne'er been spoken.

Bentley joined our family when Christopher was two years old. In Bentley's mind, Christopher's mattress on the nursery floor was his dog bed. Bentley appreciated the fact that his new bed included a little human littermate. Seeing two year old Christopher sleeping with this golden retriever puppy goodly and truly melted our hearts.

That summer, we bought a twenty-five foot pontoon boat, with a 125hp motor, and eighteen drink holders. Since all our friends had kids the same age as ours, the pontoon was loaded with families most weekends. Our kids' favorite early childhood memories include early morning boating sessions with fresh scones from the Lake Street Deli, sunsets on Lake Charlevoix, picnics and fireworks on the Fourth of July, and summer days at Grandpa Chris and Nana's cabin in Canada. Life was perfect.

On July 4, 2007, we received a mail delivery of baby chicks I'd ordered from Murray McMurray Hatchery's catalog. I didn't even know there was someone to accept deliveries at the post office on the 4th of July! But at seven thirty that morning, I got the call saying my Mixed Breed Special chicks from Murray McMurray had arrived. We were in love. What could be cuter than my three babies, cuddling twenty little chicks of every shape, size and color…on the Fourth of July, no less?

As the chicks grew, I noticed some of them seemed to be fighting. My chicks grew more aggressive by the day, the larger ones ganging up on the smaller ones. To my horror, they began to draw blood. As fall approached, the truth slowly dawned on me. The "special" part of "Mixed Breed Special" was that my little chicks shared a single gender. And that gender was male. I had ordered twenty roosters.

It got bloody. We couldn't keep twenty roosters inside a coop, because they ripped each other to shreds. Consequently, the roosters roamed the property in packs, little chicken gang-bangers, in search of their next victim.

They lurked on the guest house porch, peering in through the glass French doors. They terrorized the UPS driver when he came to deliver packages. One day, they attacked two-year-old Christopher, beating him with their wings and scratching him with their claws. I grabbed a shovel and knocked them away as Christopher lay huddled in the grass, crying.

John called our friend, Jon Foltz, who was an emergency room doctor and avid bird hunter. Jon dutifully rung the necks of every last rooster. The men boiled water behind the barn, plucking the chickens' feathers, so I could assuage my guilt by using their carcasses to make chicken soup. Due to the toughness and strong gamey flavor of the birds, the soup was entirely inedible.

I kept the children tucked away in the house, safe from the carnage taking place behind the barn. Recounting the experience later with as little rancor as possible, John said, "As I sat there plucking chickens behind the barn, all I could think about was our back patio in California, with its marble fountain and sculptured garden. I found myself wondering how in the world I ended up here!"

Much to John's dismay, I bought a new batch of chicks the very next year. These were known as Easter Eggers, which meant they laid pastel-colored eggs in various shades of pink, blue, and green. This time, they were all hens, nary a rooster to be found.

A few months after the chicks arrived, we were eagerly awaiting our first pastel-colored egg. Nana, John's step-mom, wanted to bring her grandchildren over to see the little chickens. Our kiddos were still sleeping when Nana showed up, but I told Nana and her two granddaughters, who were Gracie and Callie's age, they could go back to the coop to see the chicks while I got Gracie and Callie out of bed.

A flustered Nana returned a few minutes later with two sobbing children in tow. "It's so awful!" Nana exclaimed, looking like she was going to vomit. "Something got into your coop. There's blood all over. The chickens have been ripped to pieces. Whatever it was, it didn't even eat them. It just killed them and left them there. I'm so sorry. Make sure your kids don't go out there!" With that, she hustled the traumatized children into the car and sped away.

I was shocked. It started to rain. I grabbed my trusty shovel as protection, in case the thing that killed the chickens was still out there, and walked around to the back of the barn to view the outdoor coop. The chicken coop was an outdoor enclosure with a little door that led to an indoor pen. Every inch of the structure was either covered with wood or chicken wire. *How could something get in?*

Nana's description didn't do the scene justice. It was a massacre. There was blood everywhere. It was as if the chickens had been destroyed by a chainsaw, not an animal. Blood and feathers plastered the wall of the barn five feet up, their corpses already attracting flies.

I just fed them last night. Did I forget to close the coop? A quick inspection confirmed the coop door was securely latched. I searched the bottom of the fence line, looking for a place where the intruder could have breached the perimeter. There was no tunnel and the chicken wire wasn't damaged.

Inside the barn, the air was dark and dank. The main floor of the barn was cement, which we had poured to make it easier to move the pontoon boat in and out for winter storage. The floors of the horse stalls, goat pen, and chicken coop were still dirt.

Waiting for my eyes to adjust to the low light, I moved toward the inner coop. It was a solid wood structure at the far end of the barn. Chicken wire at the top of the coop formed a loft that was once used to store hay when the barn housed horses and goats.

The increasing intensity of rain pounding on the barn's tin roof felt ominous, bringing to mind African drums cinematically getting louder, as if something dramatic was about to happen.

A goat pen adjoining the coop was unoccupied. *Could something have dug its way in through the goat pen?* I ducked through the pen's low threshold, scanning its dimly lit interior. I couldn't see a hole in the dirt beneath the clapboard wall the pen shared with the adjoining coop. Likewise, there was no break in the wall's wooden surface. *What the hell could have happened?*

45

Now the rain was pounding so loudly, it would have been difficult to carry on a conversation, had anyone been there to talk to. I was finding it hard to hear myself think.

Staring through the chicken wire framing the chest-high door, the carnage inside the coop mirrored that of the outdoor coop. Dead chickens had been tossed about like so many bloody rag dolls, the murderer clearly enjoying his killing spree. I stooped to enter the coop. Stepping over the decapitated bodies of my little brood of chickens, I felt a wave of grief. I'd known these chickens and they had known me. I had come to think of them as pets.

Suddenly, I heard something move behind a piece of plywood, propped against the wall, beneath the nesting shelf, where the chickens laid their eggs. With no small degree of trepidation, I stoop-shuffled over to the plywood and cautiously pulled it away from the wall, exposing the body of one last chicken, who was only ninety percent dead.

Then, I heard something hiss. Pulling the plywood back farther, I was horrified to see a massive possum, standing over the chicken, teeth bared, staring at me. It hissed again. I screamed and stoop-ran out of the coop, my back grazing the chicken wire frame of the low door.

John's dad dispatched of the possum with his hunting rifle, rendering the barn safe for clean-up. Upon returning to the coop, I finally solved the mystery of the possum's entry. He'd stood on the chicken wire ceiling in the hay loft, his massive body weight pulling the metal staples from the wooden frame. I donned gloves and collected the carcasses of the dead chickens.

A while back, the girls and I had made a fairy garden at the edge of the woods, with curios purchased from thrift shops and second hand stores. We had fairy tea and cookies in the fairy garden, and were thoroughly convinced the garden had special fairy magic.

I buried the butchered chickens near the fairy garden so the fairies could watch over them. Unfortunately, something dug up their carcasses, leaving chicken bones and feathers scattered around the fairy houses. The scene brought to mind a horror movie involving satanic worship. Let me tell you, there's no better way to ruin a perfectly good fairy garden than by littering it with dead chicken pieces!

Speaking of horror, the next summer (to John's dismay) I reinforced the coop and bought yet another batch of chickens. Maniacally clinging to the dream of farm-fresh eggs, I purchased twelve Rhode Island Red chicks from the co-op store in town. They were all hens, and a single, but notable, rooster. Having raised three batches of chicks, these were the first to reach egg-laying age. Like the garden, raising chickens was a labor of love rather than a financial boon. After the cost of feed, calcium-rich grit, and the chicks themselves, our eggs ran about $9.36 a dozen.

Our third foray into chicken-rearing was a grand success. Gracie and Callie named each of the baby chicks and hand-fed them grasshoppers from the yard. As the chickens grew, the girls cradled them like babies, painting the hens' beaks and claws with fingernail polish so they would look pretty for the rooster.

When the hens wanted to go on dates with the rooster, Christopher provided transportation with his a little electric John Deer tractor. Solemn-faced, Christopher would rip around the property with a hen tucked under his left arm, another bouncing along in the trailer behind. The rooster just stood back and watched, awaiting his ladies' safe return.

CHAPTER 5

Much as our family loved to travel during the colder months of the year, we stayed home as much as possible during summers in Michigan. Often times, summer at the farm revolved around the pond. For this reason, nudity was a central childhood theme, particularly for Callie.

The farm was our little Garden of Eden, and the kids were seemingly oblivious to the fact that most people wore clothes for anything other than warmth. In fact, Callie eschewed clothing, not just in the summer, but all year long.

Callie has always been a kid who was comfortable in her own skin. Literally. Just her skin. There were several years where scant few Christmas tree decorating photos could be shared publicly, due to the fact that Callie was naked in nearly every one of them.

After school, one warm day in late spring, a set of twins in Callie's second grade class got off the school bus at our stop. Their family lived up the road and their mother had asked if I could watch the kids after school. As the brother and sister stared in consternation, Callie began de-robing the moment she stepped off the bus. By the time she reached the end of the driveway, she wasn't wearing a stitch of clothing.

"Mom! Can we go swimming in the pond?" she called into the house.

"Sure, honey. Did Max and Madison bring their swim suits?" There was no reply. I peered out the bedroom window, and inhaled sharply at the sight of Callie marching to the pond, fully naked, in front of Max and Madison, who were following at a cautious distance.

"Callie! Honey!" I yell-whispered to her from the porch.

"What?" she exclaimed, turning around and providing her classmates a full frontal view as I threw her a towel.

On warm summer days, the kids swam naked in the pond, challenging each other to see who could catch the most frogs. Perch and sunfish became part of our little aquatic habitat, thanks to the clandestine involvement of a few fishing friends. A painted turtle, rescued as he crossed the road, found a new home in the pond as well. We delighted in spotting him each spring as he emerged from winter slumber.

The pond's most surprising occupant was a goldfish, won at the county fair by tossing a ping pong ball into a goldfish bowl. Failing to find someone to feed the fish prior to an extended family vacation, we liberated our orange and white goldfish "Flash" and two of his county fair companions, releasing them into the pond. All three fish were spotted throughout the summer. In subsequent years, Flash's comrades disappeared. But Flash grew to be king fish of the pond, outweighing all the perch and sunfish!

One summer, we added five baby ducks to the pond. That fall, ice formed, limiting the surface area available for ducks to swim. I purchased three hundred feet of extension cord as well as a ninety-five dollar industrial bubbler to maintain a patch of open water. Temperatures continued to plummet and the pool shrunk.

One morning, we noticed there were only four ducks. *Had one duck flown south for the winter?* A few days later, there were only three ducks, one mottled brown and two white. *Do domestic ducks migrate?*

Worried we were losing the ducks to a predator rather than migration, I decided drastic measures were required to save their lives. I dressed the kids in black, retrieved a massive plastic storage container from the barn, and loaded it in the back of my minivan.

At sunset, giddy with excitement, we confirmed the ducks were asleep, then drove the minivan to the edge of the pond. The kids and I snuck up, undetected, and pounced on the sleeping ducks. Gracie, Callie and I each had one.

"Grab them! Grab them! Don't let them get away!" I exclaimed as the startled ducks beat at the kids with their wings. After the girls and I unceremoniously stuffed the loudly protesting ducks into the plastic storage container, Christopher snapped the lid and held it shut.

Christopher rode in the back of the van, as his job was to prevent the ducks from escaping. Our home was less than ten minutes from Boyne Mountain ski resort. A large pond, adorned with fountains, faced the ski hill at Boyne Mountain's main lodge. The fountains ran all winter long, and I'd noticed that several wild ducks made the pond their year-round residence.

I pulled the minivan to the parking lot closest to the darkest corner of the pond. The kids giggled uproariously, as we peered around the empty parking lot, which would be teaming with cars in a few weeks, when the resort opened for the ski season. Gently prying the top off the container, the girls and I each fished out an indignant duck, and ran full-steam to the edge of the pond, chucking our ducks into the water.

We watched in trepidation, desperately hoping our pets would like their new home. The domestic ducks looked nothing like their wild cousins. The two white ones especially stuck out like two sore thumbs. They huddled in a group, unaccustomed to the luxurious expansiveness their new habitat afforded.

The kids and I nonchalantly strolled to a little fishing pier that jutted into the water. Delighted to find a little duck-food vending dispenser at the end of the dock, we coaxed our ducks over with the promise of food.

The next day, we returned to the pier, pretending to purchase duck food while surreptitiously bringing our own. I worried that someone might notice how our ducks hustled to the dock when they saw us, clearly recognizing the humans who provided their daily bread. However, nobody showed up to make us reclaim our water fowl.

Years later, after our family had moved back to Colorado (yes, we eventually moved *back* to Colorado), our friends sent pictures of our ducks in the Boyne Mountain pond at the start of each new ski season.

Reminiscing on those early days in Michigan, I struggled to recall one-on-one time with John. Before the kids were born, we used to spent hours over a cup of coffee or glass of wine, talking about life, excitedly making plans for our next big business, or dreaming up our next travel adventure.

Earlier in our marriage, we always exercised together. Even after the kids were born, we went bike riding and cross country skiing together when we had a babysitter. When did that stop?

John had been an avid reader when we met, devouring personal growth, motivational, and inspirational books. He insisted that I read them too, which I did reluctantly. It wasn't that I didn't enjoy the reading, but that I didn't like being told what to do.

After the kids were born, I didn't have time to read. Scanning my mental memory bank, I couldn't remember John reading at the farmhouse in Michigan. In fact, I couldn't find him in any of the scenes with chickens, ducks, or even the pond.

Where was John? I wondered. *We didn't have cable television in Michigan. I can't remember watching movies. It's true he traveled a lot. But when John was home, where was he? Was John on the computer that whole time?* I truly couldn't recall.

CHAPTER 6

Since gardening and animal husbandry weren't my strong suits, living off the land was clearly out of the question. Happily, I was married to a rainmaker.

In a lovely twist of fate, the helmet camera market in the United States lagged while John was working for V.I.O. His solution? To relocate our family to Europe for two months as he solidified European markets.

As part of this divinely-inspired strategy, we spent weeks traveling to Barcelona, Zurich, and Paris. And for one entire month, John rented a villa with a pool nestled in the foothills of the Dolomite Mountains overlooking Lake Garda in Italy.

In the little Italian village of Riva del Garda, you could pull up to something that looked exactly like a gas pump, but it contained wine. Simply choose your varietal, dispense the wine into a ten-liter jug, and pay at the pump. Brilliant!

Eventually, heavy travel requirements and a difference in philosophy led to John's resignation from V.I.O. GoPro was following the outdoor consumer distribution strategy John had outlined to V.I.O. However, V.I.O.'s investors and board of directors were committed to pursuing military contracts.

V.I.O.'s sales reps in the UK, having experienced similar frustration with the company's military-centered approach, launched their own helmet camera brand and asked John to join them. John agreed to become the master distributor in the Americas for their new brand, Drift Helmet Cameras.

Spectacular timing, combined with John's connections in the outdoor industry and Drift's unique set of features, created the perfect storm. Drift grabbed onto GoPro's coattails, and participated in the skyrocketing growth of the helmet camera industry. John and I found the endeavor both exhilarating and terrifying. More than once, I hand-wrote business checks for over one hundred thousand dollars!

John and I held our breath each time we paid for a container load of helmet cameras, offering a silent prayer for safe passage, as the ship crossed the Pacific Ocean from China. We'd heard harrowing stories of outdoor manufacturers who had lost an entire season of inventory when freighters lost crates in a storm or were destroyed by fire at sea.

Our precious merchandise was not necessarily safe when it finally arrived on American soil. Consumer electronics were prime targets for warehouse bandits and internet scammers.

More significantly, we knew the consumer electronics industry was highly volatile. One single innovation in a competitor's product could render our entire remaining stock worthless overnight. It happened in the flash of an instant. One day, you're the belle of the ball. The next, you're selling pallets of inventory for pennies on the dollar.

Miraculously, Drift kept pace with market innovation, sometimes even beating GoPro to market with the latest, greatest feature. The numbers got bigger. More sales. More inventory. More warehouse space. More profit.

Being a master distributor meant that we made money on every single Drift Helmet Camera sold, from Argentina to Alaska. We were living on Cloud 9, although we knew that

cloud could become a hurricane, wiping out our entire life's savings in the blink of an eye.

I was responsible for maintaining MyPOV360.com, which was our retail website. I also handled accounting, spreadsheets, marketing materials, and sales letters. John took care of the forward-facing part of the business while I handled much of the backend activity. Sometimes I hired a babysitter. But more often than not, we weaved business into the fabric of our chaotic little domicile.

In addition to cash free-flowing into our bank account from a wildly successful (albeit highly volatile) helmet camera business, John's grandmother started sending annual monetary gifts to avoid inheritance taxes.

John's grandfather had been a vice president of Kraft Foods for twenty-five years. A quarter of a century of prudent investing yielded a fortune that would be divided between to two children, and eventually, two grandchildren. John and his cousin would eventually receive the entirety of the family fortune.

With the influx of money from helmet cameras and generous relatives, we suddenly found ourselves in need of financial guidance. Fortunately, we had Todd, a CPA (certified public accountant) who had been working with John in his father's rep business for years. Todd's competency was unmatched. If accounting was an Olympic sport, I'm fairly sure he would be a three-time medalist. Todd is the only accountant I've ever met who makes house calls.

Twice a year, Todd arrived at the door of our ramshackle farmhouse wearing a full three-piece suit. He donned shoe protectors over his expensive, highly-polished shoes. I often wondered whether the shoe covers were meant to protect our carpet from his shoes or his shoes from our carpet. Todd drank Diet Coke, which I kept at the back of the fridge just for his visits.

We escorted Todd through a nursery and playroom (littered with assorted toys), past Christopher's bed on the floor (that doubled as Bentley's dog bed), past our walk-in closet (with clothes waiting to be returned to their drawers or

hangers), past our bed (hastily made in anticipation of his arrival), to a long desk with two computers rising like trees atop a mounded hill of papers.

Todd was a master at bringing order to chaos. He provided a beacon as we navigated the churning waters of United States tax law. Despite Todd's best efforts, our tax bill swelled to three times our average annual salary. One day, he looked around our disheveled master bedroom as if seeing it for the first time and remarked, "I don't think I've ever seen this volume of money flow through someone's bedroom!"

"I'm guessing you don't get a lot of high-end prostitutes!" I quipped.

A booming helmet camera distribution business meant more travel for John. Again, he was largely absent for blocks of time. Though I had a very supportive network of family and friends, I was ridiculously negligent when it came to asking for help.

One morning when the kids were in elementary school, I got an early morning notification that school was closed due to a late-season blizzard. I smiled, knowing how happy the kids would be to receive the news when they got up.

John was in Denver on a business trip, and I was capitalizing on early morning, kid-free time to get computer work done. A couple hours later, I heard little feet padding into my bedroom. I turned to see Christopher. He had a concerned look on his face.

"Mama, Callie said her stomach hurts."

I was in the middle of something that felt important at the time. "I'm sure Callie's fine. Tell her to sit on the potty chair," I replied, offering the panacea for ninety percent of childhood stomach pain.

Minutes later, Christopher returned. "Callie said she needs you to come now. She said it hurts so bad she just wants to die."

Time seemed to stop. Though I'm sure I was moving at lightning speed, it felt like I was moving through quicksand. My vibrant, sunny, perpetually happy child would never use those words. Never. Something was horribly wrong.

I passed Gracie in the kitchen. "Callie's in a lot of pain," Gracie confirmed.

"I know, baby," I replied. "I want you to pack an overnight bag for you, Callie, and Christopher. Remember to pack underwear and a charging cord for the iPad. I think we're heading to the hospital."

I took the stairs to the kids' upstairs bedroom two at a time. Callie was clutching her stomach and crying. A call to our family doctor confirmed that the location of the pain indicated the possibility of an appendicitis. We were to go straight to the emergency room in Petoskey.

As a blizzard was raging outside, I worried my minivan might not make it out of our long driveway, which was barricaded with snow drifts. Gunning the engine, I punched through the drifts, and slid out onto a vacant country road.

Snow plows hadn't gone through this rural part of the county, making our trip to the hospital a harrowing journey. I called John en route to let him know what was happening.

"Do you think I need to come home?" he asked. From the sound of his voice, I could tell he thought I was overreacting. After all, there was historical evidence to support this theory.

When we lived in Denver, Callie had slipped in the shower at the swimming pool. I'd called John to say we were on our way to the emergency room, because Callie's fall had caused a massive lump on her head.

"There's a chance she's got a cerebral hemorrhage," I'd said shakily.

John met us in the swimming pool parking lot. After a brief inspection, he found a similar lump on the other side of Callie's bumpy skull.

The possibility that I was overreacting was not out of the question.

"Let's wait to see what the doctor says," I replied in response to his offer to come home.

Soon after we arrived at the hospital, the surgeon confirmed that Callie did indeed have appendicitis. She was immediately prepped for surgery. Because she was so small, the surgeon said he would have to make an incision on her belly instead of going in laparoscopically. This would mean a slightly higher risk of infection and a longer, more painful recovery.

As Gracie and Christopher occupied themselves with the iPad, I gazed helplessly at my little seven-year-old girl, with an IV in her arm. I called John.

"Well, it looks like our girl is going in for surgery," I said as nonchalantly as possible. "It's not worth booking a flight home, since the surgery will be done before you even make it to the airport. We'll be spending the night at the hospital. But the doctor thinks Callie should be able to go home tomorrow, or the next day."

"Okay," John said. "Be sure to keep me posted." I breathed a sigh of relief. The kids were my responsibility. If John came home, it would feel like I hadn't done my job or that I had let him down.

The surgery went well. I spent the night in the hospital with Callie while our friends, Chris and Tammie, picked Gracie and Christopher up.

The next morning, all hell broke loose. Tammie called in the early morning to let me know that Christopher wasn't feeling well. He had a low-grade fever.

"What do you think?" I asked. "Is he feeling good enough to go to school?"

"Well…" Tammie replied, "He's clearly feeling punk. I can take the day off from work and stay home with him if you want."

I recoiled at the thought. It was hard enough to ask friends to take my kids on a school night. Having Tammie use one of her valuable sick days to stay home with Christopher was out of the question.

"Oh, I'm sure he's fine going to school. Callie is supposed to be released from the hospital later this morning. If Christopher gets worse, I'm sure the school nurse will call, and I'll pick him up."

I looked at Callie, who was sleeping in a morphine-induced coma. It was hard to imagine she would be ready for release in a few short hours.

Anticipating the possibility that my presence would be needed on the home front, I cajoled the nursing staff into fast-tracking Callie's release paperwork.

"She's leaving today?" the nurse asked in surprise. "Normally, if a patient is on morphine, we keep them more than twenty-four hours. But if the doctor said Callie will be ready to go today, I'll get her paperwork processed."

Mid-morning, I received the call I'd been dreading. Christopher was indeed sick and needed to be picked up. I asked that Gracie be ready for pick up at the same time as well.

By late morning, I was heading home with Callie, who was still lethargic and heavily medicated, Christopher, who was sweating with a fever and moaning pathetically, and Gracie, who stayed in the car with her siblings while I picked up medication at the pharmacy.

The next twenty-four hours was one of the most traumatic periods of my life. When the morphine wore off, Callie was in utter agony. No amount of Tylenol with codeine or Advil would take the edge off her pain. Every sob elicited a corresponding cry of agony.

I sat in the middle of the couch with Christopher on my right and Callie on my left, curled up in a ball, with her head in my lap.

"Mama, please don't move," she whimpered pathetically. "And don't breathe. When your chest moves, it hurts my belly."

"Maybe you'd do better just laying still on the couch by yourself?" I suggested.

"Please don't leave me, Mama! I need you here. Just please don't move."

Meanwhile, Christopher sat on my other side, looking alarmingly listless. His motor skills were slow. His temperature was climbing.

I told Gracie I would pay her ten dollars an hour to be my nurse. She had to supply Christopher with ice chips and keep a cold compress on his head. She was also responsible for administering alternating doses of Tylenol and Advil to Christopher and Callie, tracking times she'd given them medication.

John called. "How is Callie doing?"

"Well, she's in a lot of pain. I had to get her released from the hospital because Christopher needed to be picked up at school. He's sick, and I didn't want Tammie to have to use a sick day." I did my best to keep the strain out of my voice.

"Do you need me to come home?"

Why did those words seem like a challenge to me? As if having John come home would be admitting defeat...

"No, no. I've got this, sweetie. Again, it would probably all be over by the time you got here. There's no reason to interrupt your business trip. We'll be fine."

A little later, I called my parents with an update and repeated the same mantra to them. "Don't worry. I've got this."

Despite Tammie's insistence, I refused her offer to help, when she called later that evening. "I've got it under control, sweet lady. You guys have already done more than enough. If you came over, I'd feel like I needed to turn my attention to you and Chris instead of the kids. We've got it down to a system. We're fine."

But we weren't fine. Callie was in excruciating pain. Christopher was near-catatonic. His high fever likely caused the onset of OCD weeks later, a condition that plagued him for years. I spent a gut-wrenching night attending to two babies who were both in severe discomfort.

In the early morning, just before sunrise, I was shaking with exhaustion, when I heard movement in the front entryway of the house.

Hearing the strain in my voice the previous evening, my parents had gotten in the car and driven ten hours through the night from Minnesota to Michigan to be with me. Seeing them. I burst into tears. Callie cried out in torment as my heaving chest caused stabbing pain in her gut. My parents pried her little body from my chest and I collapsed into a dreamless sleep.

My martyr complex created a lot of suffering. Why did I feel like I needed to do every soccer shuttle, without a single exception, for all three kids? Every doctor's appointment, dentist appointment, parent teacher conference, music lesson, sporting event, band concert, school play, and vocal performance? Nighttime reading sessions, help with homework, birthday parties? It's true that John traveled a lot when the kids were little. When he was home, was it John who didn't want to be inconvenienced or me who didn't want to do the inconveniencing? Either way, for years, I played the role of a single parent.

CHAPTER 7

If business travel pulled our family apart, it was family trips that brought us back together. Away from home, John took more time away from work to enjoy morning coffee, ice cream, and sunsets. Life was more relaxed, more fun. The kids got to know an earlier version of John, one that was more attentive and carefree.

One year, our family accidentally took a trip to Thailand. Whether the accident was a good one or a bad one is subjective, weighed against the merits of the alternate path, a path that would have taken us to India...had nine-year-old Gracie's Indian visa been approved.

The month-long journey through India would have included a week-long train ride across the subcontinent in a first class rail car, a visit to the Taj Mahal, connecting with my parents in Amritsar near the border of Pakistan, and traveling to a small village in the northernmost part of the country to attend an Indian wedding. At the wedding, we were to be guests of one of Drift's founders who was from that little town in the Punjab province, many of whose residents had never seen a white person. The girls and I would have worn the opulent, handmade Indian wedding attire that had been special ordered for the occasion.

Though Gracie's Indian visa was ultimately denied, I didn't go down without a fight. The Indian consulate used an intermediary agency to accept visa applications. In the weeks leading up to our departure, I called the visa processing agency daily. Each time, my entreaties were met by a thickly accented Indian voice that I'm sure was intended to sound reassuring, but actually sounded quite condescending to the practiced ear.

"Mrs. Rounds. Please don't worry. The Indian government is famous for its bureaucracy. The rest of your family's Indian visas have been issued. I'm sure Gracie's will be approved as well. Just have patience."

Five days before departure, the agency official began to squirm. "Highly unusual. Not sure what's wrong…" In the end, Gracie's visa was never processed. The visa agency had to battle the consulate in Chicago just to get Gracie's passport back in time for our flight to Dubai. By a stroke of good fortune, the visa agent assigned to secure said passport had nerves of steel.

Despite the fact they'd had Gracie's passport for two months, the Indian consulate refused to release it, saying the visa was still "in process." An employee from the visa agency was dispatched to the Indian consulate in Chicago.

"Sir, a US passport is property of the US government. You have no right to hold it," the visa agent politely informed the Indian consulate official.

"Yes, but the Indian consulate is considered foreign soil. You have no jurisdiction here."

"That's all well and good," the plucky visa agent replied. "But when you go home to see your family tonight, I will see that the police are waiting outside the consulate gate."

An hour later, at four o'clock in the evening, precisely twenty-four hours prior to our departure from Detroit to Dubai, India's Chicago consulate general released Gracie's passport to the courier. Since we lived in northern Michigan, the passport was send via Fed-Ex express first overnight to a hub in Traverse City, Michigan, where I collected the package, then hauled ass to Detroit's Metropolitan Airport for the flight to Dubai.

I am actually embarrassed for my behavior over the ensuing days. Rather than enjoying our two expansive rooms at the five star Ritz Carlton in Dubai, I agonized over Gracie's missing visa. I even went to the Indian embassy in Dubai to take up the fight again.

"We would be happy to review your daughter's visa application," the Indian official replied. "But it will take two weeks to run her background check with Interpol."

An Interpol background check for a nine-year-old? Were these people nuts? There's a good chance my heated reply left me red-flagged in India's visa processing system. Alas, there is scant hope I'll ever see the Indian subcontinent during this lifetime.

The date of our flights from Dubai to India came and went. Our stay in Dubai extended from five days to ten as we tried to figure out what to do.

John did his level best to turn lemons into lemonade. When our reservation at the Ritz ended, John rented an apartment in a luxury sky rise overlooking the Persian Gulf. The kids road a camel on the beach. We strolled the Dubai Mall, where we marveled at ATM machines with thirteen hundred dollar withdrawal limits, and Arab men buying lingerie and astoundingly expensive jewelry for their burka-clad wives.

John wanted to take us to the tallest building in the world, the Burj Khalifa. So he asked the Ritz's concierge to schedule us for high tea at the Burj. Little did we know, there are two Burj's in Dubai: the Burj Khalifa, and the Burj Al Arab, the world's only seven star hotel, which is shaped like a giant sailboat and is arguably the most iconic structure in Dubai.

Unbeknownst to us, high tea was served not at the world's tallest structure, but at the seven star Burj Al Arab. And so our children had the distinct honor of partaking in a high tea that would have done the Queen of England proud.

I'm fairly sure we were the only guests under seventy years of age. We giggled at the sheer formality of it all. The first three-tiered serving stand featured canapés, finger sandwiches, a meat pie, smoked salmon, pickled vegetables, some kind of cheesy potato casserole, and a variety of fancy hors d'oeuvres. The second three-tiered tray included scones with jam and clotted cream, lemon curd, nuts, berries, mochi, and a colorful assortment of little cookies and cakes in all shapes and sizes. And that is how we ended up with three kids under ten years of age jacked up on sugar at the world's only seven star hotel.

Though two weeks in Dubai was never part of the original itinerary, with this little "delay of game," we became more keenly aware of Christopher's unique and fascinating attributes.

From the time he was two, we called Christopher our "finder boy." If we were missing keys, sunglasses, jackets, a purse, scissors, etc., we simply asked Christopher where they were because he oddly had the answer. In time, it became so commonplace, we thought nothing of it.

The day after we arrived in Dubai, we were in a taxi, driving back to the hotel from the Dubai Mall, when five year old Christopher began telling the taxi driver where to make his turns. After four or five turns, the driver said, "Wow! You must have been living here for a long time. As much as I drive, it's still hard for me to remember all these turns!"

"No..." I replied, finally keying into what was happening. "We just arrived late last night. Maybe this is the route we took from the airport?"

"Yes, this is the same route you would have taken from the airport. But there are many turns. How does he know where to go?" the driver asked.

"I have no idea!" I exclaimed, peering around at the signs on roadways and storefronts, all of which were in Arabic. It occurred to me that it wouldn't matter if the signs used the Latin alphabet, Greek, or Chinese. Christopher had learning differences that yielded a learning delay. After three years of pre-school and kindergarten, five-year-old Christopher didn't recognize the letters of the alphabet.

"It was dark when we came in. And the flight was over sixteen hours. We were exhausted. I have no idea how he's doing this!"

Excited at the attention he was receiving, Christopher continued to call out directions. As we neared the hotel, Christopher told the driver to go straight, as the driver signaled to turn left.

"Well, it looks like you made your first mistake, little man!" the driver exclaimed. "Your hotel is this way."

"No, I didn't make a mistake," Christopher replied stubbornly. "There's construction ahead. You're going to need to turn around and go straight through that light, then turn left at the next block." Sure enough, he was correct.

As if that wasn't odd enough, Christopher had this strange habit of sidling up to women wearing burkas and starting conversations. Most kids are intimidated by adults. My three argue over who gets to sit next to the stranger on the airplane. But even my precocious girls were a bit reticent in the company of women wearing burkas.

To my surprise, nearly every woman Christopher approached dropped her face covering and responded—some in English, some in Arabic. At first, I thought it was luck, or chance.

Maybe I just haven't been paying close attention. Maybe he's getting shut down repeatedly before finding someone who will strike up a conversation. But that didn't prove to be the case. In addition to having something of a photographic memory, Christopher seemed to have the ability to consistently decipher which women were willing to chat. He could instantly create a heart-connection with people, a connection that seemed to superseded language and culture.

Witnessing Christopher interact in this new environment, I saw my son in a new light. I had to travel half way around the globe to discover what had been right in front of me all the time. Had we stayed home, I'm not entirely sure I would have gained the insight that allowed me to see the very special nature of Christopher's gifts.

Up until that point, I'd always looked at Christopher's learning delay as a setback, because it impeded his progress in school. We had spent countless hours and significant dollars on various forms of therapy to optimize brain function. These interventions included vision therapy, neurofeedback therapy, allergy testing, nutritional supplements, occupational therapy, and any cockamamie strategy I mined from the internet.

In this new environment, I realized there was absolutely nothing wrong with Christopher's brain. In fact, his ability to connect with other people (something computers can't do), might, in fact, be superior to storing and retrieving information (which computers can do). What if Christopher's mind is more highly adapted for the expansion of human consciousness?

For the first time, I began to see the world from his perspective. I learned to close my eyes, relax my mind, and actually see the world as Christopher sees it. *Christopher's secret is that he doesn't filter anything. Most people discard ninety-nine percent of the sensory input they receive. Christopher sees everything. He hears everything. He doesn't judge a thing as worth noticing or not. Everything —and everyone—is worthy of his attention.*

Whilst I was traipsing around Dubai seeing the world through Christopher-colored glasses, John was using his million mile magic status with United airlines to switch our flights from India to Thailand, since Thailand, unlike India, had no visa entry requirement for Americans.

With absolutely no planning, flying by the very seat of our pants, John booked us into two delightful little villas, overgrown with ivy and flowering vines in the very heart of Chiang Mai, Thailand.

Our family could have probably crammed into one villa. But two villas in Chiang Mai were still a fraction of the price we had paid for lodging in Dubai. I was a little nervous we weren't sharing walls with the kids. After all, Gracie, the eldest, was a mere nine years old. But the kids were thoroughly delighted to have their own space, and John and I were delighted to have a little adult privacy.

In Thailand, we continued to observe Christopher's unique ability to connect with people. The Thai culture is naturally warm and welcoming. This hospitality is even more pronounced when traveling with children. We were instantly treated as family. So much so, that it was days before the staff informed us that Christopher had been getting up at four in the morning to hang out with the night time security guard.

Apparently, the security guard would take Christopher into the kitchen to make him food. After breakfast, Christopher and the security guard (who didn't speak a lick of English), would walk around the dark, silent grounds, catching lizards, feeding fish in the pond, each chatting each to the other in his own native tongue.

The staff at the little boutique hotel in Chiang Mai doted on the girls as much as Christopher. They spent hours dressing the girls in costumes worn by traditional Thai dancers, styling their hair, and applying copious amounts of make-up. Then they clapped with delight as the girls executed dance moves or spoke Thai phrases they had been taught.

In Chiang Mai, we rode elephants through a river, held monkeys, ate insects at the night market, and even bought a piece of artwork from an elephant (a nicer thought than buying from the elephant's owner) after watching her paint a picture with a brush held in her trunk.

When it came time to leave Chiang Mai, tears were shed, both ours and those of our hotel's staff.

From Chiang Mai, we traveled to Phuket in the southern part of Thailand, where we swam with a baby elephant in the ocean and met a delightful family of world travelers with daughters the same age as Gracie and Callie. Several nights of sleepovers ensued, and we still follow each other's adventures to this day.

I was very proud of John for making that trip happen. His miraculous Thailand for India travel swap was a testimony to his commitment to our family. My strategy was to engage in a senseless battle with the Indian consulate. Meanwhile, John was concocting a "Plan B" to save his family from suffering disappointment. My heart swelled with admiration, relief...and love.

Sometimes life chooses the experience we need, rather than the experience we think we want. Though India was the destination we'd originally chosen, our family fell hopelessly in love with the culture, food, and hospitality of Thailand. More importantly, we were grateful and humbled by the soul-centric connections the Thai people inspired, both within our family and outside of it.

What if divorce ends up being like the failed trip to India: a course-correction that leads to some place richer and more impactful than our original destination?

CHAPTER 8

Our family enjoyed many other adventures, both in Michigan and abroad, thanks to the income and flexibility our Drift helmet camera distribution business provided. Drift's UK-based founders, who were previously employed with Price Waterhouse Cooper, decided to create a new North American subsidiary and hired John to run it.

John selected Eagle, Colorado for Drift's new North American headquarters. Located in the Vail Valley, Eagle's proximity to world-class skiers, mountain bikers, white water rafters, and other outdoor enthusiasts would contribute to Drift's grass-roots marketing efforts.

At least that's what John told Drift's owners. In truth, he had been itching to get back to the mountains. After attending high school in Vail and spending a few years in his mid-twenties working as a ski instructor in Vail and Beaver Creek, to John, Vail felt like home.

Thanks to the crazy success of our helmet camera distribution business, we were able to move into a million dollar log home. We purchased our house in Eagle at the precise bottom of a nationwide recession. A real estate agent, who was trying to avoid foreclosure on a house that she herself had bought out of foreclosure, sold us our home at a twenty-five percent discount. We were ecstatic.

And so on August 10, 2012, after over a decade of living dramatically below our means, we moved into a spectacular post and beam log home in the Vail Valley. Perched atop a promontory, our home had an outstanding view of a wide, sweeping gulch, populated by stunted cedar and sage brush. The following winter, we would gleefully watch the over one hundred and fifty elk who wended their way down the valley each morning, dutifully following their instinctual winter migratory pattern.

Though we were excited to move into our beautiful new mountain home, the kids and I were bereft at the thought of leaving our dearest friends. Ages ten, eight, and seven, Gracie, Callie and Christopher were in elementary school. The farm in Boyne City had been our home for nearly six years, which was the longest we ever lived in one place. Leaving our friends…again…was a heartrending experience.

Packing boxes for yet another cross-country journey, I lamented over the massive heap of belongings we'd managed to accumulate in a few short years. I pined for days of yore, when all my earthly possessions fit into a single (albeit packed) vehicle. In retrospect, all I can say is…be careful what you wish for.

John secured office space above a trendy little ice cream shop and deli in downtown Eagle Ranch, hired a few key employees, and began a highly targeted marketing campaign to solidify Drift's position in the Americas. As John managed his small team of Drift employees, the kids and I explored new passions, made new friends, and developed new skills.

Our dog, Bentley, made friends with a fox from a nearby den. We made friends with delightful human neighbors who were quick to make us feel welcome.

We moved to Colorado just before Gracie started fifth grade. At the ripe age of ten, Gracie had already inherited John's foresightedness, determination, and keen business acumen.

Gracie's peers recognized her leadership skills, as evidenced by the fact that, after just two weeks at her new school, she was elected president of her fifth grade class (though perhaps the fact that she promised iPads to every kid in her grade had something to do with that...).

In any case, Gracie had a strong, confident, entrepreneurial spirit. When the teacher announced the school would be hosting a fifth grade economics fair, Gracie was ecstatic. "Mom! We get to buy and sell things with real money!"

The rules were simple. Each student was allowed to spend ten dollars. Whoever made the most money from their ten dollar investment was the winner. Gracie and I brainstormed ideas.

Suddenly, I thought of our goldfish. "Hey!" I exclaimed. "Remember how you guys won Flash and the other two goldfish at the county fair? I said it was stupid to pay a dollar for the goldfish ping pong game because you can just buy a goldfish for nineteen cents at Walmart. What if we run a goldfish ping-pong game like they do at the county fair?"

Now, Gracie had always had a heightened respect for life in its many forms. This sensitivity even extended to mosquitos, who she verbally encouraged to leave as opposed to swatting. If someone killed a mosquito in her presence, Gracie recoiled in horror, imbuing an odd sense of shame in the perpetrator.

As a rule, Gracie isn't a big fan of keeping any animal —even a fish—captive for pleasure. Though the prospect of this highly lucrative idea was tempting, her practical-minded, conservationist tendencies were triggered. "Oh, I don't know, Mom. What if people don't have fish food?"

"We could take a little hit on the profit and buy some food to give away with every fish!"

Reader, please note the use of the pronoun "we."

Gracie was still dubious. "But how do you know the kids will take care of the fish?" she wisely asked.

"These are feeder fish," I said brazenly, caught up in the brilliance of my own idea. "By offering them as pets, we are actually saving their lives!" A voice in my head said,

Helicopter mom, coming in for a landing! But I brushed the thought away like an annoying fly. After all, what could be more personally validating than having my fifth grade daughter, the newly elected class president, win the school's economics fair?

In honesty, I don't know how many of the details I left to Gracie and how many I took upon myself. But I do remember bagging fish, scooping them out of a huge bucket of water, in the bathroom tub. And I remember bringing those bagged fish and all the supplies to school, where a teacher watched in horror as Gracie set up her little game. And I also remember the panicked voicemail from Gracie's teacher with a parent's voice in the background saying, "These bags are leaking! Who's the idiot who decided it was a good idea to bring fish to a school economic fair?"

To my credit (and Gracie's, I suppose), our family was instantaneously known to every parent at Brush Creek Elementary School—a feat not easily accomplished when you're new in town!

As we settled into our new home, we discovered a fantastic single track mountain bike trail that descended three miles through the dewy, sweet-scented sage to the very door of Brush Creek Elementary School. In the blink of an eye, our three children became skilled mountain bikers, often choosing the winding mountain bike path over the more direct, paved bike path. John and I were fiercely proud.

Eagle hosts Colorado's annual high school mountain biking state championships and has several highly developed mountain bike trail systems. I'd become a decent mountain biker in Michigan. But the trails in and around Eagle took my technical biking skills to a whole new level. After accompanying the kids on their single track ride to school, I continued to bike through sunlit sage and cedars. The brown dirt hills and golden native grasses of the high desert became my church, my sanctuary, my home. I soon took the shape and form of a Colorado mountain mama.

When winter arrived, we enrolled all three kids in the prestigious Ski Club Vail ski racing program. Gracie wanted to become the next Mickaela Shiffrin and in my heart of hearts, I believed she could do it.

In a supreme display of commitment and discipline—both mine and Gracie's—Gracie left elementary school at noon on Wednesdays and Fridays to attend optional ski club trainings that were above and beyond the normal Saturday and Sunday practices. The season spanned half the year, stretching from November through April, with ski camps in the summer. My Honda Odyssey quickly became our second home.

Ten-year-old Gracie knew I was not to be trusted to remember all the gear she needed for practices. I was continually befuddled by which skis were used for free skiing, giant slalom, or slalom. Sometimes she needed padding, sometimes she didn't. Then there were race suits, helmets, chin guards, goggles, mittens or gloves, snow pants, neck gaiters, poles, ski boots, thermal layers, etc. With a diligence that reminded me of the Roald Dahl character, Matilda, Gracie dutifully managed her own scheduling, kept track of a small mountain of gear, and somehow maintained straight As in school.

Vail ski resort was a forty-five minute drive from our house in Eagle. Zipping up and down the I-70 corridor for ski club trainings and races in the winter, club soccer in the fall, 4-H soccer in the spring, as well as forays into lacrosse, hockey, voice lessons, and theater, I came to identify with the little red ball attached to a paddle ball paddle. However, my time spent driving carpools was far from idle. In the car, my relationship with the children blossomed and unfolded.

Our chaotic schedules rarely left time for family dinners around a dinner table. The car became the backdrop for nearly every meaningful conversation with the kids. It was the place where I would first hear about struggles with friends, school, or a new romantic interest. It was the place the kids were most receptive to receiving input...or at least that's what I liked to think. After all, where else could they go?

I soon realized that carpools were the most entertaining, enjoyable parts of my day. When there were other kids in the car, I was nearly invisible, like an NPC in a video game. Fading into the background, I was a fly on the wall, listening to the kids chatter about topics not normally discussed in adult company. Over time, I accumulated valuable intel that allowed me to offer guidance, not only to my own kids, but to their friends as well. The car was sacred space where we established a bond of trust.

Car rides also played a foundational role in Callie's music career. Most people know what it's like to get a song stuck in their head. Callie had earworms on steroids. She sang Adele's "Rolling in the Deep" over and over every time we got in the car for three. Solid. Months. To this day, Christopher twitches every time he hears "Rolling in the Deep."

As Callie's ninth birthday approached, she discovered there would be an audition for *America's Got Talent* in Denver. "Mom! That's what I want for a birthday present! I want to audition for *America's Got Talent!* I don't need another birthday gift. Just that. Please, please, please, please, please?"

"Wow, honey. *America's Got Talent?* That's kind of a big ask, don't you think?" Nevertheless, I researched the audition process, and found that it wasn't expensive or even complicated. It just required a full day in Denver. "Okay!" I exclaimed. "Let's go for it!"

I found a full length, fuchsia silk dress listed on Ebay as the "Girl's Pageant Party Long Dress Princess Wedding Bridesmaid Maxi Gown." It fit Callie's personality perfectly! I also had one hundred "I heart Callie" buttons made.

Upon arriving at the *America's Got Talent* auditions in Denver, newly nine-year-old Callie grabbed the box of buttons along with a package of Oreos we'd brought to hand out and dutifully began canvasing the room, as if *America's Got Talent* contestants were chosen by popular vote.

Up to this point, most of the other *America's Got Talent* performers had been standoffish and a little cagy, like CIA agents guarding trade secrets. But even the most stoic couldn't keep from smiling, when this little fuchsia-clad girl with tight blonde curls bounded up, offering an "I heart Callie" button and an Oreo cookie.

Conversations spontaneously broke out as Callie's effervescence bubbled over. Many fellow auditionees were flattered and happy to indulge when Callie asked, "Can I have my picture taken with you? Just in case you become famous?"

Callie befriended a girl named Aaliyah Rose, who was just a couple years older than her. Neither of the girls made it on *America's Got Talent*. But a few months later, we were watching an ad for the Disney Music Awards on the Disney Channel, when we saw Aaliyah Rose singing "Let It Go" from the movie *Frozen* in an ad promoting the upcoming awards!

"That's what I want to do, Mom! I want to be a singer on the Disney Channel, like Aaliyah Rose!" Callie proclaimed wildly.

My personal validation indicator started pinging. *Imagine! We could be famous!*

With that, we upped the mileage game. Callie began taking voice lessons from Stuart Whitmore at All That Entertainment, two and a half hours away in Denver. The voice lessons paid off. Callie sang the national anthem at Denver's Mile High Stadium for the opening of a professional lacrosse game. She cleaned house at talent shows the following summer, earning five hundred dollars in prize money.

I took helicopter parenting to new heights by writing Callie's first recorded song, "Always Mountain Time," for a talent contest. The contest was being judged by a local country music radio station, whose tag line was...wait for it... Always Mountain Time!

We had the song professionally recorded at a studio in Minturn, Colorado.

Again, reader, please note the use of the pronoun "we."

To Callie's immense chagrin, "Always Mountain Time" is still up on YouTube and her friends occasionally find it.

Our life in Colorado was really good. We had multiple circles of friends. Surrounded by three hundred and sixty degree views of the Colorado Rockies, our house was perfect for entertaining. We had a movie room downstairs where kids congregated on a regular basis. I loved hosting parties and having dinner with friends.

In addition to developing a large social network of parents whose kids participated in the same soccer, lacrosse, and ski programs as our kids, we formed an additional socially active group of neighbors in our little Highlands sub-community of Eagle Ranch. These friends were well-traveled and had fascinatingly diverse backgrounds. I was co-president of the middle school PTO (Parent-Teacher Organization) and an active member of the elementary school PTO. For me, life was hectic, but good.

Our foray into the helmet camera industry ended when Drift Helmet Cameras was crushed by the force of GoPro's tidal wave, and Drift was squeezed out of the few sponsorship opportunities John's team had managed to finagle. The Drift founders opted to close up shop in the United States, retreating to European markets to lick their wounds.

For over a year and a half after the Drift Americas project ended, our family stayed in Eagle. John dabbled in minor real estate investments, and I sold advertising for a local magazine publication.

Years of ski racing and a questionable genetic legacy had left John with premature deterioration in his hips. For a decade, he'd been attempting to fend off hip surgeries with every alternative treatment on the planet. All were for naught.

Eventually, John made the decision to have both his hips replaced in two surgeries that were six weeks apart by one of the most reputable hip surgeons in Denver. Little did we know...when it comes to surgery, the anesthesiologist is nearly as important as the surgeon.

I was incredulous to discover that hip replacements were considered outpatient procedures! We arrived at the surgical center early in the morning as John's hip replacement was one of the first surgeries of the day.

Prior to surgery, John told the anesthesiologist that he didn't respond to novocaine and that dental work required several times the normal dose to get him numb. He also had a history of needing high doses of painkillers to take the edge off pain.

"I'm a big guy. You're a big guy. I get it," the anesthesiologist replied in a thick Russian accent. "We big guys need a lot of drugs. No problem. I've got you covered."

I stopped him. "I don't think you understand. It's not a size thing. My husband's mom has the same issue. Their bodies don't seem to process pain medication the same way as other people."

The anesthesiologist shook his head and said, "I've got him covered. He won't be feeling any pain. I promise."

After giving John a kiss goodbye, I went back to my hotel room across the street to wait for news that he was in recovery. Two hours passed. John's mom called to see how he was doing, and I promised to call when he got out of surgery.

Another half hour passed, and the anxiety was building. I called the surgical center.

"Oh, Mrs. Rounds. Your husband is in recovery. The surgery is done, but they're having a little trouble getting his pain under control."

The anxiety grew. I sensed there was something the woman on the other end of the line wasn't telling me. "Is he okay? Was the surgery successful?"

"Ah...yes...but it's still going to be a little while before you're able to see your husband."

I hung up the phone and immediately walked across the street to the medical center.

"If he's in recovery, there is no reason I shouldn't be allowed to see my husband," I said to the woman at the front desk.

She was visibly uncomfortable. "Yes. Well, let me check with the doctor."

What's wrong? Why don't they want me to see him?

The woman returned and gave me a little reassuring smile. "Your husband is fine. Like I said, they're just having trouble managing his pain. I'll take you to see him now."

I followed the woman to the recovery room, which was lined with beds. There were a couple patients sitting propped up with pillows or hesitantly walking around the room using a walker.

I was aghast when I saw John. He was sitting in bed, propped up with pillows. His face was swollen and ashen white, completely drained of color. He didn't look like the same person.

I took his hand. It was freezing cold. "Hey, baby. How are you doing?"

"I'm in a lot of pain." Two health care workers stood at the base of John's bed and nodded empathetically.

"We've given him all the pain medication we can. If we were at a hospital instead of a surgical center, we might have other options. But we can't give him more painkillers without risking cardiac arrest."

"Oh, honey." Seeing him in so much discomfort made me feel panicky. Instead of wanting to hold him and comfort him, I was fighting the urge to run.

When the health care workers were out of earshot, John told me that the anesthesia hadn't worked. He had felt the surgeon cutting into his hip and screamed in pain. The anesthesiologist's solution had been to "knock him out." But when John regained consciousness, the pain was still there waiting for him. The experience had been excruciating.

I struggled to comprehend what John was saying. "Are you telling me they performed hip surgery on you without anesthetic? You weren't numb at all?"

"I don't know if the anesthetic had little effect or no effect. All I know is that it was the worst thing I've ever gone through in my entire life. And afterwards, the drugs they gave me didn't take the edge off. It's been all I can do just to keep it together."

I was appalled. "Is there anyone we can talk to?"

"At this point, they've given me everything they can give me. There's nothing more to be done."

One patient after another arrived in the recovery room and was discharged mere hours later. As the medical staff struggled to manage John's pain, we spent the day in the recovery area, reluctantly leaving at eight that night when the surgical center closed for the day.

The ensuing days and nights were sheer misery. John needed care through the night. We'd rented a portable pneumatic compression device that used ice water to reduce swelling. The ice needed to be replaced every couple hours. Pain medication also needed to be administered every two hours, day and night.

To complicate matters, Gracie and I had to get up at four forty-five in the morning for spring ski trainings at Beaver Creek the entire week following John's surgery. Near the end of the week, I was so tired, my hands wouldn't stop trembling. I performed my daily duties. But there was little energy left for true empathy.

Years later, sitting in the parking lot at the base of the ski hill and at the brink of divorce, I asked myself, *When being a mother was my highest calling, the deepest love I could possibly access, why wasn't I able to "mother" John when he was hurting?* With that question, the numbness gave way to an ache that grew stronger, rising up through my chest, clutching at my throat.

I'm sorry. I'm so sorry I wasn't fully emotionally present for you when you needed me. I'm sorry for the times I was distracted by the kids sporting events, or voice lessons, or theater performances, or meetings at school, or the endless shuttles, or my parents, or mountain biking, or volunteer activities, or social obligations. I'm sorry I wasn't more attentive.

Sitting in the passenger seat of the truck on that cold misty day in January 2020, I knew the apology was too late. Besides, it was only spoken in my head. I simply didn't have the energy to form the words. Too much time had passed now. Too many layers of scar tissue covered wounds to hip and heart.

CHAPTER 9

After Drift pulled out of North America, John struggled to find a career path that would solidify our family's financial future. Much of our savings was tied up in our home and commercial real estate investments. Though each real estate investment was lucrative, the uncertainty of the real estate market made John nervous.

In August of 2015, exactly three years after moving to Colorado, John the crazy idea to return to his hometown in western New York and re-open his parents' outdoor store... for a single weekend event.

Ellicottville, NY boasts not one, but two ski resorts. Holiday Valley was ranked the third best ski resort in the east by Ski Magazine. Holimont, which is fifty percent Canadian-owned, is the largest privately held ski resort in North America and regularly attracts a very cosmopolitain clientele from the Toronto area.

John intended to return to his quaint little hometown of Ellicottville to briefly re-open Adventure Bound, the outdoor store his parents owned in the 1970s when he was a child. The building that housed Adventure Bound was still owned by John's mother, and the retail space was vacant. John planned to create an Adventure Bound pop-up store for Ellicottville's Fall Fest weekend.

During Fall Fest, an annual event which takes place during the second weekend of October, Ellicottville's population of less than fifteen hundred full time residents swells to thirty-five thousand. John proposed the idea of reaching out to sales representatives, retailers, and manufacturers in the outdoor industry to fill the retail space with discounted outdoor gear.

The concept had some merit. It was an opportunity to leverage industry relationships and his mother's prime retail location. John flew to Ellicottville at the end of August to begin preparations.

I was a little suspicious when John sent pictures of fairly significant renovations he was making to the store's structure.

"Wow, honey. It looks like you are investing a lot of time, energy and...money?...for a Fall Fest pop-up project."

"I'm just doing it to help my mom. These modifications will make the space more rentable," John assured me. "My mom is covering all the expenses."

A couple weeks later, John sent me paperwork for new vendor applications. "We can get better margins if we open accounts with a few key manufacturers that are a good fit for the Fall Fest crowd. Don't worry. We won't order more than we can comfortably sell over Fall Fest weekend."

Though I wondered whether all this was worth the hassle, it was't until I received a video of the kid John hired to chip mortar off the walls ("To expose the building's old brick structure!") that I truly became alarmed.

"Hey. There is no *way* you are just doing that to improve your mom's building!" I exclaimed.

"Here's the deal. My mom hasn't had any luck renting this space. It's one of the best retail locations in town, but it's been vacant for a long time. The space will look more attractive if it's occupied, rather than vacant. In addition to Fall Fest, there are two major events in Ellicottville leading up to Christmas: the Christmas Stroll and Christmas in Ellicottville. We can fill the store with outdoor gear we buy at a discount. We'll have a prime downtown retail location for a few months, and my mom will hopefully have more luck attracting a tenant. It's a win-win for everyone."

There was a long…pause.

"Why do I feel like I'm being tricked into opening a retail store?" I asked.

"That's not what's happening!" John exclaimed. "Nobody is tricking anybody into anything. There are no good deals on real estate in the Vail Valley right now. This will give us the chance to generate some cash while we wait for the market to swing back in our direction."

"Gracie is really happy in Colorado," I said.

I'm *really happy in Colorado*, I thought.

"We're not moving," John replied in exasperation. "I'll just spend a couple months here making some cash. You and the kids can come out for Fall Fest, then head back to Colorado. Hopefully by Christmas, my mom will have found a new tenant for the retail space. See? Everybody wins."

In October, after nearly two months of separation, the kids and I were reunited with John. We fell in love with the charming little community of Ellicottville. The town looked as if it had dropped straight out of a Norman Rockwell painting. Its main street was lined with tall brick buildings, featuring brightly lit store windows that were colorfully decorated to attract the onslaught of visitors that would soon swell the streets in a flood of Fall Fest fervor.

We stayed in a high-ceilinged luxury apartment over the store, where John's mother and step-father had lived. Decorated to look like a French chateau, the apartment captivated the imagination. The main living area was referred to as the garden room. With vaulted post and beam ceilings, European-inspired terra-cotta tile floors, and a wall of windows that provided sunlight to feed a prolific collection of decades-old jade trees, Christmas cactuses, and Irish shamrocks, the garden room was a place that inspired people to congregate.

There were three bedrooms. One was in a little nook, accessed by climbing a hung staircase and crossing a suspended balcony over the Harry-Potteresque library. The library itself was in a location that reputedly once served as the town's basketball court.

A dark, heavy-paneled hallway, with antique chandeliers, cut through the apartment at an odd angle, bringing to mind secret rooms and hidden passages.

The kitchen featured an expansive island, covered in hand-painted European tiles. Its most prominent feature was a massive medieval fireplace. Reminiscent of an old world European castle, swinging wrought iron arms supported a huge iron cauldron, and a large cast iron vessel for heating water. There was a functioning dumbwaiter next to the fireplace, which would deliver wood from the basement, three floors below, at the push of a button. Though the apartment had been unoccupied for most of the previous two decades, the kitchen still carried the faint scent of fires of yore.

A few days after arriving in Ellicottville, Gracie announced, "I could really see myself living here." John and I were shocked. Of our five family members, Gracie seemed most entrenched in her life in Colorado.

"What about your friends in Eagle? What about skiing and the soccer team?"

"Ellicottville has two ski resorts! And I'm sure this school has a soccer team. I'll still have my friends in Colorado. But I'll make new friends here too. I really love this town. It's got great energy," Gracie replied confidently.

Admittedly, I too was feeling the town's magnetic pull. Looking back, I recognize the fact that as charming as Ellicottville was, its magnetism wasn't strong enough to lure Gracie and I from the fabulous home, lifestyle, and friends we had developed in Colorado. There was another dynamic at play, one that had been influencing our family's decisions from the start: we were restless, likely due to some nomadic gene in our DNA.

After three years, our time in Colorado had run its course. Our family's collective internal clock was indicating it was time for a change. With no other option presenting itself, Ellicottville was destined to be our next stop. It had nothing to do with choice. Like mice who reached the next bend in the maze, only one turn led forward. And there was no turning back.

I was fully in support of the decision to move our family from Colorado to New York in early December, 2015. So I had no one but myself to blame when it became woefully apparent that our chateau-like luxury apartment shared another characteristic common to old European castles: it lacked central heating and air conditioning.

Having moved from Ellicottville when he was thirteen, John was largely unaware of the apartment's heating and cooling deficiencies. An archaic, hugely unreliable pellet stove in the garden room provided the apartment's primary source of heat.

Too ancient to be serviced by local appliance technicians, I wrestled with that damnable pellet stove several times a week. Scouring the internet, I watched several hours of YouTube tutorials and managed to replace the pellet stove's motor, which provided two weeks of heat before the new motor burned out.

Compounding my misery, the apartment's high ceilings prevented antique light fixtures from adequately lighting its vacuous rooms. In the gloom of winter, our quintessential French Chateau had the bearing of a cold, dark, abandoned castle.

Like John, mourning the loss of the Petaluma mansion's marble patios and fountain during his chicken-plucking endeavors, I found myself wondering how I'd gone from toasty in-floor heating in a four thousand, five hundred foot luxury home nestled in the mountains of Colorado…to living in a frigid, poorly lit, medieval apartment in western New York, coaxing a few meager BTU's from a reluctant 1970s pellet stove.

Our options to heat the fricking European chateau were limited. The garden room's floor to ceiling windows were made of single-paned glass, the interior surface of which was often covered in crystalline ice. Running electric heaters would cost a small fortune. With high ceilings and a wall of windows, we would barely raise the temperature more than a few degrees in the garden room. And heat from the garden room would never make it to the bedrooms at the back of the apartment. The estimate to install central heat was a staggering sixty thousand dollars.

For that first winter, John or I got up every morning before school to build a fire in the kitchen's massive walk-in fireplace. The kids huddled around the fire, miserably eating their gruel in the company of the fireplace's cast iron menagerie.

"Listen!" I exclaimed, "None of the castles in Europe had heat. Stop feeling sorry for yourselves. You're living like kings and queens!" Secretly, I crossed my fingers that Child Protective Services wouldn't find us out.

As the rest of us struggled to regain our footing, it appeared the big winner in the move was Callie. A socially background person in Colorado, Callie suddenly found herself surrounded by an active network of friends. This was largely due to her prowess in music and theater.

At Callie's middle school in Colorado, music and theater took a back seat to athletics. For a small, rural school, Ellicottville had a surprisingly robust arts program, and Callie was delighted to finally take center stage.

At fourteen, her voice was starting to lose some of its chipmunk-like quality. Rather than a fan base of one (namely me), her music began attracting the attention of her peers. She joined Matt's Music Vocal Performance Team in Buffalo, which provided options to perform at Buffalo's Strand Theater, the Hard Rock Cafe in Niagara Falls, and local Jazz festivals.

When it came to singing, Callie had a ferocious work ethic and insane talent. She also had a mother who scoured the internet for music camps, vocal instructors, performance opportunities, and vocal competitions. Just as I'd dedicated an exorbitant amount of time, money (with John's blessing) and effort to Gracie's ski racing and Christopher's learning differences, there was no limit to the energy I would expend to help Callie achieve her dream of becoming a world-renowned recording artist.

As a result, Callie attended summer singing and songwriting camps in New York City and Los Angeles. At a music camp in New York, she met Mia Litzenberg, who co-wrote the song "Escape Bound," this book's namesake. Mia has since factored heavily in Callie's life story as they traveled together in Costa Rica, Hawaii, Washington state, Bali, and twice in Peru.

Callie also had the opportunity to write and record two songs with a professional singer-songwriter in Brooklyn, auditioned for *America's Got Talent* twice, and even got an offer to become a background vocalist in a local rock band that was in the process of negotiating a touring agreement with Canadian singer-songwriter Avril Lavigne.

Meanwhile, John and I discovered that owning a retail store had its pros and cons. At no time was this statement more valid than during spring mud season in western New York.

Con: The weather sucks. Nobody comes to town. Therefore, the store loses money if we keep it open.

Pro: The weather sucks. Nobody comes to town. There is no down side to closing the store and going somewhere warm.

So in 2017, John and I pulled the kids out of school for the month of April and headed to Lake Atitlan in Guatemala. Nestled into wild, rugged hills surrounding Lake Atitlan, our house, Casa Colibri (Hummingbird House), was only accessible by water.

A large master's suite occupied the entire top floor of the three-story, Tuscan-style home. A hammock on the balcony offered a spectacular view of volcanos, rising from the shore, at the opposite end of the lake. When we needed a ride to town, the kids would run to the end of the dock, arms flailing, to catch the attention of a passing water taxi.

Obtaining food was a near daily concern on Lake Atitlan. Produce goes bad much faster in third world countries than it does in the United States. This has little to do with the heat.

I was continually mystified by carrots. A three pound bag of organic carrots in the United States could sit in the fridge for six weeks with barely a change in firmness and texture. Even when refrigerated, my Guatemalan carrots—straight from the farmer's market—would shrivel within days after purchase, and look barely edible after a week!

Thanks to the highly perishable nature of produce in Guatemala, we made forays to the small lakeside community of San Marcos La Laguna several times a week.

San Marcos had a prolific population of stray dogs, and Christopher seemed morally inclined to care for all of them. When I finished shopping at the market, I had no trouble finding Christopher. I simply looked for clumps of dogs hungrily wolfing down the piles of dog food he purchased with his own money.

The kids were enrolled in Spanish lessons in San Pedro La Laguna, which was one town away from San Marcos. The morning commute across the lake was usually calm. But as the wind kicked up in the afternoon, the ride back home was turbulent. Several times, I found my hand in the death-grip of an old, indigenous Guatemalan woman. Our family was shocked to learn that many of the people who spent their lives in the communities surrounding Lake Atitlan never learned how to swim.

One day, when I was accompanying the kids to school, we saw a man's corpse laying on the dock, as we disembarked from the water taxi in San Pedro La Laguna. Though the man's eyes were closed, there was nothing covering his face. His arms had been neatly folded over his chest. Two elderly woman were wiping away tears as an official-looking man stood awkwardly nearby.

Seeing a dead body came as a such a surprise, the kids didn't know how to process what they were seeing. To my horror, their natural response was to giggle. Herding the kids down the dock, I was suddenly aware of the fact that our culture hides death from public view, as if it's something abhorrent and unnatural. Here in Guatemala, no one was attempting to shield children from the sight of death.

I remembered seeing my paternal grandmother at her funeral. She had spent ten years battling colon cancer before it finally consumed her. Standing in front of her casket, I noticed that Grandma had none of the deep wrinkles that had lined her face for as long as I could remember. Her cheeks had lost their sallow pallor. Ironically, in death, she looked far healthier than in life.

One of my aunts commented, "They did a good job on her."

I knew the blood had been removed from her body, replaced by an embalming solution to prevent deterioration. Gazing at the waxy plasticized skin on my grandma's face, I felt a sense of detachment, as if an alien had replaced the body that had once belonged to my grandma. Her life's struggles had been erased from her face. Those were the struggles that made her human.

Standing at the end of the dock on Lake Atitlan, I felt a sense of intentionality in the moment. During Dia de los Muertos in San Miguel de Allende, Mexico, death was viewed as something normal and natural. I wanted to teach my children to face death with compassion and grace, not shy away from it. Leading the kids back to the corpse, we offered our respects and said a little prayer over the man's body. The women nodded gratefully as the kids blew kisses and walked away.

The great success of our April mud-season escape to Guatemala in 2017 prompted us to plan a trip to Nicaragua in April 2018. The entire country celebrated our arrival with nationwide protests and rioting. One might wonder why we didn't cancel the trip, especially since United Airlines was voluntarily offering a full refund on our flights.

The honest answer is that John and I were travel-hardened and a little jaded. I'd worked as a tour guide during the fall of Communism in Eastern Europe. John had survived a half dozen nation-wide strikes in Latin America. We thought the civil unrest in Nicaragua was just another run-of-the-mill political uprising to blow off steam. We soon learned it was more serious than that.

Gracie and John flew from Colorado to Managua. Callie, Christopher, and I were to join them later that night on a flight from Buffalo. I delayed our departure when John called to tell me that he and Gracie had troubles getting to their hotel.

Their taxi had been stopped by men wearing bandanas across their faces, who demanded money every few kilometers. John and the cab driver acquiesced, as failure to do so could have resulted in the taxi being bludgeoned by bricks and bats. The taxi also had to skirt piles of burning tires blocking the road. Gracie said she could feel the heat from the fires through the taxi door.

"You're going to want to switch your flight to tomorrow morning," John's voice sounded strained. "Taxi drivers won't come to the airport to get you at night. We'll come get you at the airport tomorrow. Fortunately, our taxi driver is ex-military. Even though all the roads are barricaded, he knows a route out of Managua. Once we get to San Juan del Sur on the coast, everything should be fine. Most of the rioting is contained to the city."

Any remaining bravado disappeared as we flew into Managua the next day. Across the city, I could see smoke rising from piles of debris left burning in the streets. There were very few people or cars on the roads. With the exception of a band of men walking along the outside perimeter of the fence surrounding the airport, with a military troop in pursuit, the streets were largely vacant. More troops guarded the airport parking lot.

But just as John promised, once we left Managua, the tranquility of the pastoral Nicaraguan countryside bore little evidence of a country in conflict. On the empty beaches in San Juan del Sur, it was easy to forget the country was embroiled in civil unrest.

John spent the vast majority of his days in San Juan del Sur on the computer, presumably working on social media projects for Adventure Bound. I prepared food, spent time with the kids exploring the town, beaches, and markets, and attempted to escape Nicaragua's stifling heat by swimming in the villa's pool.

John joined us for some of our most memorable moments in San Juan del Sur, which included evenings watching sunsets together, happily licking ice cream. On those nights, we sat on a cement wall overlooking beach volleyball courts, where barefoot Nicaraguan youth laughed and cajoled each other below. We gazed quietly as the sun neared the horizon, where the ocean met the western sky. As the very edge of the sun disappeared into the water, we watched, transfixed, and as a family, said "ploop."

Unbeknownst to us, that month in Nicaragua would be the last trip we would take with just the five of us. The following year we would all gather in Peru, but Gracie's boyfriend would be with us, yielding a completely different dynamic. A rich, vibrant chapter of family travel had come to an end.

CHAPTER 10

I suspect we missed our exit cue. When our life's script indicated change of setting, as it predictably did every one to three years, we remained rooted to Adventure Bound in Ellicottville. I'm pretty sure the rest of the cast and crew went on without us—a cast that included new friends on distant horizons, in that "somewhere else" where we were supposed to be.

Left to our own devices, no longer sticking to the script, we struggled to find our role in the next scene. Apparently, none of us knew how to improvise. Unbeknownst to any of us, we were in the final countdown —our last year together as a family.

Gracie, who was seventeen, struggled with depression and anxiety and became entangled in deeply unfulfilling, co-dependent relationships. *Note to Gracie's younger self and her previous boyfriends: it wasn't your fault. You did the best you could. I love you.*

Callie, who was fifteen, was surrounded by friends, most of whom drank heavily, vaped, and smoked copious amounts of weed. *Note to Callie's younger self and her friends: Yes, of course I knew. I love you.*

Christopher, who was fourteen, spent ninety percent of his free time on his phone, in bed, eating candy, and gaining weight. *Note to Christopher's younger self: It's okay, buddy. Your life is going to get much, much better. I love you.*

John and I weren't doing much better. We drank. A lot. My libation of choice was red wine. John's was tequila.

I went on a spiritual journey, a ten day soul quest in the Inyo Mountains, just east of the Sierra Nevadas in California. The experience left me with more questions than answers.

In one of life's maddening mysteries—a phenomenon I refer to as "The Pendulum of Connectedness"—I became even more disconnected than my pre-soul-quest-self. The process may sound familiar: first, a person has a profoundly transformative spiritual experience, like a transcendental out-of-body encounter, words imparted directly from the divine, a visit from angels or spirit guides, or a vision where they seemingly see the very face of God. A miracle is declared! There is awe. There is wonder. There are tears of gratitude.

Then, faster than you can say "namaste," that same individual—who just moments earlier was the recipient of divine grace—exhibits irrational anxiety, fear, or even anger. Shouldn't powerful spiritual encounters have more sticking power?

Since contemplating my soul quest was emotionally disruptive, it seemed safest to disregard the experience altogether.

Adventure Bound became a soulless venture. Once an outlet for our joint creativity and passion, the store had been relegated to a series of mundane daily routines, that comprised monthly routines, that comprised seasonal routines. Our store failed to yield personal joy, financial glory, or professional fulfillment. Rather than being yoked to the same harness, John and I were continually pulling in different directions.

The tectonic plates on which our beautiful world had been built had indeed shifted. The plates moved in new directions. Lava and scalding geysers boiled up from fissures I never knew existed. Had they been there all along, tiny cracks that widened over time? Or were the fissures newly formed in the aftermath of my soul quest? Either way, the plates were now at odds, threatening to buckle and break what I'd assumed would always be a strong, happy home.

John spent six months in Peru with Callie and Christopher, with the rationale that by establishing Peruvian residency, he could expand our options in the burgeoning world of crypto currency. Taking high school classes online, Callie and Christopher reaped the benefits of a rich cultural experience in Peru. Not wanting to leave her boyfriend, Gracie stayed with me in Ellicottville, while I ran the store.

In the drear darkness of those winter months in Ellicottville, I struggled against melancholy. My days were bookended with two activities that made me feel less lonely: meditation and drinking.

Each morning, I got up at five for two hours of meditation. In meditation, struggling fiercely to stay awake, I experienced moments of ascension, spiritual connectivity, and even glory. But those moments were fleeting. It felt like meditation wasn't making me a better person, or even creating a lasting shift in perspective. It simply provided temporary relief from gray.

Gracie and I visited the rest of the family in Peru. As always, travel rekindled a sense of connectedness, both for John and I as a couple, and for all of us as a family. In Peru, I continued to meditate for two hours a day…and drink wine as well. But the space between meditation and happy hour didn't feel as colorless.

"Maybe we could just live here," I said to John, feeling hope bloom in my chest. "We could rent a super inexpensive apartment, hire a manager to run the shop…"

Even as I spoke the words, hope withered. It just wasn't practical. Gracie still had a year and a half of high school and she would never leave her boyfriend. The shop was only moderately profitable. Without our sweat equity, it would likely lose money. Besides, Pisac was a town of hippies and spirit-seekers, many of whom came in search of indigenous plant-based medicines. It wasn't a place most people would consider "family-friendly."

In an effort to expand Adventure Bound's reach in the local community and create a consistent, four-season business, we added Ellicottville Coffee Company to the store in the fall of 2019. Though I'll never know the long-term financial ramifications of that decision, it certainly added more stress than money to the equation in the short term.

Somewhere along the way, John and I had lost our intuitive style of communication. Frequent misinterpretations created anger and resentment. We developed negative narratives that left us feeling isolated, abandoned and utterly alone. We scrutinized each other's words for veiled insults. Every disparaging comment felt like a slap in the face. Wilting in the hot glare of criticism, a spark of defiance ignited.

In the span of a few short months, we burned the place down.

CHAPTER 11

January 30, 2020 was the day of reckoning. Mulling over the events of the previous months, John's grounds for divorce were a little clearer. While it's true that we'd had two decades of happy marriage, the previous year and a half had been spiritually and emotionally draining.

Post soul quest, I felt as if I was being called to rise to a challenge. But for the life of me, I couldn't figure out what that challenge might be. There was an undercurrent of defiance, a refusal to continue playing the role of habitual capitulator. (Say that three times fast!)

The night after the conversation with John in the truck, I climbed into a king sized bed that seemed ridiculously big for two people and downright obscene for one. Previously blessed with the gift of sleeping soundly and effortlessly, I suddenly panicked at the thought that I might never be able to fall asleep again. Visions of a succession of sleepless nights strung out in an endless parade in my mind and I felt my throat begin to constrict. But tears never came.

In the morning, I realized with chagrin, it had been years since John and I laid in bed together in the morning. That thought finally elicited a single, precious tear that leaked out of the corner of my eye, a tear I was loathe to wipe away, not knowing when the next one might come.

I wanted to save my marriage. I knew people who had become bitter through divorce: precious souls, damaged in the hurricane of separation, digging through the rubble in the aftermath, struggling to find the lost or broken pieces of their hearts. Frightened at the prospect of losing yet another piece of the soul I'd worked so hard to restore during my soul quest, another tear leaked out of the corner of my eye.

John and the kids had dominated my mindshare for the better part of two decades, while Inner Guidance was relegated to the shadows. As my domesticated life began to crumble, I felt the pressing need to become attuned to Inner Guidance again.

"You are worthy of love. Though John may have forgotten it, he truly loved you. Reach for evidence of that love," the voice of Inner Guidance whispered.

He used to make my coffee for me in the morning.

"Good. That's good. Keep going," Inner Guidance prompted.

He used to clear snow from the windshield of my car. And plow the back parking lot with the tractor.

"Nice work. Keep going."

I realized that recently, much of my inner dialog had been focused on what John didn't do, as opposed to what he did.

He was so patient and encouraging when he taught me to ski. And it made me feel special when he carried my skis for me. He never got frustrated when I was learning to sail. He's a really good teacher.

I thought about the many cups of coffee we shared in far-flung corners of the planet, where we eagerly discussed new business strategies or envisioned the exciting places we would live.

We dreamt of sailing the world with the kids or spending a year living abroad.

"Yes," Inner Guidance replied. "You were happy. You were loved."

I wondered if there was a way back to that love. Maybe it wasn't too late.

Getting out of bed, I felt lighter. I undressed, ran hot water, and stepped into the shower. Like removing layers of clay, the remaining clods of heaviness melted with the steam, as hot water ran in rivulets down my body. Sighing deeply, I finally relaxed.

"You attracted this. Everything that's happening right now…it's not happening *to* you. It's happening *for* you." The voice that spoke these words in my mind was protective, like part of me, but different. It had a deep, abiding quality.

As this voice continued to show up with guidance, wisdom and insight in ensuing months, I came to refer to it as the Big Guy. In my mind's eye, the Big Guy was simply my own Inner Guidance in masculine form.

"I attracted this," I repeated out loud. On some level, I knew those words should have made me feel culpable, guilty for the role I'd played in the destabilization of our marriage. Instead, they felt like a lifeline. Though on the surface, it seemed that John was at the helm, there were unseen forces at play, and they were working on my behalf.

Maybe if I'm attracting this, I can fix it! I'll do better. I'll be better. I'll focus on the things John does instead of the things he doesn't do. I'll be more mindful of my wine consumption. I'll be more playful and less stressed. Maybe this whole thing is a much-needed wake-up call that will end up strengthening our marriage.

And so began an email assault to win my husband back.

At the end of February, I flew from Western New York to Minnesota to help my mom recover from a knee surgery. From the safe space of my childhood home in Two Harbors, Minnesota, I launched a barrage of emails intended to convince John our marriage was worth saving.

I got sucked into buying a forty-nine dollar ebook called *His Secret Obsession*, which teaches the lonely and forlorn to win back lost love. Even using the masterfully manipulative text and email techniques described in the book, my electronic love campaign was met with firm resistance.

I was grasping at a thought dancing at the edge of consciousness just out of reach, a puzzle waiting to be solved.

John asked for a divorce at the end of January, then flew to Peru two weeks later over President's Day weekend. It seemed absurd at the time, because apart from Christmas week, President's Day weekend was the busiest winter weekend in the store. Then I remembered President's Day weekend had coincided with Valentine's Day.

The wheels in my head turned painfully slow. On our very first date, at the January Outdoor Retailer show, John insisted on breaking up with his girlfriend before consummating his relationship with me...over Valentine's Day in Chicago.

Seemingly out of the blue, I called John to ask if he was having an affair.

John did not confirm it, nor did he deny it. I knew my husband would have been morally outraged at the insinuation, if he hadn't been guilty.

So there it was. He had a lover.

Instead of feeling hurt, angry, or even jealous, I felt nothing. It wasn't my fault the marriage fell apart, nor was it John's. It wasn't my responsibility to put the pieces back together, nor was it his. The broken glass that once contained our marriage was simply beyond our ability to repair.

Attempting to maintain a death grip on my rose-colored glasses as one event after another threatened to rip them from my face, I took a hard look at myself. Pre-marriage Christy was confident, adventurous, and brave. Marriage had eroded my sense of worthiness. I continually felt guilty for not working hard enough and not being enough. Like the donkey chasing the carrot, I was chasing an elusive, undefined benchmark just out of reach. It had become impossible to live up to John's expectations.

But what if that was my own fault? What if the foundational basis of my validation, the ruler I was using to measure myself, was too reliant on the expectations of my husband and children?

Pre-marriage Christy received validation from her own achievements. Post-marriage Christy received validation from joint business ventures, family travel experiences, and kids' accomplishments.

When it came to expressing my own talents and abilities, did I have enough skin in the game? Or had I gotten lazy?

Sequestered at my parent's house in Minnesota, as my mother recovered from her knee surgery, I got up at five in the morning to write, pray, meditate, and receive insight from the Big Guy.

One morning, in the darkness, just at the edge of waking, I once again sensed the deep, abiding presence of the Big Guy and felt the words, "Your true purpose is to live a life of peace, harmony, laugher, love, joy, gratitude, surprise, and delight. Joy is life's purest form of expression."

That sounds nice. But joy doesn't pay the bills. I need to do something. And I need to find a place to live!

"When the Israelites left Egypt, God provided for their daily needs. They wandered the desert for forty years before finally entering the land of Canaan. The Israelites learned to develop trust. This is your time in the desert. It's not a punishment. It's a blessing. Your every wish, your every want, your every need, your every desire will be provided," the Big Guy replied. "You simply need to trust."

In the absence of a plan, I made the decision take the him at his word, allowing him to meet my short-term needs. After all, what choice did I have? There were rumors of lockdowns and stay-at-home orders on the horizon. A job search would be pointless. Besides, I was pretty sure the Big Guy would offer a great benefits package.

In my mind, the arrangement was kind of like having a cosmic sugar daddy. His presence was deeply personal, protective, and masculine. Even amid the chaos and uncertainty, I felt safe.

I continued to hold up my end of the bargain, getting up at five each morning to listen. His daily directives were simple and gentle. Write a blog post. Meditate. Journal. Exercise. Rest. Heal. Easy peasy lemon-squeezy. During my daily runs, he provided insight into negative narratives and limiting beliefs that were holding me back.

In time, I came to think of the Big Guy as a personal concierge, cruise director, and best friend, all rolled into one.

Investing in Bitcoin and other cryptocurrencies was one of the games we played…one that proved to be as lucrative as it was entertaining.

It was a match made in heaven. Literally. As I listened to the Big Guy's voice, my own shortcomings were gently and lovingly revealed. There was never condemnation—only patience and compassion.

But what about John's shortcomings? What about his role in the divorce?

"That is none of your concern, precious one," the Big Guy replied tenderly.

Much as I wanted to trust him implicitly, my financial prospects seemed cause for concern.

John's mom owns the Adventure Bound building and our apartment. She's not going to let me stay. John had already made it clear there will be no alimony and no valuation for the business. Where are the kids and I going to live?

I felt tension rising in my throat as panic built in my chest.

"Stop," the Big Guy instructed gently. "It's time to go for a run."

On that late February afternoon run, words formed in my mind, following the cadence of feet hitting the dirt, *I am safe. I am guided. I am protected. I am loved.*

"More…" the Big Guy's voice challenged.

I picked up the pace and repeated the words: *I am safe. I am guided. I am protected. I am loved.*

"Keep going," his voice encouraged.

Flat grey clouds filled the sky. I could smell the pine trees that bordered the dirt road. Relaxing into the rhythm of my feet on the gravel, I took a few deep breaths, savoring the fresh, cool, northern Minnesota air as it filled my lungs. Then the words came in a rush, as I spoke them out loud:

I am embracing the Universe's wealth as it rains down in an avalanche of abundance, flowing through me.
My every need, my every want, my every wish, my every desire is instantaneously met by Infinite Intelligence.

That part reminded me of Tony Robbin's words from "Not Your Guru."

I am Source energy and Source is everything.
I feel the Universe's wealth and abundance in the love of my family and friends.
I feel the Universe's wealth and abundance in the creativity and inspiration I receive each day.
I feel the Universe's wealth and abundance in the health in my body, my physical beauty, and my strength.
I feel the Universe's wealth and abundance in the money that comes to me so easily, like a river flowing through me.
And now I feel the Universe conspiring on my behalf, that I might be, and do, and have, anything that I desire.

I spoke the last sentence out loud, like an incantation, and a wave of power rolled over me. "Woah! Holy shit!" I exclaimed.

In a panic, I began to repeat the mantra, afraid I would forget it. But words were there in my head, clear as a bell, as soon as I reached for them. I was flabbergasted. Me... the woman who couldn't even memorize her own children's cell phone numbers, was suddenly able to recite this whole mantra, effortlessly, over and over, word for word.

Arriving home after the run, my cheeks rosy from the cold, I had the sensation of being bathed in light and warmth. With deep gratitude and awe, I kept repeating my mantra, just to prove I hadn't forgotten it.

Unbeknownst to me, that mantra would be repeated hundreds, if not thousands, of times, providing comfort in my darkest hours. It was my magic sword, wielded in the face of anxiety, to banish thoughts of lack or limitation.

CHAPTER 12

After two weeks in Minnesota, my mother's knee was healing nicely, and I returned to a very uncomfortable domestic situation in Ellicottville. John avoided being in my presence whenever possible. The kids sensed tension and acted out.

John didn't want to tell the kids that our marriage was ending until after the final paperwork was signed. As that process could take months, especially during Covid, I insisted we tell them sooner. John was adamant. So was I. In the end, I unilaterally informed the kids that John and I were getting a divorce. John was livid.

In early March 2020, global epidemiological chaos mirrored the chaos in my personal life. Covid was wreaking havoc on the country. The media's overuse of the word "unprecedented" was unprecedented.

On March 15, our family sustained a direct hit from the category five shit-storm of 2020. New York State declared a state of emergency, closed schools, and announced a stay-at-home order. John was scheduled to leave for Peru at midnight that night. But Peru's president announced that a fourteen-day quarantine would go into effect immediately. John cancelled his flight to Peru, preventing him from being reunited with his lover.

Then, on that very same day, my mother called with the news that my father had gone to the emergency room with chest pains. X-rays revealed that the pain in his chest was not related to his heart, but a mass of tumors they'd discovered pressing on his lungs. The tumors were cancerous.

At the brink of a global pandemic, I found myself on my parents' doorstep. Christopher and I made the twenty-hour drive from Ellicottville to Two Harbors while the girls took flights to meet us in Minnesota. Though I didn't know where the kids and I would live, staying with my parents while Dad was going through chemo was impossible.

My parents wrapped me in a warm embrace that lasted just a little longer than their normal hugs. "We're so glad you're here," my mom said, with great warmth in her voice. My dad's eyes teared up a little.

You know those people who volunteer at school, help out at church, deliver groceries to the home-bound, bring meals to the elderly, and contribute generously to just about every charity that bothers to asks them for money? That describes my mom and dad. But my parents take selflessness to a whole new stratosphere.

As I'd already mentioned, they flew to cities far and wide, at their own expense, to offer assistance when we needed a babysitter. They also worked tirelessly on a multitude of building, remodeling, and repair projects for all of their children. Most recently, my parents and my brother, Curt, spent nearly two weeks of twelve hour days to help build the coffee shop...and refused compensation of any kind. I was ashamed that I wouldn't benefit from their kindness.

Stepping into my mother's kitchen, I inhaled deeply. Mom was always baking something. That day it smelled like apple crisp. A pile of mail sat on the kitchen counter next to a kitschy homemade napkin holder and a bottle of pills dad was taking in preparation for chemo.

The night after collecting Gracie and Callie at the airport in Duluth, I overheard the girls talking tearfully behind a closed bedroom door and picked out the word "homeless."

"Hey!" I exclaimed, opening the door. "We are *not* homeless! We're nomadic. There's a difference! Just because we don't know where we're going to live at this exact second doesn't mean we won't have a place to live. We just need to relax into this stage of not-knowing. It's all going to work itself out. Maybe we'll take a roadtrip this summer!"

At this, the girls stopped sniffling. Always the practical one, Gracie said, "Mom! We're in the middle of a global pandemic! In case you haven't heard, there's a stay-at-home order! Grandpa has cancer. If we stay here, we put Grandma and Grandpa at risk of getting Covid. It's too cold to travel. Even you have to face it. We're homeless!"

"A temporary state of transition doesn't make you homeless," I replied. But she was right on one point. It wasn't safe or practical to stay with my mom and dad, since my presence—not to mention that of three teenagers—put my dad at risk of contracting Covid.

"Listen. A roadtrip will be really good for us. Maybe we'll head to California and see if that's a place we'd like to live." I knew Callie would love that idea. She hated the cold. "It will be great! You'll see."

Though my entire adult life could be characterized as an unending cycle of planting and uprooting, I'd always managed to maintain my footing, providing a constant sense of "place" for John and the kids.

For the first time, I really didn't belong anywhere. No place felt like home. Not a single longitudinal-latitudinal position on the globe called to me. Like a dove sent from Noah's arc, there was no safe place to land.

And with that simple thought, the decision was made. I'd promised the kids a roadtrip. Who was to say when…or if…the roadtrip needed to end? The freedom that concept evoked was intoxicating.

I needed space to rediscover who I was outside of the context of marriage. It would be like my own, private, traveling ashram, with plenty of room for self-refection and personal growth. For first time in a long time, I felt hopeful.

I had no idea that the roadtrip would become a three month endeavor covering over eighteen thousand miles, where we never knew where we would sleep from one night to the next. Though all three kids joined segments of the trip, my primary partner-in-crime would be Callie, whose drive to become an Instagram travel influencer would dictate our route, based on seventy-two points of interest she wanted to visit.

At the time I made the decision to embark on this journey, I certainly had no way of knowing that at summer's end, the roadtrip would continue in Costa Rica, with not only my own three kids, but other people's kids as well.

CHAPTER 13

In April, 2020, with whispered encouragement from The Big Guy, I borrowed eight thousand dollars from my parents to buy a pop-up trailer, which would be light enough to tow with my Honda Odyssey Touring Elite minivan.

The kids and I were itching to hit the road. However, there were a couple problems. For one thing, April was too cold for glorified tent camping in most parts of the United States.

For another, there was a lockdown order in most states, and nobody seemed to know what that meant. Would police prevent us from crossing state lines? Would campgrounds and hotels be closed?

My dad was starting chemo treatments. It was time to leave Minnesota. Since I couldn't think of anywhere else to go, I packed up the minivan, hitched up my new pop-up trailer, and drove back to Ellicottville. With the help of a dear friend and property manager, I was able to secure a month's lodging in a ski chalet, owned by Canadians who were not able to cross the border due to Covid.

The ski chalet was beautiful. Just a few houses down from the main entrance of the now-vacant ski resort, it offered blessed sanctuary in the midst of tumultuous waters.

April in western New York is characterized by thick, heavy clouds that occasionally settle to earth in a damp, depressing fog. Rain actually feels somewhat cathartic, a final release of all that pent-up moisture in the atmosphere. The air has a damp, organic scent, promising rich, earthy nutrients to any plant willing to brave the risk of a late-season freeze.

One morning, I woke up feeling deeply unhappy. Amid the chaos, I'd never really processed the fact that something precious had been lost. I mentally reached for the Big Guy, but couldn't feel his presence.

Though reciting my mantra provided a brief respite from the sadness, the pain soon returned, and the downward slide continued. By mid-morning, sadness turned to crushing despair. Nothing alleviated the solid weight that had settled on my chest.

I grabbed my rain jacket and ventured out into a cold, blustery drizzle. Just across the road lay hundreds of acres of private land, owned by a friend. I found the nearest access point and was a soon lost in a maze of trails that wound through an old hardwood forest.

Wandering aimlessly, grief overwhelmed me, making it hard to stand. I felt the need to drop to the ground. Scanning the forest, I noticed a massive hardwood tree whose energy reminded me of something old, wise, and motherly.

Dropping to my knees in the thick blanket of leaves at the base of the tree, a primal urge surged through me, a desire to press the entire length of my body as close to the earth as possible. I grasped clumps of cold, wet leaves, tossing them aside as I dug through the layers, until I reached the thick, loamy earth at the base of the tree's trunk.

Pressing my cheek to the dirt, I inhaled deeply. Sobs finally gave way to tears of gratitude as the scent of rotting leaves dulled the knife edge of despair. I pressed my body deeper into the earth, willing myself to become something dead and composting, yearning to become one with fungus and mycelium.

I awoke an indeterminate period of time later, cold and stiff from sleeping on the ground. Feeling for the sadness, it was nowhere to be found. I kissed the tree and thanked the Earth Mother for offering healing.

In the days that followed, despite the chaos in my personal life and the world at large, I could sense new life on the horizon. The height and breadth of possibility was uplifting. My dialogue with the Big Guy became clearer, more pronounced, and more reliable.

The seclusion of empty, muddy dirt roads, criss-crossing forlorn ski runs that had been filled with skiers just a six weeks earlier, called to me. Skeletal trees braced themselves against the cold, damp wind, patiently awaiting their time to bud. They made me aware of the sap running in my own veins, inspiring thoughts of rebirth and new beginnings.

One day, I felt the presence of the Big Guy. I'd been thinking about the roadtrip, wondering what the kids and I would do in the fall when the weather got too cold for traveling in a pop-up trailer.

Where will we go?

"Keep traveling," the Big Guy replied. "At this point, your journey has no end date."

Again, the prospect of endless travel sent chills of excitement up my spine.

But how will we pay for that?

In a spark of inspiration, the Big Guy impressed an idea in my mind.

Before Covid, online schooling represented a tiny segment of college education. During Covid, every educational institution in the United States had to figure out how to offer classes online. Online education went mainstream, virtually overnight.

I could negotiate a deal with low-end hotels or high-end youth hostels in Latin America to provide flat-fee monthly housing for all those online college kids.

At some point, international travel would resume. And in lieu of a traditional semester abroad, kids would be able to move freely between any of our lodging partners by continuing to take their classes online.

Brilliant! That's absolutely genius!

A global flat-fee monthly housing program would not only meet the needs of students, it would provide a way for the kids and I to travel cheaply as well. A world of possibilities stretched out before me.

It will be the world's first global dormitory! I'll call it "Nomaditudes!" We'll have hundreds of partners across the globe with thousands of students traveling through our programs every year.

"Slow down," the Big Guy cautioned. "This isn't about meeting your need for validation by setting up some grandiose business plan. It's just a way to cover travel expenses. You just earned your freedom. Don't trade it for a set of golden handcuffs."

That's ridiculous! Nomaditudes will be scalable. I can keep it small during the pandemic, then go for global expansion once travel resumes. It's a fabulous idea. I need to live up to the potential that idea offers.

And of course, Nomaditudes was the perfect vehicle for the validation I so desperately craved, a way to prove to the world that divorce hadn't gotten the better of me!

Nomaditudes felt like coming home to an earlier version of myself, a girl who was inquisitive, daring, and adventurous, a girl who didn't believe in limits…or boundaries.

In my earliest twenties, I'd worked for an organization called Friendship Ambassadors, a non-profit that was originally funded by the venerable Readers Digest Foundation.

The mission of Friendship Ambassadors was to sponsor cultural exchange between Eastern Europe and the United States at the height of the Cold War. To my delight, three years of Russian language classes and a degree in International Relations with an Eastern European focus landed me a job as international programs coordinator with Friendship Ambassadors.

I spent my summers shepherding American high school and college students on their performing group tours throughout the Soviet Union and Eastern Bloc. The rest of the year, I toured the East Coast with inbound Eastern European performing groups.

On one particular tour of Buda Castle in Budapest, Hungary while traveling with an energetic choir from a college in California, I tired of answering the prevailing question of the day (and every day, for that matter): "Where is the bathroom?"

Leaving the group in the hands of our capable local Hungarian tour guide, I descended a staircase facing the Danube River and soon found myself alone, gazing at a sloped terrace skirting one of the castle's lower walls.

A big fan of James Michener's historical fiction novels, I'd recently read his book, *The Source*, for the second time. It was utterly enthralling to learn that many of these ancient structures were built one on top of another for centuries upon centuries.

What if Buda Castle was sitting atop its fourteenth century counterpart? How would one find the original castle? Hmm…How indeed?

I jumped the staircase's the marble railing and dropped to the grass below, then quickly sought cover in the thick vegetation along the castle wall. The bushes created a little tunnel, making it easy to travel along the base of the castle wall, while staying entirely concealed. I felt like Indiana Jones!

A little path through the tunnel of bushes led to a cement opening, covered with a metal grate. My heartbeat quickened as I noticed the grate didn't have a lock. With trepidation, I gave it a tug and was surprised when it came off easily. Peering into a dark horizontal tunnel that receded into the underbelly of Buda Castle, it almost felt as if I'd been led to this place.

Barely able to contain my excitement, I scurried back to the group. Though I was their tour guide, some of the college students were only a year or two younger than me. Assembling three of my favorite kids, I swore them to secrecy and told them about the hole in the wall of the castle.

We made plans to meet later that night for an exploratory mission.

I purchased a flashlight and returned to the wall with my little band of outlaws. Stomachs pressed to the earth, we shined the flashlight through the opening in the wall, casting its beam across the tunnel's interior. The floor of the tunnel, which was filled with water, was a couple feet below the edge of the hole in the wall. The prospect of dropping into water of unknown depth and origin prompted my three companions to throw in the towel.

"C'mon! Don't be a wuss!" I exclaimed to the biggest, and presumably bravest, kid in the group. "How often do you get the chance to explore a fourteenth century castle? And maybe it was built on something even older!"

"There is no way I'm walking through castle sludge!" he exclaimed.

"It doesn't even look deep!" I huffed. "Fine. But at least help lower me down. And stay here while I check it out."

Shimmying backwards on my stomach until my legs dropped over the lip of the cement opening, I grasped the upper arms of two boys who lowered me another several inches before my bare feet made contact with the murky water. The wall was at chest height when my feet hit the tunnel floor. As it turned out, the water was just a few inches deep.

"You guys! The water isn't even deep. Look. It's barely over my ankles! Come on!"

But I didn't get any takers.

I took the flashlight and moved into the tunnel alone, making the kids swear not to ditch me. A dozen feet from the tunnel's entrance, a metal ladder ascended through a vertical tunnel. I cast the flashlight beam upward, but couldn't see where the ladder ended. I continued on. Old wiring ran along the top of the wall, and I wondered if this tunnel had been used as a bunker in World War II.

Then I saw something that looked like blood on the wall. *It's just rust,* I told myself. Closer inspection revealed that it was indeed blood or some liquid that looked very much like blood. Scared out of my wits, I ran.

"Look who's the wuss now!" the big kid exclaimed, as I lurched through the cement opening, feet scrambling for purchase.

A year later, I returned to Hungary, this time with my European trekking companion, Elizabeth. I took delight in the fact that, like me, Elizabeth loved to wear skirts when she traveled. We both felt it made us look elegant and poetic.

Elizabeth and I had met four guys—an American, two Australians and a New Zealander—while looking for lodging near the train station in Budapest. They offered to let Elizabeth and me to crash with them.

Three of the boys were exuberant, eager to regale us with tales of wild adventures. But one of the Australians, a man named Danilo with broad shoulders, grey-brown eyes and a wild tousle of brown curls, was more reserved. He was content to listen, bemused by the antics of his traveling companions.

"It sounds like you're the kind of guys who might be up for an adventure. Can you keep a secret?" I challenged the boys. Elizabeth clapped her hands in excitement, as I'd already told her about the tunnel in the castle wall. "We're going to need some flashlights."

Our team of six spent over an hour exploring the tunnels under Buda castle. The most exciting discovery was a large room that looked like a high-ceiling chamber. A crumbled stone staircase rose to the ceiling above and ended abruptly. One by one, our flashlights began to go dim. By the time we made it back to the entrance, there was only one dim flashlight between the six of us.

Danilo and I were at the back of the line, following the others in pitch darkness. "Hold up, I have something for you," I whispered in the darkness, just loud enough for him to hear. I felt him stop in front of me. Running my hands up his chest to his face, I pressed my lips to his and felt his arms circle around my waist, pulling me into an embrace.

Though a cold April wind blew across the empty Ellicottville ski slope, memories of passionate, often mischievous, antics from early travel adventures spread like heat through my veins. There was the tryst with a Serbian engineering student on a train from Leningrad to Tallinn, a month spent exploring the Irish countryside with an energetic young lad from Dublin, the weekend flight to England I accepted on a dare when a wealthy American businessman offered to take me to the London theater; so many intriguing men I'd loved, then dismissed in pursuit of my soul mate, who now had the audacity to serve me divorce papers!

Travel had provided the backdrop for so much excitement, growth and adventure. Nomaditudes harkened back to that freedom of yore, fertile soil for the achievements that would play a foundational role in reestablishing my personal and professional validation. I just needed to find business partners who would share my vision.

CHAPTER 14

Whilst I enthusiastically schemed plans to create the world's first global student dormitory, my own lodging situation became somewhat dire. The Ellicottville ski chalet rental ended in April. May was still too cold to camp.

Making Boyne City, Michigan the next stop on our pre-roadtrip journey seemed somewhat poetic. It was the place John and I started our married life together. It was the place to which we returned after Christopher was born. And it was home to some of our dearest friends.

As the kids had fond memories of their childhood on Lake Charlevoix, they were in full support of my decision to return to northern Michigan. Boyne City had a moratorium on short term stays during the early stages of Covid. Gracie offered to lead the charge in finding a defunct AirBnB for a six week rental, and negotiated a deal on a four bedroom, three bathroom, neat-as-a-pin cottage that was almost too good to be true.

The day before leaving Ellicottville for good, I struggled to decide what to take and what to leave. All my worldly possessions needed to fit in the van and the pop-up trailer's tiny front storage compartment. Downhill skis? Cross country skis? Back country skis? Snowshoes? Mountain bike? Fat tire bike? Tent? Sleeping bags? Stand up paddle board?

The rocking chair Gracie just bought me for Christmas? Pictures of the kids? Shoes? Jackets? All my winter clothing? I asked John if I could store some things in a corner in the basement under Adventure Bound. He said, "No." With no other option, I rented a storage unit on the spot, and spent the day filling it with things I would never have considered taking, things that would feel familiar to the kids once I decided to land. I took Christopher's mattress and log bed, Callie's speakers and equipment for recording, Gracie's books, two log chests of drawers, a huge antique armoire I'd found at an antique store in Colorado, and matching bench.

My brain clicked into survival mode. Recalling the image of a dove, with nowhere to land, the minivan and storage unit became Noah's arc, and it was starting to rain. I needed to save everything I could. All living things needed to come with me. This included all three kids, a hundred pound. golden retriever, a very pissed off cat, a crested gecko, and an aquatic frog. In my mind, John had been prepared to abandon us on the brink of a pandemic. He wasn't to be trusted with life. I agonized over the plants that would be left behind.

I packed food and supplies for the pets, as if pet food stores might suddenly disappear. I purchased dried goods in bulk at a restaurant supply store, and loaded a twenty pound bag of lentils and forty pound bag of rice in the car. Then, realizing I couldn't leave John and Ty without food, I bagged up five pounds of lentils and ten pounds of rice to leave behind.

As hysterically funny as all of this seems in retrospect, I have deep compassion for that earlier version of myself, who had clearly hit rock bottom. The eight hour drive from Ellicottville to Boyne City calmed my nerves. Exhaustion replaced the anxiety that had nearly overtaken me, as I left the life I'd spent twenty-three years building.

In Boyne City, Nomaditudes provided a welcome distraction. Having spent the better part of two decades living in other people's shadows, I contemplated the kind of light that might emanate from my heart now that I'd finally made the decision that my validation would come from my own achievements.

Contacting northern Michigan's Small Business Development Center (SBDC), I was assigned a business consultant and was provided access to a student research team, who compiled a contact list for college and university international study program.

After building a fairly complex website, securing social media assets, and buying the toll-free number 888-886-6623 (888-88-NOMAD), I was finally ready to reach out to prospective lodging partners.

Selina, a high-end youth hostel chain that caters to digital nomads, was my first (and only) choice. When John and I had traveled as a family, we typically rented a luxury home, condo or villa through AirBnB. In recent years, we'd added a brief youth hostel stay to the start or end of our trip. No surprise...our kids liked the youth hostels better than the luxury villas.

Selina was our go-to hostel chain. Their reliable wi-fi, amenities, and moderate pricing attracted a diverse, somewhat affluent clientele. Selina's properties had a high energy, cross-cultural vibe without the noise, debauchery, and occasional bedbug infestation one finds at cheap party hostels.

Personally, I loved the fact that each Selina hired local artists to paint bright, intense murals that captured the area's cultural traditions and values of the region. Public spaces featured whimsical structures like treehouses, teepees, old-fashioned VW beetles or vans, and other edgy artistic elements that inspired playful social media pics. Most importantly, Selina had recently received a ninety-two million dollar investment from WeWork to upgrade their network capabilities. Strong wifi would be important for Nomaditudes students taking classes online.

After thoroughly researching Selina's mission, values, history, and founders, I was ready to reach out to their corporate headquarters to propose a partnership. The head of Selina's corporate sales department, a British gal who lives in London, immediately caught the vision.

"This is all really quite amazing," she said in her charming British accent when I described my plan. "We were just discussing the idea of a program of this sort in our meeting last week! With Covid, more people are working and studying from home. Why not spend a month or two living somewhere warm? We would be very open to the idea of creating a flat monthly fee for your online students."

Over the next month, she and I exchanged emails and frequently connected via Zoom. Together, we created Selina's first flat monthly fee program, called the Nomaditudes pass, which provided students access to thirty-one Selina locations in twelve Latin American countries for less money than most students would pay for room and board at their college in the United States.

There was only one problem. The entire world was in lockdown. Nobody knew when travel would resume, especially international travel. Though I knew in my heart of hearts that travel bans would be lifted in the near future, promoting student travel was a tough sell.

Our idea was such a good one, I was worried someone might steal it. Nomaditudes had to be first-to-market. I needed a spin doctor, a person who could effectively navigate the intricate interplay between the current epidemiological climate and this future opportunity for student travel.

I was emboldened (perhaps a little cocky) when the Selina partnership came together. In a fit of stark-raving ambitiousness, I hired a hotshot public relations gunslinger from Lafayette, Colorado who had once been part of a larger PR firm that catered to outdoor brands. This was a mistake that would prove to be both premature and costly. His $1,750 monthly retainer, though well-warranted for an established business, was truly obscene for my stage in the game. After all, Covid travel restrictions prevented travel to eleven of the twelve countries on my Nomaditudes pass, a fact that didn't play well in press releases.

But in May, 2020, Nomaditudes wasn't the only project occupying my attention. We had three high school graduations to celebrate!

Gracie was a high school senior. Callie, having taking high school classes online for two years, had earned enough credits to graduate...at the age of sixteen. Callie's friend, Cyrene, had elected to make a quarantine jailbreak to join us in Michigan and was a senior as well.

Part of me thinks that Gracie never really trusted me after the goldfish debacle at the economics fair in Colorado. So, as was the case with her ski race training in Vail (and researching AirBnbs in Boyne City), Gracie took charge of things she deemed important, which included her own graduation celebration.

In a ceremony that was attended by Gracie, Gracie's boyfriend, Callie, Cyrene, Christopher, and me, the girls made their gradation a one-of-a-kind event by making speeches (in dresses and skirts that would have gotten them sent home from school) and danced to a lurid rap song that has *never* been played at *any* graduation in *all* of history...and never will be.

Pet shenanigans also occupied significant mental energy. Remember that metaphor comparing my van to Noah's arc? Thank heavens the fate of the feline race wasn't in my hands. Left to me, cats would have disappeared from the face of the earth.

My severe cat allergies initially precluded our family from cat ownership. But on Christmas, 2014...a superbly fluffy, nine hundred dollar Siberian named Jingle was acquired and given to the children as a gift due to a characteristic unique to the breed: Siberians produce saliva free of allergens.

In Ellicottville, six years later, our family's sentiment towards Jingle would be akin to the way one feels about a crotchety relative who bathes infrequently. Despite his high-brow pedigree, Jingle made regular forays to the dumpsters of neighboring restaurants, often returning home with fur

119

clumped, matted, and smelling of sticky substances of unknown origin.

Jingle's unpleasant smell matched his character. For though he was prone to scratching (or even biting) a human family member when they offered an unsolicited display of affection, Jingle was extremely persistent in his cloying demands for attention when he felt the urge for a pat. This usually happened whenever someone opened their computer.

Still, just as one feels guilty for uncharitable feelings toward an ill-tempered relative, our family felt badly for not loving Jingle more. And when he went missing from our rental house in Boyne City, I couldn't help but think I didn't do enough to make him feel wanted. The kids heartily agreed.

My penance was paid in the signs I posted for our missing cat…and the hours spent roaming the streets calling for him by day and night. But alas, despite my efforts, Jingle was never found.

The subject of Bentley is much more painful, both for me and for everyone else in our family. I doubt there is a purer soul on the planet than the soul of a golden retriever. And Bentley was one of the purest goldens I've had the pleasure of knowing.

When we left Ellicottville, Bentley was thirteen years old. For four years prior, Bentley loved spending time greeting customers in Adventure Bound. But with the addition of the coffee shop, the new espresso machine produced noises that made Bentley yelp and beg to go outside. Consequently, he spent his days alone in the apartment. Bentley's aging hips made it difficult to get up and down the long flight of stairs leading to the back parking lot, where he went to the bathroom. So when I left Ellicottville, I took Bentley with me.

I made arrangements for Bentley to stay with our friends, the Kuhns, since they had one of Bentley's brothers. The Kuhns' kindness exceeded the metes and bounds of friendship, in both scope and scale. Since I wasn't sure how long the roadtrip would last, leaving Bentley (and the crested gecko and aquatic frog) seemed more like pet abandonment than pet sitting.

For their part, Chris and Tammie Kuhn tried to make me feel as if dumping my pets in someone else's lap was the most normal thing in the world. I suspect the fact that I was willing to take them up on their generous offer was, in fact, evidence of a deeper character flaw. Perhaps I was like unto those who lived too much and loved too little.

In the days and months that followed, I suffered more angst over the fate of our pets than the fate of my marriage. Losing Jingle and leaving Bentley felt reckless and irresponsible, the result of moral failure. I was deeply ashamed.

Boyne City had been my fifth move in four months. After traveling to Minnesota in February, ping-ponging between Ellicottville and Minnesota in March, back to Ellicottville in April, followed by a six week short term rental in Boyne City, I was ready to be done with four solid walls and white picket fences. The open road was calling.

As the roadtrip lacked a destination or an end date, it became apparent that the term "roadtrip" was a thinly veiled attempt to conceal itinerancy. This observation was not lost on the kids and elicited mixed responses.

Callie was thrilled. Like me, when it comes to fight or flight, Callie is a runner. With the artistic eye of a gifted photographer and the physique of a runway model, Callie's goal was to create content to launch her career as an Instagram travel influencer. The roadtrip fit Callie's agenda perfectly. She took the helm as trip navigator, painstakingly researching hundreds of Instagram-worthy spots in the western half of the United States. She mapped a route that included seventy-two destinations. Each of these points on the map indicated a jaw dropping backdrop for her photo shoots and drone videos.

Gracie, who despises social media, wasn't keen to embark on a trip whose itinerary was dictated by Callie's Instagram agenda. That, plus the fact that Gracie had a boyfriend with whom she was unwilling to part, prompted her to borrow money from me to buy an old Subaru Outback and embark on a roadtrip of her own.

Gracie turned her Subaru—as well as a beat-up Yakima Rocket Box rooftop carrier she found on Craig's List —into a super-economy tiny home, parceled into spaces representing each room of a traditional house. There was an area of her vehicle dedicated to toiletries, a living room, and a sleeping area. She even had a little library in the spare tire compartment.

My parents helped Gracie pad her makeshift bed with foam to make it more comfortable and cut bug netting to fit her windows, securing it to the car's frame with magnets. The Subaru would be Gracie's home for the foreseeable future.

That left Christopher. Of the three kids, Christopher was the least impacted by the divorce. Like Gracie, Christopher wasn't excited at the prospect of being sucked into Callie's ambitious social-media-driven agenda. Plus, he gets car sick easily. So we all decided it would be best for Christopher to return to Ellicottville with the promise he would fly to Los Angeles at the end of summer to join Callie and I for the cross country trip home.

Sometimes life surprises us with unexpected twists and turns that bless our lives in delightfully unforeseen ways. The fact that Gracie and Christopher wouldn't be joining Callie and I on the roadtrip left room for Mia, Callie's friend from summer music camp. I was thrilled to have Mia join us for the first couple weeks of the journey, partially because she would keep Callie distracted and partially because she would keep me distracted.

Callie and Mia are kindred spirits, sharing a passion for adventure and a knack for getting into trouble. When they were fourteen, the girls got kicked out of music camp in Los Angeles for breaking out of a second story dorm room window in the middle of the night. The goal of the midnight foray was to watch the sun rise from the top of a hill nearby.

Intending to use pool floaties as mattresses, the girls threw their inflated floaties out of their dorm window. Then they climbed down a tree and ran through the dark streets of

LA, using their phones for navigation. There is a good chance they would have made it if they'd inflated the pool floaties at their destination rather than in the dorm room. Apparently, two fourteen year olds walking through LA in the middle of the night carrying pool floaties is something that draws police attention. They were returned to campus in a squad car.

The night before we headed west, just before dropping off to sleep, I realized it had been a long time since I'd listened for the Big Guy's voice. Introspective blog posts and meditation had given way to business plans and to-do lists. Though I missed the peace, safety, and stillness I felt while communing with the Big Guy, it felt good to have goals, a sense of purpose, and independence.

CHAPTER 15

The roadtrip was never about reaching a destination. But I'm not sure it was even about the journey. In truth, it had more to do with home—losing one, yearning for one, the shame of not having one, the quest to find one. I really hoped to fall in love with a place somewhere along the way, a place that would satisfy that hole in my heart for "home."

Mia's parents met us at the campground in Boyne City for our big send-off. I nuzzled my goodbye to Christopher, unsure of when I'd see my boy again.

Electrical issues plagued the trailer lights, necessitating a last minute scramble to find a repair shop. In honesty, I was grateful for the distraction from the pain of saying goodbye to Christopher and our pets.

A repair shop quickly identified the issue. The faulty fuse was replaced, trailer lights were restored, and we were on the road in short order. Our first stop was Madison, Wisconsin.

I've always been drawn to academia and love the idea of living in a college town. I can just picture myself sipping lattes in a trendy coffee shop or drinking wine on a widely acclaimed scholar's front porch, embroiled in scintillating conversations on a wide range of fascinating topics, like the theoretical basis of string theory, or how trees communicate using a fungal network of mycelium.

Due to my fascination with college towns, Madison became the one and only destination I added to Callie's seventy-two points of interest. I selected Madison because it's home to the University of Wisconsin, it's surrounded by lakes (according to Google maps), and "Outdoor Magazine" ranked Madison as one of the best outdoor towns in America. Plus it was just one state away from my parents. In my heart of hearts, I secretly hoped that Madison would be a place I could call home.

Traveling through the Upper Peninsula of Michigan, I happily conjured idyllic images of Madison in my mind, images I later realized were based on the town of Stillwater, Wisconsin, which is nothing at all like Madison.

So eight hours later, emotionally drained from our goodbyes in Boyne and physically exhausted from the drive, I was shocked to find Madison to be far more city-ish than I'd envisioned. Maybe it was the modern concrete block buildings downtown, or maybe Madison was just having a bad hair day. Either way, I wasn't catching Madison's groove.

We drove by a marshy lake that smelled of things more dead than living. And though I kept a keen lookout for my beloved academics, in early July, there were none to be found.

However, the community boasted a sizable vagrant population that congregated in front of empty frat houses. Both people and buildings suffered from deferred maintenance. After one night in Madison, I was happy to hit the road.

Our next stop was Omaha, Nebraska. In Omaha, I lost Mia and Callie. As it turned out, they weren't lost so much as misplaced…for twelve hours.

We rolled into a hotel just off the highway around nine at night. Callie and Mia informed me that there was an Instagram-worthy lookout less than twenty minutes from the hotel. I was dead tired, so I tossed the keys to Mia and admonished her to drive safely.

I then inserted earplugs, slapped an eye pillow over my eyes, and was fast asleep before the girls changed clothes, fixed their hair, applied makeup, and walked out the hotel room door.

My alarm rang at eight the next morning.

Wow. I didn't even hear the girls come in.

But even as the words formed in my head, my mama-sixth-sense told me their bed would be empty. Removing the eye pillow, I visually confirmed the presentiment. Their bed was still perfectly made.

Oh…this is bad. This is really bad.

I grabbed my phone. No messages. No missed calls either.

Oh…This is can't be good.

Though watching sunrise was archetypal for these two, failure to communicate was not. Both girls were careful not to to cause worry.

I grabbed my phone again and realized, to my horror, that the little icon in the corner indicated no signal.

I'm in middle of fricking Omaha, just off the interstate! How can this be in a no cell zone?

Scrambling to grab the hotel room receiver, I barked into the phone, "What's the wifi password?" As soon as I punched in the code, texts started coming through. Twelve missed calls. Four voicemail messages.

"Mom! We went to the lookout, but we can't remember which hotel we're staying at. Call me when you get this."

I called Callie's phone. It went straight to voice mail. I listened to the next message.

"Hey, Mrs. Rounds, it's Mia. Callie's phone is dead. I think you must have taken your charger out of the car. We're low on gas and we didn't bring any money. Anyway, we've been driving to random hotels, but we can't find the one where you're staying. Call me when you get this."

I called Mia, praying that by then her phone wasn't dead too.

"Oh my gosh! We're *so* sorry," Mia gushed when she answered.

Whew! I thought they were going to be furious with me for not answering my phone!

"Hey, sweet girl! I'm so sorry. Can you believe my phone doesn't get cell service at the hotel?" I gave her the name of the hotel.

"Okay," Mia replied. "I put the hotel into my GPS. We aren't far away. I think I have enough gas to get there."

"Alright, I'll see you guys in a bit." I listened to the two remaining messages while waiting for the girls to arrive.

"Mom! This is Callie on Mia's phone. Why aren't you picking up? Oh my gosh! We've been driving around for three hours and the car is almost out of gas. We left our wallets and we don't have any money."

"Hey, Mrs. Rounds, Callie and I just want to make sure you know we're safe. We're spending the night at a McDonald's parking lot. It's supposed to be open all night, but there is a line of cars that's been here since, like, two in the morning. Everyone's out of their cars because they've been here over an hour, waiting for someone to take their order. So it's like a big party in the McDonald's parking lot! But don't worry. We're safe."

I drew the girls into an embrace when they walked through the door and sheepishly asked, "You're not going to post this story, are you?"

"Too late," Callie replied.

Miles passed in silence as Mia and Callie busied themselves with their phones. The car's thermometer indicated an outside temperature of one hundred and four degrees.

Wow! That's really hot for sleeping in a pop-up camper!

"What's the agenda when we get to Denver?" I asked.

"We need to be at Lookout Mountain by sunset," Callie declared. "Then tomorrow morning, we'll head to Red Rocks for sunrise. Sunrise is at five forty. So we need to leave by five."

I winced. "Ugh. That's going to be a short night's sleep."

With a sigh, I realized our timeline would be largely dictated by the sun's rising and setting, as colorful skies provided the best fodder for Instagram.

Gracie used to make Callie leave her phone inside when we watched sunsets together from our back deck in Colorado. "Take a picture with your eyes," Gracie would say. Then together, the girls murmured, "Click."

Musing over the magnetic attraction between sunsets and teenage girls, I remembered a sunset I'd watched when I was seventeen.

It was fall semester my freshman year of college. Newly arrived on campus, I was seeking a sunset viewing spot on the western side of the Gustavas Adolphus College campus. Standing alone in an open field behind the college's athletic center, I was suddenly overcome with melancholy. As the sun sank low on the western horizon, tears of sadness were streaming down my face, but I had no clue why.

In ancient Egyptian mythology, Isis was able to gain power over Ra when she divined his true name. Maybe if I name the sadness, it will lose its power.

I peered into the sadness.

Are you just stupid teenage hormones?

But even as the thought surfaced, the words failed to ring true.

Are you homesickness?

After completing enough credits to graduate after my junior year, I'd bypassed my senior year of high school and enrolled in college a year early. Maybe the sadness stemmed from leaving home at seventeen. After a brief pause for introspection, I knew the sadness was more than homesickness.

Are you loss?

I paused.

Yes, loss. But what did I lose?

As the last rays of the sun faded in the distance, I felt the pain sharpen.

Childhood.

I was mourning the loss of childhood and couldn't shake the feeling that something precious was being forgotten.

And then I saw an image of myself as a child, standing before the setting sun. I wasn't just watching the sun set, I was setting with it. In a flash of intuition, I remembered. As a child, the feeling of sun on my skin sent tremors of pleasure through my body. Turning my face to the sun, I felt pure bliss as its rays exploded in a kaleidoscope of red patterns behind my closed eyelids. I didn't just witness sunrises and sunsets, I experienced a visceral connection to the sun's rising and falling. Like knowing the words to the music, I actually knew the sun's setting song.

At the gloaming hour, standing amid waves of grass in a field in southern Minnesota, I reached toward the sun with all my heart. But I couldn't remember the song. Watching the colors fade from deep orange to indigo, I struggled to find words the sunset evoked: awe, gratitude, warmth, magic, power, inspiration, safety. None of those words matched the feeling the sun elicited when I was a child. Like losing the ability to see a spectrum of light, it was as if there was an entire range of emotions that slipped away with the magic of childhood.

To this day, sunsets are tinged with melancholy, because in witnessing the setting sun, I sense something precious that was lost.

Driving toward Colorado, I suddenly realized that Callie and Mia could still feel the sun set. Their nearly maniacal drive to view sunsets was driven by more than photo shoots. They felt a deeper connection than I did. My throat choked with envy. I pressed my foot on the accelerator, urging my iron horse forward, speeding its westward journey.

We blasted into Denver riding a one hundred and five degree wave of heat. By my calculations, the pop-up trailer's canvas walls would add about ten degrees to that temperature, rendering a campfire superfluous since we could most likely roast marshmallows on our skin.

Our campground was in a municipal park called Bear Creek Lake on the west side of Denver. I'd chosen the campground due to its proximity to Red Rocks, the location of our impending sunrise.

Our nice wide camping spot at Bear Creek Lake had nary a bush or tree to navigate around (or provide much-needed shade). When I first got the pop-up, my dad taught me how to back a trailer. The secret is to put your hand on the bottom of the steering wheel instead of the top. Then you simply turn the wheel in the direction you want the back of the trailer to go.

Callie stood on one side of the campsite's parking pad, while Mia manned the other. They called out directions, as I expertly swung the trailer into place. I took solace in the thought that, though I was totally incompetent when it came to keeping track of two teenagers, at least I could back a trailer!

"Hurry! Hurry, hurry, hurry!" the girls exclaimed. "We've got to get to Lookout Mountain before sunset!"

"I want to set up the camper now so we don't need to do it in the dark," I replied. "It will only take fifteen minutes if we all work together."

In a harried frenzy, Callie grabbed firewood to block the trailer's wheels while I cranked the trailer jack off the Honda's trailer hitch. Mia went to work cranking down the stabilizer jacks and Callie ran around the trailer, releasing the corner latches that allow the camper to open. Meanwhile, I rummaged through the trailer's front storage compartment, looking for the crank handle used to raise the pop-up. The longer I searched, the more an ominous suspicion took up residence in the pit of my stomach.

Where is that handle?

A quick inspection of the crank shaft yielded certain knowledge that the pop-up would not be popping up without that handle. I emptied the storage compartment, dropping the inflatable stand up paddle board, paddle, pump, fishing rods, and firewood onto the ground next to the trailer. No handle. Suspicion became a solid knowing. I'd failed to take the handle out of the shaft after collapsing the trailer in Michigan. The handle was lost somewhere along the 1,344 miles of highways and byways between. A Google search revealed the fact that all camping and outdoor stores were closed.

"Maybe someone else in the campground would let you borrow their handle," wise Mia suggested.

We peered at the RVs around us. To our chagrin, there was not a single pop-up in sight. After all, who would be stupid enough to camp in a pop-up trailer in hundred and five degree heat? I rapped on the door of the campground host's trailer.

The door was opened by a man holding a plate of something that smelled absolutely divine. My dinner plan was Progresso vegetable soup, unheated, eaten straight from the can.

"How can I help you?" he inquired pleasantly.

I sheepishly explained our predicament and asked if he, by extraordinarily odd chance, had a spare pop-up trailer handle.

"Nope," he replied. "And I don't think there are any pop-ups here right now." He kindly curtailed the temptation to finish the sentence: "Because most folks have more common sense than that!"

After a moment's hesitation, he continued, "Why don't you take a drive around the campground, just in case there's a pop-up I don't know about. I'll finish my dinner. Then I'll head over to take a look at your camper. If nothing else, I have a couple sections of stainless steel tube. With any luck, we'll find one that's the right diameter for your crank shaft. The campground has a little welding and fabrication shop. I can have the guys jury-rig something up for you."

I stared at him in surprise. The fact that there was even the remotest possibility he had stainless steel tubing in the correct size for my lifting jack was odd enough. The prospect of a county park campground with a steel fabrication shop seemed absurd. "Wow. That would be great!" I exclaimed.

The girls were nearly frantic in their panic to see sunset. "Stop it!" I hissed. "This is more important! Get in the car. The faster we find a handle, the faster we get to the sunset spot."

A thorough search of the campground failed to reveal a single solitary pop-up camper. Returning to our site, we were met by the kind campground host. "No luck?" he inquired. I despondently shook my head. Taking careful measurement of the shaft, he replied, "No worries. We'll get you squared away. The boys in the shop have welding tools. I'll have them whip you up a replacement handle. But it might take an hour or so."

I thanked the campground host profusely. By now, the sky was showing the faintest hint of pink and the girls were dancing around like they had to go pee. "I'm going to take the girls to watch the sunset," I called back to the campground host. "We'll be back soon!"

Scrambling into the car, I realized the minivan's gas gauge was pointing at empty. The girls begged me not to stop for gas as colors streaked across the western sky. By the time we'd wound our way up the tight switchbacks to Lookout Mountain, perched atop the eastern flank of the Front Range of the Rocky Mountains, I was totally stressed out. Convinced the car was running on fumes, I said, "You girls go. I'm going to find gas."

"What's the difference between getting it now and just waiting until we can all go down together?" Callie asked reasonably. "Stay and watch sunset, Mama. It will make you feel better."

"What would make me feel better is *not* running out of gas in the dark on a mountain road while a very kind campground host is back there waiting for us with a handle he just made!" I barked irritably. Callie and Mia silently exited the car and walked off in the direction of the sunset as I fought back tears.

Where is this meanness coming from? The girls just want to watch sunset.

I switchbacked down the mountain, took a wrong turn, and got hopelessly lost. I grabbed my phone. Apple Maps displayed an empty grid. No cell service.

"Selfish," a voice in my head said over and over. At first, I directed that word at Callie, though on some level, I was actually chastising myself.

After twenty minutes, my car was miraculously still running, in spite of a fuel needle deeply buried below empty. I caught a bar of cell coverage. The map revealed that I was nearly back at the spot where I'd dropped the girls.

An elated Callie answered the phone when I called.

"Mama! Mama! It was one of the most beautiful sunsets I've seen in my entire life! Where are you? Did you see it? Come to me now! Mia and I found the perfect place."

Callie shared her location and I tracked my way to her. Deep golds, purples, russet reds, and oranges raced each other in streaks across the sky, melted the ugly cobwebs that shrouded my heart.

Callie took me by the shoulders. "Breathe, sweet Mama. Look at the sunset. It's there just for you. Let go of your worry." I took a tight breath and did my best to relax the knotted rope of muscle that used to be my shoulders.

The sky darkened and we got back in the car. Now that I had internet, I plugged the location for the nearest gas station into the GPS and was dismayed to see it was fifteen minutes away.

"I really don't see how we can make it," I informed the girls.

Switch-backing down the mountain, I coasted whenever possible, conserving every precious drop of fuel. The girls cheered when they saw the lights of the gas station ahead. Pulling up to the pump, my car spluttered and died before I had the chance to turn off the ignition.

"Oh my gosh!" Mia exclaimed. "That was totally a miracle!"

We returned to the campground to yet another miracle. The campground host's steel tubing was the right diameter to fit the shaft of my pop-up trailer. Like an angel sent straight from heaven, that sweet man stood holding a brand new, make-shift crank handle. To my delight, it worked like a charm. Our pop-up was popped up in no time.

I was overwhelmed with gratitude as we were the benefactors of yet another miracle, our third of the day. Not only did we make it to the gas station by getting sixty miles out of our last gallon of gas, not only did people and events conspire perfectly to provide a new crank handle for the pop-up trailer, but the temperature dropped nearly thirty degrees, making it perfectly comfortable for sleeping. Enshrouded in darkness, we opened the windows, allowing a cool evening breeze to blow through the camper.

CHAPTER 16

To most folks, the 4,480 miles we'd traveled since leaving Ellicottville in mid-March would certainly qualify as a roadtrip. But to me, pulling out of Bear Creek Lake municipal park in early July was when the adventure truly began.

Up until that point we were always driving towards a specific destination with a specific purpose: driving to Minnesota to see my mom and dad, driving back to Ellicottville to pack up my stuff, driving to Boyne City to connect with friends.

After Denver, we had no agenda, no itinerary, no purpose-inspired northern star to guide our path. Instead of driving to get somewhere, I was simply driving because staying wasn't an option. Callie and I were incapable of standing still.

I stared at a scattered constellation of Callie's seventy-two dots on the map, trying to discern a recognizable pattern, a zodiac symbol that would provide some inkling of what lay in our future. The only clarity I received was a nagging suspicion that my woeful lack of planning might come back to bite me in the ass.

We didn't have a single reservation, which meant that each day, we'd need to figure out where to spend the night.

This proved much more challenging than the #vanlife Instagram accounts made it look.

For one thing, most state and national park campgrounds booked up months in advance. For another thing, many private campgrounds were closed due to Covid, putting even more pressure on the ones that were open. Finally, I had scant little money to pay for either public or private campsites, since over half the money I'd budgeted for this adventure was eaten up in fuel costs.

Callie discovered an app called Campendium that lists free, dispersed (back country) camping spots on public lands. Use of these free camping spots is known as boondocking. The Campendium app is populated with user-driven content, which often provides little more than a GPS coordinate.

Boondocking proved to be both boon and boondoggle. It featured many creative, off-the-beaten-path campsites with awe-inspiring vistas of nature in all her splendor. There were two major caveats:

1) "Off the beaten path" sometimes meant a potholed road, filled with deep, muddy ruts…or no road at all. Both proved challenging for my little Honda minivan pulling a pop-up trailer, especially when a lack of pull-outs made retreat difficult, or impossible.

2) Campendium's second shortcoming was the fact that some spots listed on the app were of questionable legal standing (if not outright illegal) for overnight camping.

Blissfully unaware of the challenges inherent in boondocking, we bid farewell to the inventive campground host at Bear Creek Lake campground and embarked on our westward journey.

After savoring a decadent sunrise at Red Rocks, where sky and rocks exploded in shades of garnet, russet, and gold, we went out in search of the campsite Callie had chosen to be our inaugural Campendium destination: Magnolia Creek Campground near Nederland, Colorado.

Callie had selected Nederland (known as Ned to locals) due to its proximity to Estes Park and Rocky Mountain National Park. Plus Ned had something called the Carousel of Happiness. If there was anything that seemed really, really worth riding, it was the Carousel of Happiness!

Gracie and her boyfriend, who had been working their way west in Gracie's Subaru, were to join us at Magnolia Creek Campground the following day. Our plan was to explore Rocky Mountain National Park together.

My Honda Odyssey Touring Elite minivan performed marvelously while towing the pop-up trailer across the mostly flat plains of the central section of the United States. Now it was time to test her mettle (my car was most certainly a stalwart "her") on the steep, winding switchbacks of the Rocky Mountains.

Just outside Denver, I-70 climbs the winding Floyd Hill corridor for ten steep miles. Not wanting to strain the engine, I stayed in the far right lane, as cars zoomed by on my left at seventy miles an hour. Keeping constant, steady pressure on the gas, I was delighted to discover I could avoid putting the engine into overdrive on the steep uphill grade.

Just before Idaho Springs, we took the exit for Central City. Similar to the old fashioned lettering at the entrance to an old west amusement park, a massive sign announcing the "Central City Parkway" arched across the highway, bringing to mind gold-seekers of the wild west. It soon became clear that attempting Central City Parkway's steep, winding grade with a minivan towing a pop-up trailer required the same foolhardy ambition as mining for gold in days of yore.

After twenty minutes, the van crested over a rise, entering one of the few downhill sections we encountered during the near-steady uphill climb to Nederland. I had just rounded a hairpin turn when the road dropped again sharply, then loomed like a wall in front of me. Cursing the civil engineer who thought it was okay to design a road with a near-vertical ascent, I pressed hard on the gas to capture a last burst of momentum from the short downhill grade.

Barreling down the hill, I could feel the weight of the pop-up trailer pushing us from behind. Half way up the next side, our momentum gone, the trailer pulled us back like a sea anchor. My Honda's engine strained to pull the excess weight. Callie and Mia sat frozen in silence as I dropped the car into first gear, hoping the extra power would be enough to eke us over the top.

As the car continued to slow, it occurred to me that the minivan might not be up to the task. What would I do if we just stopped? There was no shoulder. My backing skills were limited, at best. How could I possibly back down this ridiculously steep two-lane road that afforded zero visibility to cars coming from either direction?

The girls were muttering words of encouragement, hoping their affirmations would bolster the car's courage and mine as well. Oblivious to the fact that the accelerator was touching the floor, the car continued to decelerate. My hearty little minivan slowed to a near-crawl: walking, I could have kept pace with it. Then, miraculously, we crested the lip of the hill, amidst cheering and a rousing round of high-fives.

Greatly relieved (though still somewhat traumatized), I followed Campendium's coordinates for West Magnolia Campground. At West Magnolia, I learned that "campground" is a term loosely used by the US Forest Service to describe a broad range of venues where one might opt to spend the night on public lands. Following a washboarded dirt road for a few miles, we came to a place the map indicated was our turn off.

"This can't be it!" I exclaimed. There were no signs indicating a campground. I turned onto a road that was even more deeply rutted and potholed than the last.

"According to the Campendium map, this is Magnolia Creek Campground," Callie declared.

The trailer hitch bottomed out hard. Getting out of the car, I saw that the impact had disengaged the trailer brake, but mercifully hadn't damaged the trailer's electrical system. Draping the trailer brake over the hitch, I moved forward with caution. Mia got out of the car to guide me over the roughest patches. Despite our best efforts, the hitch bottomed out two more times, as I desperately scanned the surrounding high alpine landscape, looking for a place to park.

After hitting a particularly deep pothole that nearly swallowed the trailer whole, we stopped to get the lay of the land on foot, exploring dirt trails branching off from the road ahead. Callie shouted a few minutes later, "Oh my gosh! I found it! I found the perfect spot! You guys have got to see this!"

Just around the corner, a small clearing with a fire grate backed up to a stand of aspen trees and high alpine conifers. Just beyond the clearing was a field of wildflowers, set against a dramatic backdrop of the Rocky Mountains.

Mia and I stood with our mouths open. Then we turned to each other in excitement. "No way, no way, no way! This place is amazing! How did we get so lucky?" Navigating the remaining few hundred feet to the campsite, I successfully backed the trailer next to the fire pit and we settled in for the night.

The next morning, we went into Nederland to ride the Carousel of Happiness and get cell phone service. Ironically, the Carousel of Happiness was closed due to Covid, an ominous portent to the events that followed.

A perusal of text messages revealed the fact that Gracie and her boyfriend had run into trouble on Vail Pass. En route to join us at Magnolia Creek Campground, Gracie's Subaru's engine blew up when it ran out of oil. The car had to be towed to a Subaru dealership in Silverthorne.

I dialed Gracie's number. After a few rings, she answered the phone and burst into tears.

"The technician thinks the entire engine needs to be replaced, Mom. What will I do? I'm on a roadtrip without a car!"

My heart dropped. Gracie had borrowed five thousand dollars from me to buy the car just six weeks earlier. Further complicating matters, the immobile Subaru held all her worldly possessions.

"We'll just have to take all this as it comes, baby. Everything happens for a reason," I said, with little conviction.

I made plans to collect Gracie and her boyfriend from the Subaru dealership, which involved driving back down the mountain to Idaho Springs, and continuing up I-70 to Silverthorne. The Honda minivan felt perfectly buoyant without the trailer.

Gracie and her boyfriend were waiting by the road outside the dealership when we arrived. I held Gracie as she erupted in a fresh bout of sobs. The Subaru had been more than her first car. It was her home. She spent her entire two thousand dollars of savings, as well as the loan from me, to purchase it. The dealership's mechanic presented an estimate of over eight thousand dollars to repair the vehicle. Gracie's Subaru was totaled.

"Well, let's get some lunch and head back to the campsite. You guys can spend the night with us in the camper. We'll come up with a plan from there," I suggested ruefully.

Returning to Magnolia Creek Campground a few hours later, something felt off. Callie and I looked at each other. "Is this the right place?" Callie asked. The turn looked the same, but the road itself was different. It had been completely bulldozed. Heaping mounds of dirt lay directly in our path.

I stopped the car. In the silence that ensued, the truth slowly dawned on me. The road was being repaired. Hard-packed potholes had been replaced by deep, soft mounds of dirt, freshly churned by a bulldozer. Forward progress was impossible.

Stunned, I emerged from the car. Skirting one of the dirt heaps, I walked around a bend in the road and came face-to-face with a massive bulldozer. Panic rose in my chest. I stared at the point beyond the next rise where I knew my pop-up trailer was parked.

Peering past the bulldozer, the road was torn up as far as I could see. Even without the pop-up trailer, my Honda Odyssey would have a tough time making it through.

I marched up to the bulldozer and the driver opened the cab door. "Hey! My trailer is parked up the road," I declared, hoping to mask the panic in my voice. "Any idea how I can get to it?"

The driver barked something into a walkie talkie. Within a couple minutes, a small skid steer scooted into view.

"Sorry for the inconvenience, ma'am," the skid steer driver said. "You're in that pop-up over the hill? It'll be about fifteen to twenty minutes, but I'll get you there."

Walking back to the car, I suddenly realized how Gracie felt. No matter how modest our accommodations had become, her car and my pop-up trailer provided sanctuary, a moving sense of place. It was alarming to feel like your home was in danger, no matter what shape or form "home" might take.

Back at the car, I started the engine, pulled forward, and informed the kids of the skid steer driver's promise to reunite us with the pop-up trailer in twenty minutes. The kids burst out laughing. "No *way!*" They declared. "There's no *way* that's going to happen."

But the skid steer driver skillfully used his bucket to back-blade a rough path through the churning ocean of dirt. When he was done, it was just the width of my car. Bucking like a bronco, I raced down the narrow trail, attempting to keep minivan's wheels from getting mired in the soft, freshly tilled soil.

"Wow. That's a lot of drama for one day!" I exclaimed. "I think we all need to take fifteen minutes to meditate and calm our nerves." The kids heartily agreed.

As we each walked in different directions, seeking a spot that would inspire us to settle into the space inside our minds, I was occupied with a nagging thought.

When good things happen, I feel blessed. When bad things happen, I don't feel blessed. Challenges make me doubt my worthiness.

I found a rock in a high alpine clearing. Relaxing into meditation, the Big Guy was ready with a reply. "Your challenges aren't punishments. In fact, it's just the opposite. Each challenge is a precious gift, chosen with care just for you. These gifts are beautifully wrapped. They shape you into the person you need to become in order to accomplish your soul's purpose."

Those words rang true.

Challenges aren't random. Gracie's engine could have blown up anywhere between Boyne City and Denver. The fact that it happened when I was just an hour away was no coincidence. I was there to help her when she needed me.

We were fortunate the bulldozer driver was still there when we arrived, so he could plow a path to the trailer. And we were so lucky that it hadn't rained, which would have made the road impassable.

I lost the trailer's crank shaft just before arriving at a camp ground with welding supplies to rebuild a new one. I ran out of gas just as I pulled up to the pump.

These challenges were specially crafted for a single purpose: to teach me to trust*! Even in the midst of challenge, events are unfolding exactly as they are meant to unfold, and this divine timing is perfect.*

"You're not alone. You've never been alone," the Big Guy affirmed. "Your challenges have always been specifically designed for you to underscore how very much you are loved. You are, and always have been, worthy of the many blessings you receive. Your challenges are lessons to trust, not only in God's power to guide and protect you, but that you are *worthy* of that guidance and protection."

Sitting in an alpine field, surrounded by wildflowers, I watched the sun's rays dancing on tree-studded mountain slopes in the distance and felt deeply grateful. Grateful we made it back to the trailer. Grateful Gracie and her boyfriend weren't hurt when the Subaru's engine blew up on Vail pass. Grateful to have both my girls with me. Grateful for the food that filled our bellies. Grateful for the awe-inspiring natural beauty all around us. Grateful for the freedom to chart my own course. And yes, grateful for the challenges that taught me to trust divine guidance.

CHAPTER 17

Our next stop was our former home town of Eagle, Colorado. After the harrowing experience getting into Magnolia Campground, I was loathe to venture into the mountains above Eagle with the pop-up trailer. There was free camping along Hardscrabble Road, but having explored that road on several occasions, I knew it lived up to its rough-and-tumble name. Instead, I paid ten dollars a night to camp at a Bureau of Land Management (BLM) rustic campground near the Eagle River in Gypsum.

While Gracie attempted to discern her next move, I struggled to hold my equilibrium. The contrast of living in a pop-up trailer in a place where we'd once occupied a million dollar home was surreal. I was embarrassed to return to my old stomping grounds without a home...or a husband.

Two nights in a row, I showed up on the doorsteps of dear family friends, wearing the same dresses I'd worn when we'd lived in Eagle. I even brought the same bottle of wine to the parties. But I wasn't the same me.

My friends were warm, welcoming and so incredibly supportive. But I felt like an alien in a world that was once mine. I suspected that if they knew how I really lived, they would be shocked and a little repulsed. A voice in my head whispered, "Phony. Imposter."

While the kids eagerly accepted invitations to enjoy warm meals, comfortable beds, and warm showers, I declined their offers to stay. Instead, I passed four chilly nights in the pop-up trailer, bathing naked in the cold water of the Eagle River.

I was nervous that a momentary return to a life of comfort might open an aching longing for domestication, a willingness to accept the yoke of complacency in exchange for the warmth and safety of hearth and home. But like it or not, that yoke was broken beyond repair. And there was no hearth and home to return to, whether I ached for it or not.

Due to the loss of Gracie's vehicle, we stayed in Eagle longer than we'd planned. Though Callie and I were on the road for an indeterminate period of time, Mia was not. We had only two weeks before Mia would fly home from Las Vegas to Michigan. The girls were anxious to cover as much ground as possible.

With great angst, Gracie and I wrestled with the pros and cons of various options, desperate to determine her next move. I deeply wanted Gracie and her boyfriend to come with me. She flatly refused.

Gracie and Callie were very close, especially after a soul-bonding ceremony in Peru two years earlier. They share sister secrets, like sneaking out to get tattoos in Cusco or getting their noses pierced together in Nicaragua.

That being said, the sisters fought like feral cats. Stress from knock-down-drag-out sibling brawls would have likely put all of us over the edge. In light of this fact, wise Gracie declined my many pleas to join our roadtrip adventure.

"My boyfriend is thinking of getting a new truck," Gracie said. "If he can find something here, we can use that to continue on our roadtrip."

"Interesting thought. But the Subaru had a bed. Where will you guys sleep?"

"I don't know, Mom. Maybe we'll get a tent," Gracie replied in exasperation.

I knew Gracie was frustrated and overwhelmed. In truth, neither she nor her boyfriend had money for a new vehicle. She was having horrific struggles with John and his entire side of the family. Staying with relatives on that side of the family was entirely off the table.

"Just make up your mind, Gracie!" Callie exclaimed. "We've got to get going. We're already two days behind schedule."

"Do you really think your stupid Instagram profile is more important than my car? In case you haven't figured it out, my car is my home! Without a *car*, I have no place to *live*!" A storm was brewing over Gracie's head. It was time to diffuse the situation or take cover.

"Listen, Grace. Why don't you guys just come with us to Vegas. I'm guessing vehicle prices will be lower there than in the Vail Valley," I suggested.

"Mom! For once and for all, I am *not* getting sucked into the social media influencer tour!" Gracie declared.

"For your information, social media influencers focus on bikini shots and modeling. I want to be a travel influencer and inspire other people to travel," Callie exclaimed defensively. "Besides, this roadtrip is a once in a lifetime experience, and I've been planning it for years—way before I wanted to be a travel influencer. We are doing some major backcountry hikes. Every day we're stuck here is another hike that drops off the list!"

We'd already spent four days in Eagle, which was two days more than we'd intended. It was time to go. Paralyzed by indecision, Gracie and her boyfriend were stuck. Unwilling to come with me, with no clear path forward, they took up residence with our friends, the Conklins.

My throat tightened as I pulled away from the curb in front of the Conklin's house. The Honda minivan bucked wildly as it tugged my pop-up trailer over Eagle Ranch's speed bumps a little too fast. Tears blurred my vision.

You just left the Conklins to figure out what to do with Gracie. Again.

Less than three years earlier, it was the Conklins who came to our rescue when Gracie was struggling with the depression and anxiety. While I stayed in Ellicottville to run the store, Gracie moved to Colorado to live with the Conklins. Passing the baton to the Conklins again was like admitting yet another parental defeat.

Go ahead and leave. That's what you do best. You left Adventure Bound without even asking for a share of the business you spent five years helping to build. You left your parents to deal with Dad's cancer on their own. You left the Kuhns to deal with the gecko, aquatic frog...and Bentley. What about all the failed chicken experiments? Ditching the ducks in Boyne Mountain's pond? You left Christopher. Now you're leaving Gracie.

In my heart of hearts, I knew much of that rant wasn't fair. Each accusation involved a complex web of factors. Still, taken as a whole, the picture was clear. When the shit hit the fan, I ducked and ran.

Callie, Mia, and I were quiet as we crossed south-central Colorado en route to Great Sand Dunes National Park. The sun had just dipped below the western horizon when we pulled into the sand dunes' parking lot.

The girls planned to hike to the top in the dark, where they would camp out and watch the sun rise from the top of the dunes. I wasn't keen on this plan, as camping on the dunes was prohibited.

"I don't know..." I hedged, feeling the weight of civic propriety. "What if you get caught? I don't think either of us will have cell service."

My voice lacked conviction. After all, if I was Callie's age, I would *absolutely* spend the night on top of the sand dunes. I was even half-tempted to do it now.

Waving her arms in a sweeping gesture that encompassed the entirety of Great Sand Dunes National Park, Callie exclaimed, "Who the heck is going to search for us in all that?" She quickly packed a tent and sleeping bag into her backpack.

Taking advantage of a lack of park service patrols didn't seem fair.

But crawling through a hole in the fence doesn't mean I created the hole, does it? After all, I'm not even the one crawling through the hole. I'm just letting the kids crawl through it. That's okay, right?

Taken aback by the feral lawlessness of this line of thinking, I felt the voice of societal judgement rising in rebuttal. But societal judgement was no friend of mine, so I quickly stomped it back down. After all, I'd berated myself enough for one day.

Light was fading. Not waiting for my permission or even a reply, Callie chirped, "It's almost dark. We've got to go!" She gave me a peck on the cheek before she and Mia scampered off.

I hesitated, standing under the glaring lights that illuminated the visitor's center parking lot as the girls' forms retreating into the shadows. Then I climbed back into the minivan, hoping to finding a place to camp before all light was lost.

Campendium listed a free campground with electrical hookups just over ten minutes away at the San Luis State Wildlife Campground. I was skeptical. How could a state campground—much less one that includes electrical hookups—be free? According to their website, the state park status changed to a state wildlife area on May 1, 2017. Colorado Parks and Wildlife "provides free electrical hook-ups at some sites and will continue to do so until costs become prohibitive."

During the short ten minute drive to San Luis State Wildlife Campground, I began to worry. What were the odds that there would be space available in a campground with free hookups? Electricity was a rare luxury. It had been over a week since I'd camped in a spot with electrical hookups.

It was pitch black by the time I arrived at San Luis Campground. The minivan's headlights had trouble penetrating a low-lying mist. Scouting the area with my cell phone's flashlight, I was delighted to find an empty pull-through spot. I set up the pop-up trailer, plugged the camper into the electric box (Yes! There was working electric!) and enjoyed the rare opportunity to read by the trailer's electric lights.

The next morning, the early morning desert beckoned, enticing me to wander over hard-packed stretches of cactus-studded land that stretched out expansively for miles in every direction. It amazed me that this barren expanse of dry cracked clay, barely supporting sagebrush, would be considered a wildlife refuge.

Venturing a mile or so from the campground, I began to notice long trails through the dirt, some as narrow as my finger and some as wide as my arm. The trails criss-crossed all over the desert floor. It slowly dawned on me that these trails were made by snakes…lots and lots of snakes. I high-stepped the mile back to the camper and packed up to meet the girls.

The Great Sand Dunes, which rise seven hundred and fifty feet from base to crest, are the largest dunes in North America. Though it was only eight o'clock in the morning, it was already hot. Ascending the steep mountain of sand, I met the girls as they were running down.

"Mom!" Callie exclaimed excitedly, "You should see the pictures we got. They are absolutely amazing." She scrolled through a couple pictures on Mia's professional camera.

I hadn't realized the girls had brought long flowing dresses with them. In the photos, the girls looked like exotic desert trees, standing atop the dunes at daybreak, with nothing but sand as far as the eye could see. Scrolling through the stunning pictures, I felt very good about making the decision (it was a decision, wasn't it?) to let them spend the night on the dunes.

From the Great Sand Dunes, we drove to Telluride, stopping to swim at Pagosa Hot Springs. It was a hot day. The river was so refreshing. I remembered a family trip John and I had made to Pagosa Hot Springs when the kids were young. They loved swimming over the small waterfalls, their little bodies buoyant in the current. We used mud from the river bottom to paint our faces and bodies.

Smiling at the memory of the kids covered in mud, I looked up to see Mia emerging from the cool water. She reached for her towel.

To Mia's dismay, her phone, which had been sitting on her towel when she unfurled it, fell into the river and was swept away by the current. Mia and I locked eyes, unable to process what had just happened. The search for Mia's phone was short-lived, as we both accepted the futility of the effort. The device was gone.

In an attempt to assuage Mia's guilt and pain, I promised her the universal teenage panacea...a hamburger, milkshake, and fries. After existing mostly on fruit and bagged salads from Walmart, the promise of a hamburger had the desired effect.

Steamies Burger Bar in Telluride managed to surpass our wildest expectations, delivering the best burger I've had in my entire life.

Eagerly anticipating our food's arrival, I tried to distract my grumbling stomach by placing a long overdue call to the public relations specialist I'd hired for Nomaditudes. A twenty minute conversation revealed the fact that absolutely no headway had been made during his first month (and $1,750) on the job. Media outlets were not remotely interested in risking backlash from covering a story about student travel when a global travel ban was still in effect.

Only one month into a three month PR contract, I sorely regretted my bad timing and bravado. In the end, I agreed to send the media guy a check for one month's work, and he agreed to abandon a PR initiative that was doomed to failure. In truth, I think he was as relieved as I was.

Feeling abashed, I arrived back at the table which was piled with food. The sight was cheering. Just as the name implies, Steamies steams their burgers as opposed to charbroiling or grilling. Supposedly, steaming makes their burgers healthier. I can vouch for the fact that it makes them delicious-er!

I ordered the Yeti Burger, which the menu said was voted the number one burger in Colorado. I'm not sure who counts the votes, but I'd personally cast my ballot for that Yeti Burger. "All Natural Colorado Beef topped with Cheddar Cheese, Applewood Smoked Bacon, Crispy Onion

Strings, topped with a housemade BBQ Ranch Sauce served on a Golden Toasted Brioche Bun." Oh baby!

The great thing about existing on a diet of bagged salads and canned soup is that just about any other food is a delicacy. In the case of Steamies burgers, our meal was simply decadent.

Though it took weeks to stop fantasizing about Steamies burgers, it took a single hike to burn the calories. After spending the night camping at a free roadside parking lot just outside Telluride, the girls and I were ready to tackle Telluride's iconic Blue Lake Trail.

At the start of the three hour hike, Mia and Callie were happily chatting away, clearly breathing easily and therefore unaware of my impending heart failure.

To keep from getting dropped, I practiced a hiking technique I used to keep up with people (like John) whose legs were longer than mine: two normal steps, one *long*, two normal steps, one *long*. I also calmed my mind, willing myself to breathe through my nose at least half the time, to trick my parasympathetic nervous system into thinking I wasn't actually dying.

The girls stopped for a mini photo shoot, giving me the chance to gain valuable ground. Even if my heart and lungs didn't allow me to keep up with two ultra-fit sixteen-year-old girls, I was proud of the fact that my muscles and joints were strong enough to handle the strenuous hike.

When their photo session was over, the girls launched past me, continuing to climb in altitude with the ease of a helium balloon. I abandoned all of hope keeping up. Relaxing into an easy gait, I inhaled deeply. The scent of fresh pine melted on my tongue like a lemon drop, dissolving with my breath as the miles passed.

The hike provided space to reflect on the mental tongue-lashing I'd given myself when leaving Eagle.

"You bear the full weight of responsibility when things go wrong, while failing to take credit when things go right," the Big Guy remarked. "It's time to let go of that self-criticism and disapproval. This is your time to focus on self-love."

I took a deep breath and relaxed into the steep climb to Blue Lake.

The scene at trail's end took away what little air was left in my lungs. Draped in a skirt of scree, Mt. Sneffels rose dramatically above a surreal turquoise lake that God already photo-shopped. As I walked to the far end of the lake, wildflowers ran rampant in the meadow, embroidering the base of the mountain's skirt. Peeking shyly from behind the great mountain's legs, a little marmot stared at me inquisitively.

Callie and Mia, who had arrived at the lake long before me, were happily snapping pictures of each other. After spending over an hour at the lake, I reminded the girls that they were hoping to make it to Utah by sunset.

Mia's flight from Las Vegas was just five days hence. The distance we needed to cover (both by car and on foot) to reach the rest of Callie's Colorado, Utah, and Nevada destinations was not simply impractical; it was utterly impossible. With no small amount of disappointment, the girls crossed several stops off the list. This still left a highly aggressive itinerary, one that required us to witness sunset in one location and sunrise in another.

By the time we descended the Blue Lakes Trail, I was utterly exhausted. It was late afternoon when we arrived back at the car, and we still had a four hour drive to Mexican Hat, Utah. Callie wanted to stay at a free campsite in Goosenecks State Park because it was close to the Valley of the Gods, our next sunrise photo spot.

We arrived at Goosenecks State Park well after dark. It was actually more of a pull-off, a place where the dirt road we'd been traveling widened into a parking area.

"I think we're here," Callie said, eyeing the map on the Campendium app. "It looks like this is it. But be careful. One of the comments says that there is a steep drop just to the right as you enter this pull-off."

Dead tired, we set up camp in the dark, hoping to catch a few hours of sleep before heading to the Valley of the Gods for sunrise.

Waking at daybreak, I opened the camper's door and my jaw dropped in awe. A gooseneck, the geological feature for which the nearby state park was named, is a sinuous canyon or valley formed by moving water. Horseshoe Bend, one of the most iconic landmarks in Arizona, is a famous example of a gooseneck.

We were parked right at the brink of a canyon that dropped a thousand feet to the San Juan River. Three hundred million years of moving water created this U-shaped canyon, exposing layer upon layer of red sandstone in the process. We stood rooted to the spot, basking in the glow of our good fortune—not just for the beauty of the landscape at our feet, but for the fact that we didn't accidentally drive another fifteen feet in the dark and plunge to a fiery death in the canyon below. "Thank you, Universe," I whispered.

Witnessing the Valley of the Gods at sunrise was mystical. This was Navajo country. A blanket of reverence shrouded towering spires in sacredness. For two hours, we drove through an alien landscape where earth mirrored sky. The rising sun streaked the heavens with colors mimicking the color spectrum of the rocks: glowing shades of gold, orange, and red.

We were entirely alone. With the exception of a single car parked far off in the distance, we did not encounter a single person or vehicle. Wending our way through the landscape, I imagined the Creator playing in a sandbox. Red earth looked as if it had been dumped from a sand bucket. Giant russet sandcastles had been sprayed with a hose, forming sun-hardened spires in a multitude of shapes, colors, and sizes.

By the time we returned to the camper at nine that morning, the air was already oppressively hot. Sweat was pouring down our faces in the few minutes it took to take down the pop-up trailer. We decided our next stop would be Lake Powell. The weather forecast indicated the town of

Lake Powell would see temperatures in excess of one hundred degrees over the upcoming days, a fact that didn't bode well for camping.

After a late morning breakfast in Mexican Hat, suffocating heat prompted us to tarry a while beside the San Juan River.

The water of the San Juan River was a milky, grayish-brown. The cool liquid felt luxurious on my burning hot skin as I knelt in the slow-moving flow at river's edge. Though stifling heat of the parking lot made it hard to breathe, the air above the river smelled rich, damp, and earthy.

I slipped off my swimsuit. Like an insect newly hatched, I spread my arms and legs wide, allowing the soft maternal water to envelope every inch of my body. Bathing in the sediment-rich waters of the San Juan felt like baptism. In nature's sweet embrace, something I hadn't realized was broken was healed.

Sufficiently cooled, I braved the sun's abusive glare to view petroglyphs on the cliff walls beyond the parking lot. Broad-shouldered anthropomorphic figures shared the wall with decades of graffiti. It was difficult to determine which figures were native and which were the result of desecration. I took a short trail that led to a shaded spot at the cliff's base.

Pressing my hands against the cool stone, I wondered at the ancient people who painted the enduring images on the cliff face above me. Had their daily concerns centered exclusively on the task of survival, or had they too wrestled with thoughts of love, loss, and purpose? Were their lives really as simplistic as their nature-based art suggested? Or was their art allegorical, representing complex human experiences and deeper emotional conditions?

And what the hell would they think of this white woman with two teenage girls, traversing their ancestral lands in a minivan pulling a pop-up trailer? Something told me that if these people had the spiritual wherewithal to integrate vision quests into their rites of passage, they would understand my journey.

CHAPTER 18

After paying homage to the ancient indigenous artists who left their mark on the San Juan River valley cliff wall (and possibly graffiti artists who had done the same), I returned to the water to cool off, then quickly hopped into an air-conditioned car for the six hour drive to Lake Powell.

There were no free camping options near Lake Powell, so we crossed our fingers that the National Forest Service's Beehive campground—which was available on a first-come-first-serve basis—would have space available.

Yet again, we arrived after dark. Scanning the parking lot by headlight, we spotted an empty spot next to a picnic table.

The word "campground" implies multiple campsites, trees, and things like electrical hookups, water, bathrooms (or at least a porta-potty), and trash cans. Alas, Beehive campground had none of these. With only six parking slots and no amenities, Beehive was a scenic fourteen-dollars-a-night parking spot with a picnic bench overlooking Lake Powell.

At the height of summer, the campground was half empty due to the fact that Page, Arizona experiences temperatures in excess of one hundred degrees in July. Without electrical hookups, campers either need to have generators to run their air conditioning or suffer through sweltering summer heat. For two nights, we did the latter.

After exploring Horseshoe Bend and seeking respite from the heat in the cool water of Lake Powell, we hobbled into Las Vegas with a van and trailer in desperate need of maintenance. The minivan's tires were showing significant signs of wear, and though the van's brakes were fine, I wanted get the trailer's brakes checked after the grueling mountain descents.

Similar to Colorado mountain roads, Walmart parking lots proved to be detrimental to the pop-up trailer's health. On more than one occasion, the dip at the entrance of a Walmart parking lot caused my hitch to bottom out, disengaging or damaging the trailer's electrical harness. As a result, my tail lights would flicker, or stop working altogether. In Vegas, I made much-needed service appointments for both the Honda and the trailer.

Mia's parents had graciously offered the use of their timeshare in Las Vegas, and we were all fantasizing about warm showers and air conditioned bedrooms. After weeks in the pop-up trailer, a real bed felt like true Vegas-style decadence.

The car was quieter, more gloomy, in anticipation of Mia's impending departure two days hence. Callie and I were a little nervous at the prospect of being alone in each other's company. Mia's energy buoyed us up, keeping dark clouds at bay.

I'd rarely cried after the divorce and hadn't seen Callie cry either. I worried there might be hell to pay for what must surely be a shit-load of emotional repression. At any moment, our psyches might launch a mortar attack against those walls of mental masonry.

In Mia's presence, Callie and I held it together. What would our post-Mia dynamic look like? The roadtrip didn't have a defined end date. Based on the number of destinations on Callie's list, we were looking at another two months of travel; just the two of us, covering thousands of miles without Mia's levity, wisdom, and companionship.

Pulling off the highway, we drove past empty hotels and casinos near the famous Las Vegas Strip. The scene that met us was shocking, bringing to mind post-apocalyptic images from a Mad Max movie. The glaring lights of casinos were dark and the air inside was tepid as casino owners attempted to alleviate sky-high utility expenses. Having spent weeks in the wilderness, we'd forgotten that a global pandemic had dried up the rivers of tourists that normally thronged these streets, draining the life blood from Sin City.

Vegas was pathetic without her makeup. There were no fancy shows, no expensive restaurants, no limos or crowds cruising the Strip. Without the hoards of tourists she wears like a fancy party dress, Vegas just looked old, tired, and seedy. Her remaining inhabitants, those who had nowhere else to go, were drug-addled prostitutes and vagrants, precious children of God living the hard-knock life. My heart went out to them as they shuffled in aimless circles, clinging to the shade. Every few minutes, we heard police sirens. Twice, we witnessed altercations with the police.

Parking sideways in the parking lot, I backed the trailer up to a cement wall, disconnected it, then parked my minivan in front of the hitch at a right angle, forming a T. This made it impossible for someone with a hitch to snip the lock and steal my pop-up.

The sobering reality was that I felt a sense of commonality with the homeless people in Las Vegas, a fact I found disconcerting. When we were little, my mom used to teach empathy by saying, "But for the grace of God, there go I." Those words hit dangerously close to home.

I was fortunate to have parents who lent me money to buy my eight thousand dollar home. I was grateful to have money for gas, but I was keenly aware of each dollar I spent on food and camping. However, spending $1,750 for a PR guy was a business expense (albeit a truly foolish one), and therefore, in my mind, allowable.

Though my basic needs were met for the foreseeable future and I was hopeful that Nomaditudes would provide income in the fall, I felt financially vulnerable. Callie could feel it. My anxiety was contagious. I tried to convince her that my fears were unfounded. Still, I worried. And she worried that I worried. Vegas fueled the flames of worry into full-blown anxiety. Its itinerancy was raw and brutal.

I needed a distraction, a shift in focus. Aside from gambling, what is Vegas's distraction of choice? Sex!

Despite the fact I'd been an adult for a full thirty-three years, my shadow had never darkened the doorway of an adult store. Even t-shirts with sexually suggestive slogans gave me the heebie jeebies.

But visiting a sex shop in Las Vegas was at the top of the girls' to-do list. We figured, if you're going to do it, you might as well go big. Callie's internet research led us to a huge sex superstore.

What would people think if they knew I was allowing the girls to visit a sex shop in Las Vegas?

The Big Guy asked, "What is this audience that is still judging you? Who are you still performing for? Do you feel like you are doing something wrong?"

No. It's lighthearted and fun. The girls and I need that right now. Besides, I don't want my kids to feel guilt or shame around the topic of sex. I want them to feel like they can talk to me freely and openly.

As the girls giggled their way towards the tawdry lingerie hanging on the back wall, I found myself awkwardly standing in an aisle amid a stunning array of rubber penises in absolutely every shape, color, and size.

In an attempt to conceal my squeamishness, I did my level best to move through the aisles with the confidence of one who regularly frequents sex shops. Reading the funny names of the sex toys, I snorted and chortled.

It reminded me of my first visit to a marijuana dispensary. Creative marketers used pot parodies when naming candy bars, such as Reefers Peanut Butter Cups in packaging that looked like Reeces Peanut Butter Cups, and Stoner Patch Dummies that looked exactly like Sour Patch Gummies.

I snickered at the Joy Stick Thruster and Tickle Me Pink Vibrator. My imagination ran wild, trying to fathom the use for items like the Mr. Swirly Glass Dildo (who the heck thinks it's a good idea to shove glass up into their nether-regions?), the Clone-a-Willy vibrating dildo kit (what's in the *kit?*), the double-ended dildo (hmm…), strap-on dildos, and the enigmatic rabbit vibrators.

"Can I help you?" a sales woman asked, startling me out of deep contemplation.

"Oh! I, um…Think I might be interested in…um…a product of some kind."

What the heck am I doing?

"Certainly," the woman replied, exuding confidence. "What kind of toy are you looking for?"

For some reason, her use of the word "toy" made me giggle.

This isn't anything serious! It's just a toy.

"Well, I don't know. What do you recommend?"

She looks normal. Not like someone who would be into anything painful or kinky.

"Depends what you're looking for," she replied. "Do you want clitoral or vaginal stimulation?"

Again, I giggled.

How can a person ask a question like that with a straight face?

"Or anal," another sales clerk piped up helpfully. I guffawed, then blushed.

"I have no clue," I replied honestly.

That response drew a crowd. Apparently, a fifty-one-year-old sex toy virgin isn't something you see every day in Las Vegas. Customers, nonchalantly eavesdropping, stepped forward to extol the virtues of their favorite toys.

I was quickly overwhelmed and somewhat terrified. I scanned the room to make sure Callie and Mia weren't witness to the sudden attention being lavished on me. To my relief, they were safely in the dressing room trying on teddies.

A male sales clerk pulled a massive dildo from the locked display case behind the counter, holding it out for my inspection.

I must have let out a little, "Eep…" because my original sales lady said, "Woah there, cowboy. We don't want to scare the lady!"

She handed me a small innocuous box. In it was a tiny, purple, lipstick-looking device, not much bigger than my thumb. After being exposed (figuratively) to much more intriguing toys, the Screaming O Vooom seemed somewhat underwhelming. I looked at the sales lady dubiously.

I'm clearly a novice, but this little guy looks like a waste of money.

"This will get the job done without risking bodily harm," the sales woman said with a Cheshire grin. The other customers and attending salespeople nodded knowingly, several having personally experienced the Screaming O's purple pleasures. "And it's waterproof," she added brightly, bringing to mind a fresh flurry of naughty thoughts.

Ready to be done with the ordeal, I paid for the vibrator along with a ridiculously overpriced spray bottle of toy cleaner.

"I'll be waiting for you in the car," I called to the girls, who were still snorting with delight in the dressing room.

Sadly, my sweet little tube of purple passion was *stolen* at a hotel in Peru several months later. It was on the bedside table when I left for a hike. When I returned that afternoon, it was gone. I searched everywhere for it. But alas, my Screaming O Vooom was no where to be found.

What kind of person steals another woman's vibrator, I ask you? More odd than the circumstances surrounding the loss of my vibrator was the fact that I felt a tinge of jealousy that I'd never felt over John's affair. Weird, right?

After all, unlike husbands, vibrators are easily replaced.

CHAPTER 19

We bid farewell to Mia with heavy hearts. Callie and I traveled most of the distance between Las Vegas and Zion National Park in silence. The empty space wasn't simply vacant. It was occupied by something solid and sad. Callie and I felt as if Mia, with her upbeat enthusiasm, had been replaced by another silent traveling companion—one who was the mirror opposite of her.

By the time we arrived at Zion, we didn't have the mental energy to search for a place to spend the night. I prayed we'd find a place to stay without effort.

According to Campendium, Zion's Watchman Campground was one of the nicest National Park campgrounds in the United States. It filled up months in advance, especially during the summer.

Sure enough, the sign at the campground's entrance said, "No Vacancy." I pulled up to the campground's registration cabin anyway. The park ranger was just finishing up a phone conversation.

Hanging up, he asked, "You checking in?"

"Um…I know it says no vacancy, but I just wanted to see if you happen to have any cancellations?" I asked sheepishly.

He glanced from me to Callie, then leaned out the window to view the pop-up trailer. "Hah!" He exclaimed. "This must be your lucky day! I literally just got off the phone with someone who cancelled their spot for tonight. It wouldn't fit a big rig, but it's the perfect size for your pop-up trailer. And it's right along the river. I think you ladies will be really happy with that spot!"

"Thank you, Universe," Callie and I whispered.

Gratitude pierced the gloom for a moment. But it wasn't long before the heaviness returned. Like a melancholy pigeon temporarily shooed from the eves, it stubbornly re-alighted and set up camp.

That evening, as we went to watch sunset at Zion's famous canyon overlook, Callie hiked up for a better view and dropped the camera Mia had given her for her birthday. The camera was broken.

Returning to the car, Callie realized she didn't have her phone. A frantic search revealed the fact that the phone was indeed missing. She'd left it sitting on the hood of the car as we rushed off to catch sunset. When we returned to the car, the phone was no longer on the van's hood.

Gloom turned to despair as we spent the next three days half-heartedly exploring Zion and Bryce Canyon. It was becoming abundantly clear that the use of drones was prohibited in most of the locations Callie was hoping to visit. How would she become an Instagram travel influencer without her iPhone or camera? My antiquated phone's outdated camera could never produced the high resolution images Instagram devotees had come to expect.

The fact that we were immersed in such dramatic scenic glory made the sadness feel all the more tragic. This spectacular display of natural beauty was wasted on us. The fact that it couldn't elicit the awe and appreciation it so richly deserved made us feel petty and self-absorbed. And so the heaviness accumulated like noxious fumes settling into the pit of our stomachs.

Sans phone and camera, Callie struggled to regain her equilibrium. Seeing her pain broke my heart. Whether it was because we couldn't stand to see the other sad or because we didn't want to contribute to each other's sadness, Callie and I spent most of our time in Bryce Canyon hiking independently.

I lingered at overlooks, gazing at the magnificent artistry of sunlight on towering spires in shades of scarlet, orange, and vermilion, willing the beauty of the place to move me, shape me, inspire me.

Make me feel something, *damn it!*

But my soul failed to respond. I was bone dry. Empty.

Staying still made us both feel anxious. We were running just ahead of a tidal wave of sadness. If we stopped too long, it might overwhelm us. So we kept moving.

As the miles rolled by, Callie attempted to mitigate the gloom by whiling away the hours editing drone footage. After all, the drone was the only camera she had left.

Callie had a knack for portraying her subjects from new, innovative perspectives. She began shooting pictures with the drone like most people would shoot pictures with a camera, interspersing the pictures into her drone edits.

En route to Salt Lake City, Callie downloaded a trial version of an expensive video editing software program and devoured every tutorial she could find, not stopping until she'd sucked the meat and marrow from its bones.

Long after dark, we were still an hour out of Salt Lake. It was time to find a place to spend the night, preferably one that was free.

The freeway looked like any suburban freeway. There was no public land for miles. However, Callie had identified a free parking lot on Campendium that was just a little over a mile off the freeway exit.

By the time we arrived, Callie was asleep. I crossed my fingers that there would be space for a pop-up camper at this time of night.

Taking the highway exit, I plugged the coordinates into my phone's GPS. Freeway lights quickly disappeared from view as I wound up a steep gravel road. The minivan's engine strained against the weight of the trailer and its wheels spun out a few times.

Cresting over a rise, the GPS indicated we had arrived at our destination. But there was no parking lot in sight. I continued to wind up the road and came to a sign. Reading by headlight, the sign indicated overnight camping regulations for the parking lot beyond. It was pitch black. I couldn't see a thing beyond the beam of the van's lights.

As I drove through the lot, my headlights illuminated a few skeletal vehicles hovering in the shadows, scattered around the outside edge of the parking lot. I parked in a wide open space. Not wanting to wake Callie, who was still fast asleep in the passenger seat of the minivan, I wearily set up the pop-up trailer alone.

Even in sleep, Callie's heaviness was contagious. Sorrow settled like a wet blanket on my shoulders as I blocked the wheels, disconnected the trailer, cranked up the pop-up and cranked down the stabilizer jacks. Once the trailer was set up, I shuffled Callie inside and dropped into my own bed, asleep before my head hit the pillow.

After what seemed like a few short hours, the sound of car engines shutting off and car doors slamming nudged at the edge of consciousness. But I couldn't bring myself to wake fully. Then I heard voices calling to each other in loud whispers. Cracking an eye, I was surprised to discover the darkness was softening into daybreak. Light was just starting to seep in through the camper's canvas exterior.

"Who the heck is up at this hour?" I wondered aloud.

Unzipping a canvas window, I saw more cars arriving. Some were parked just behind the camper. Scanning the lot, I realized all the overnight vehicles were parked at the opposite end of the lot. It seemed we had inadvertently camped in the middle of a spot where cars were arriving in droves, at an ungodly time in the morning.

What the hell?

Perplexed, I noticed people, mostly men, were opening the trunks of their cars and extracting huge backpacks that looked like body bags.

More voices were coming from an open field on the other side of the camper. I opened another canvas window in the direction of the field and inhaled sharply.

Huge, brightly colored parachutes billowed in a light morning breeze as paragliders silently took to the air like so many silent, graceful birds, lifting effortlessly skyward and away.

"Callie! Callie! You've got to see this!" I shook her awake and unzipped the canvas window at her feet.

"No. *Way!*" she exclaimed. Paragliding was an activity at the very top of Callie's bucket list. I boiled water on the stove. We had our morning coffee, listening to the paragliders pre-flight banter, and shared in their delight as they soared on favorable air currents.

"Thank you, Universe," we whispered.

We continued on to Park City, where Callie's closest childhood friend, Kaila Kuhn, was training for the Olympics.

Callie and Kaila were inseparable as children and they had both followed paths that deviated dramatically from the norm. Callie traded prom and football games for international travel, online school, and graduation at sixteen. Kaila had been living away from home since she was thirteen, spending her high school years training to be a world-class ski jumping aerialist.

The combination of waking to paragliders, savoring a perfect sunny day in Utah, and seeing Kaila helped Callie and I shake any of the remaining gloom we'd felt in Zion and Bryce Canyon.

With a rekindled sense of adventure, we set out to find an elusive landmark, Spiral Jetty, on the northeastern side of Utah's great Salt Lake. Spiral Jetty was built in 1970 by artist Robert Smithson. Using six thousand tons of black basalt rock, Smithson made a fifteen-hundred-feet-long coil of rock in the shallow waters of the Great Salt Lake.

Using the satellite view on Google Maps, we located the Spiral Jetty earthen sculpture and zoomed in. Google's satellite image revealed an unimpressive shadowy spiral in the exact middle of nowhere. There was no indication of a road to get there.

"You're sure it's worth the trip, Cal?" I asked dubiously. "It looks like a whole lot of nothing."

Callie was determined. "This one is important. There aren't many shots of it on Instagram. But the ones I've seen are incredible. In some pictures, the water is actually pink! And I can use my drone there."

We zoomed into the map, trying to identify a single road amidst open desert and expansive dried up salt flats. We finally decided to attempt to reach the GPS coordinates by dead-reckoning.

Though this strategy never got us remotely close to Spiral Jetty, we came across shallow pools of water on the eastern end of the Great Salt Lake, sectioned off in rectangular plots of bright gold, deep umber, cerulean blue, and emerald green.

Callie flew her drone, capturing images of water laid out like a patchwork quilt, an expansive tapestry of color that grew more spectacular as the drone flew higher. Callie returned to the car, breathless with excitement. "Mom! If these are the images I'm getting here…imagine what it's going to be like when we find the Spiral Jetty!"

I gave a moody huff. "Really? We are still looking for that thing? We've been driving all morning and it still looks like it's hours away."

"Please, Mom," Callie begged. "I just have a feeling about this. We need to get there!"

Since our road dead-ended nowhere close to Spiral Jetty, we back tracked out to the freeway and dropped the trailer at a drug store parking lot off the next freeway exit.

After hours of searching, a dubious mom and elated daughter finally rounded the last bend leading to Spiral Jetty. We had been traveling over two hours on an entirely deserted, bone-jarring, dirt road. I was trying to ignore the gas gauge, which indicated we had less than a quarter tank of fuel. Cell service evaporated miles ago.

My jaw dropped when Spiral Jetty and the Great Salt Lake finally came into view. I blinked, my brain attempting to process its ocular input. Pink. The water was actually pink—not just the beach's sand…but the water itself!

In fact, the beach wasn't made of sand at all. Rather, it was alabaster white, crystallized salt. But the water was bright, oyster shell pink! And smack dab in the middle of the pink water was Spiral Jetty, a massive rock structure that strongly resembled a gigantic nautilus, surrounded by pink water. The visual effect was breathtaking.

"Come on, Mom!" Callie cried excitedly as she grabbed her drone from the back of the car. There were a few other people milling about, similarly mystified by the surreal landscape. Pink water stretched off in the distance as far as the eye could see, getting fainter in color as it left the shore.

We pattered across a great frozen saline beach, its hardened salt abrasive as our feet broke through its crusty surface. Minutes later, we were cautiously high-stepping into the warm, shallow, pink water of the Great Salt Lake. On closer inspection, I realized the water was teeming with millions, perhaps billions, of tiny, bright red, brine shrimp. It was the bodies of these little creatures that gave the water a pink hue!

"Callie!" I exclaimed. "This is spectacular! Why don't more people know about this?" I asked.

Callie was busy preparing her drone for launch. "I don't know!" she replied excitedly. "Maybe it's just a seasonal thing!"

The drone buzzed to life like a giant insect taking flight. Callie used my phone to control the aircraft, as we marveled over the images the drone's camera was capturing. Swooping whirls of pink swirled in varying degrees of vibrancy for miles in every direction. Callie found a salt island, stripped down to her swimsuit and began capturing some of the most stunning drone images I've ever seen.

"When can I see your video?" I asked excitedly.

"You need to wait until it's done, Mom! I'm not posting the videos one at a time. By the end of our trip, I'm going to put together the best travel video on the internet. It will blow you away. My Instagram account will go viral overnight!"

"But can I just post a few pictures on Facebook?"

"That's not the way it works, Mom. This needs to be fresh content. Something nobody has seen before. You'll just have to wait."

Sometimes, I got bored as Callie drained not one, but two drone batteries, trying to capture the perfect shot.

But I also understood that for Callie, Instagram wasn't just about personal validation. Aware of the fact that social media eroded her self worth, Callie spent very little time on social media. Her desire to become an Instagram travel influencer was driven by an aspiration to create income while traveling the world. High quality content would make that dream come true.

Skillfully maneuvering the drone into position, Callie would hide the controller as she captured footage, hiking the razor's edge of mountain ridges, posing in seemingly precariously positions atop thundering waterfalls or frolicking in alpine lakes.

If she was lucky, the end product would be a short clip, less than five seconds long, that was skillfully crafted to make it look effortless. Each clip was gleaned from twenty to forty minutes of footage and hours of editing. On many occasions, a full day's hike yielded no usable footage.

It was late afternoon and ominous clouds were gathering by the time we left Spiral Jetty. On our way home, I watched small tornadoes of sand spiral up towards the sky. I felt a kinship with the little dust devils, stretching towards the heavens, as they furiously swirled around with no clear path or direction. Twice, I watched them connect with a matching twist of clouds coming down from above, as if God was offering a hand to the little spirals of sand below.

We spent the night at a dark, deserted parking lot about a mile off the freeway in Wyoming. Most Campendium spots have at least one or two vehicles. This one was perfectly empty, remote, and absolutely silent. I felt a bit of trepidation after reading signs posted around the parking lot that read, "No shooting."

Unaccustomed to feeling uneasy in my cozy little camper, I tuned into the Big Guy for reassurance.

"All is well. You are safe. You are protected. Events are unfolding exactly as they are meant to unfold. Your timing is perfect," Inner Guidance confirmed.

"Thank you, Universe," I whispered, for the third time in as many days.

CHAPTER 20

After weeks of following Callie's manic agenda, chasing scenic destinations with a religious fervor, the list of stops seemed to be expanding rather than diminishing. I began to suspect that Callie was adding to the list because she didn't want the roadtrip to end.

Though I thoroughly enjoyed the open road, I longed for a break from the pressure of figuring out where to sleep each night.

"Can't we just spend a couple days in one place?" I asked Callie. "It would be so nice to chill out and just get caught up on email."

Once again, as the old adage goes…be careful what you wish for.

We rolled into Montana on July 28th, which was Christopher's birthday. It felt strange not being home to celebrate with him. Home. That word didn't mean what it used to mean. I recalled the time I'd overheard Gracie and Callie talking in tearful whispers at Grandma and Grandpa's house. "Homeless."

"Hey!" I'd replied, "We are not homeless. We are nomadic. There's a difference."

But as I thought of Christopher at home with John, in the company of Aunt Anne and Ty, who have birthdays the same week as Christopher, the line between nomadic and homeless felt precariously thin. Home was the place where my boy was celebrating his fifteenth birthday. So in that regard, I was truly homeless.

Driving north towards Yellowstone, I called Christopher. Hearing his voice made my arms ache to hold my boy. Traffic slowed to a crawl as we ended our call. We were going ten miles an hour when I spotted the culprit responsible for the slowdown: a massive bison, walking on the shoulder of the road.

"Wow! Look at that bison! We must be getting close to Yellowstone," I exclaimed to Callie, marveling at the size of the beast.

Callie, who was frantically typing a Snapchat message on my cell phone, barely looked up. After losing her phone in Zion, she would occasionally use my phone to communicate with friends or family. But that didn't happen often, and never with such intensity.

"What's up, honey?" I asked.

"Mom! Cyrene and I met some guys when we were in Boyne City. They said they were planning a trip out west. And guess what! They're in Yellowstone! They're here! Right now!"

Uh oh. I smelled heroic effort on the horizon: *my* heroic effort. I knew this aroma well. Its familiar scent is associated with traveling great distances, exuding enormous effort, and/or expending huge sums of money to make my family happy.

"Yellowstone is a big place, honey. And I really want to find a camp site before dark."

"But *Mom*! They are just outside of Yellowstone. And they're going to the rodeo tonight! Can I go to the rodeo with them, Mom? Please?"

I hesitated. Though it was true that our trip to Salt Lake City and Spiral Jetty had bolstered Callie's spirits, I had been nervous she would slip back into despondency over her lost phone, broken camera, and general state of upheaval. I was grateful to see Callie's exuberance, and probably would have agreed to build a rocket ship and take her to the moon if it kept a smile on her face.

"Okay," I said, feigning reluctance. "Find me a camping spot. I'll drop the camper and we'll go find your friends."

"*Yes!*" Callie exclaimed. After a few minutes perusing Campendium, she murmured, "Wow. Mom, I think I found the perfect camping spot. It's definitely a 'mama spot,' right on the water. And it's free!"

Twenty minutes before reaching the town of West Yellowstone, Callie directed me to turn left onto a dirt road. We wound our way a couple miles through pastoral rolling hills dotted with horses and cows.

"Turn here," Callie said, indicating a narrow road on the right. A sign at the top of the drive said, "Rough road ahead. Campers and large vehicles are highly discouraged. Caution! No turn around!"

Hmm… "Callie, maybe we should scout this one out on foot first."

"No, Mom! There isn't any time. The guys are at a store buying cowboy boots and cowboy hats for the rodeo right now. They're coming into Yellowstone to meet me. I don't want to make them wait!"

I took a deep breath and turned down the dirt road. It was indeed rough. Though I took the potholes at a snail's pace, the trailer hitch bottomed out twice in deep crevasses and I whispered a prayer of protection for the trailer's newly repaired electrical system. One section of the road was covered in a pool water. I had to drive into the bushes to skirt its edges. Slowly but surely, we made headway, and I managed to keep the electrical system in tact.

Our objective was one of three first-come-first-serve camping spots at the edge of Hebgen Lake. Campendium reviews raved about the fact you could camp free in level spots right at water's edge. We crossed our fingers and prayed that at least one of these spots would be available.

The road curved and seemed to end at a small beach parking lot. People on the beach gazed in wonder at my minivan towing a pop-up trailer. Every other vehicle in the small lot was a truck or SUV.

The lot only had room for a few cars. There was no room for the camper, no room to turn around, and there were certainly no camping spots here. A feeling of panic rose in my chest. "Are you sure we're in the right place?" I asked Callie.

"This is it, Mom," Callie said, looking around in confusion. "And it wasn't just posted by a single reviewer. There are four reviews."

I got out of the car and walked to the back corner of the lot, where I discovered the road continued. Hopping back in, I said the words we were both thinking. "Let's just hope there is a spot available! I'm guessing that entrance road would scare most people off!"

A few hundred feet farther up the shore, the road opened into another parking lot, this one larger than the beach lot. My heartbeat quickened as three pristine camp sites came into view. The one in the middle was occupied. But the other two were available. We took the one farthest from the entrance, which was the largest of the three.

Giddy with excitement, I backed the trailer onto the pebbled beach, right to the edge of the lake, carefully watching to make sure my trailer tires stayed on solid ground. I left just enough space to be able to walk around the back of the trailer without getting wet.

Wow! If the camper's screened windows opened, we could fish from the camper!

Callie and I took in the scene. Low mountains surrounded the lake on two sides. Higher mountains rose up to the east. The lake was pristine, its water cool and refreshing. It would be perfect for swimming! A few small fishing boats dotted the lake in the distance. Other than that, the large lake was empty. A small island beaconed in the near distance and I was itching to explore it with the inflatable paddle board that had been used only once on Lake Powell.

"Thank you, Universe," I whispered with excitement.

"Okay, Mom! Time to go!" Callie exclaimed. "We don't have cell service and I need to connect with the guys." I was loathe to leave this idyllic spot. But Callie was insistent. I blocked the wheels, dropped a flat piece of wood under the post of the tongue jack, cranked the coupler off the trailer ball, disengaged the wiring harness and chains, and reluctantly left my sweet little campsite at Hebgen Lake.

Despite the fact that the Honda was free from it's pop-up burden, the minivan still bucked mercilessly over the deeply rutted trail as we ascended to the main dirt roadway. Coming down this path with the trailer had been a heroic feat. How in the world were we going to get the camper back up? Even a small amount of rain would make the road impassable.

Callie worried over my phone, desperate for a cell signal. We finally got service in West Yellowstone and the phone buzzed several times as texts came through.

"Yes!" Callie exclaimed. "The guys are meeting us at Artist's Point. They should be there in forty-five minutes." Then she frowned. "They said there is no cell service in Yellowstone. They sent this message fifteen minutes ago."

"Okay. So how far is Artist's Point?"

Callie's face fell as she consulted the map. "Oh no, Mom. It's over an hour away. I tried to text them, but they're not answering. They must be in the park already. We've got to hurry!"

I followed the herd of vehicles, slowly wending their way past the smoking rivers, spluttering mud cauldrons, and surreal landscapes of Yellowstone National Park. I was dying to explore, but wanted to wait to see the sights with Callie. "Why don't you tell me about the places you want to see tomorrow."

Silence. Callie, always ready with a list of Instagram-inspired destinations, was suspiciously quiet. She squirmed uncomfortably.

My mama radar pinged. "What's up?"

"Well…" she started hesitantly. "I had no idea Yellowstone was so big. The rodeo is on the other side of

Yellowstone, and it probably won't get over until late tonight. You'll be over two hours away at your cute little campsite. And I can't ask the guys to drive me home. It would take them four hours round trip."

"Oh my gosh!" I replied in exasperation. "Why didn't you tell me the rodeo is on the other side of Yellowstone!"

"I've got my hammock!" she replied hurriedly. "I can just spend the night and be back by late morning. They are nice guys, Mom. You know Zac. He went to school with Gracie when we lived in Boyne City. And I've told you about Connor. He's the one whose dad owns a boat rental business on Lake Charlevoix. I went boating with him a few times this summer. The other two guys are friends of theirs."

"But you don't even have a cell phone! How will I get ahold of you?"

"Your camp site doesn't have cell service anyway! I'll borrow a phone from one of the guys. You can call me when you get to town tomorrow morning."

My parents had always been supportive when I took risks in pursuit of adventure. I was only a few years older than Callie when I traveled around Eastern Europe during the Cold War. And that was during a time when credit cards didn't work behind the Iron Curtain and there were no cell phones.

I needed a gut check. Taking a deep breath, I tuned in to my higher self. A green light, like a traffic signal appeared in my mind's eye.

"Okay," I replied. "I'll be in town at ten o'clock tomorrow morning. Make sure Zac's cell phone is charged and available, so you can let me know when and where I can pick you up."

"Yes!" Callie exclaimed. "Thank you, thank you, thank you, Mom! You're the best!"

We spent the next hour at the Artist's Point parking lot waiting for the boys to arrive. With no cell service, there was no way to know if we'd had a miscommunication on the time and place, or if the boys were having car trouble.

Callie was visibly nervous. Her hopes had swelled at the prospect of seeing kids her own age. I knew she desperately wanted things to work out. But I gradually began to suspect she was nervous about something else.

Callie was spending an inordinate amount of time rifling through her belongings, putting together a bag that was substantially more comprehensive than a standard overnight bag.

Why would she need multiple outfits for an overnight?

She labored over whether or not she would need a hair straightener.

"Why do you need a hair straightener at the rodeo?" I asked. She didn't reply.

Finally, a white car packed to the gills with four boys and their camping gear pulled into the parking lot. Mightily relieved, a gleeful Callie bounded up to the car, hugged the two boys she knew and beamed happily upon meeting the two she did not.

"This is going to be *so much fun!*" she exclaimed.

The boys shyly introduced themselves to me, and apologized for getting lost on their way to meet us.

"Let's go for a hike!" Callie exclaimed.

After a quick dismissive hug, Callie led the boys across the parking lot to the Artists' Point trailhead. Catching Callie's enthusiasm, their voices got louder and more energetic as they trailed off in the distance.

I stood alone beside the van, a nearly audible sucking sound having drained the parking lot of its life force energy.

After a moment of hesitation, I scrambled off after the kids, trying to avoid being seen.

It's not like I'm following them. That would be weird. But it took a long time to get here. I have just as much right as they have to hike the Artist's Point Trail!

I hung back, making sure I didn't catch up to Callie and her friends. Their voices carried through the woods, accentuating my loneliness.

You're just being dramatic. It's only one night!

But even as the words formed in my head, they didn't ring true. Callie wouldn't be weighing the decision to bring a hair straightener for one night of hammock camping. On more than one occasion, she expressed how much she missed being with kids her own age. That's why she was nervous. She didn't want to deceive me, but she couldn't afford to ask my permission to leave and be told she couldn't.

Tagging along behind the kids, listening as their voices filled the woods, I intuitively knew Callie would join the boys for part of their roadtrip. However, I didn't know that the next time I would see my daughter would be at the Bozeman airport, ten days hence!

The next morning, I woke at daybreak to prepare coffee, meditate, journal, and watch the sun rise over the verdant green hills across the lake. The lake was perfectly calm. Fish sipped bugs from the lake's surface.

I inflated the stand up paddle board and loaded it with a big red plastic bowl, shampoo, and soap in hopes of finding a private spot to bathe. The nearby island seemed to be a likely place.

Pushing off from shore, I saw large shadows moving beneath the surface of the water and was shocked to discover a veritable carpet of fish the length of my forearm.

"No way!" I exclaimed, thinking wistfully of John and our fly fishing guides.

They would love this!

Dropping to my stomach, I laid the paddle next to me and let the morning sun warm my back as I watched the silvery fish wriggle back and forth, their bodies reflecting the sunlight.

Paddling to the island, I pulled my paddle board on shore and walked to the opposite side, which was more secluded. Squirming out of my swimsuit, I dipped my toe in the water. It was deliciously cool and refreshing. I filled the bowl in the shallow water and returned to shore, sudsing and rinsing fifteen feet from the waters edge. Then I returned to the lake for a post-shower skinny dip.

The water on this side of the island was shallow, so I had to naked wade a long way out in ankle deep sludge to reach water deep enough to dunk under. Just then, a little aluminum fishing boat rounded the point and cut the motor. Two fishermen cast their lines and waited for a bite.

As a frequent skinny dipper, I knew the risk of encountering inadvertent intruders. The fishermen's voices traveled clearly across the water's surface. Though the water was still shallow, I was able to squat low enough to cover my shoulders.

Too close. They'll see me for sure if I try to get out. It's a good thing the water isn't colder!

I thought about the cup of coffee sitting on the picnic table outside my camper, patiently awaiting my return.

Fishy, fishy in the brook. Come and bite, on their hook. Fishy, fishy in the lake. Come and bite, on their bait.

My stomach growled and I remembered that I still hadn't eaten breakfast. The fishermen noticed me kneeling in the water and gave a friendly wave. I waved back.

Crap. Now it's like we practically know each other. I certainly can't go to shore at this point!

Then I remember the carpet of fish I'd seen just off shore.

Those fish were pretty big. I wonder what kind of fish they are? I wonder if they're the kind of fish that nibble toes... My subconscious paused for effect.

And with that thought, I squat-waddled until the water was too shallow to stay submerged, then marched my naked butt to the beach without a backwards glance at the fishermen.

After my paddle of shame back to camp and a hurried breakfast, I drove towards the town of West Yellowstone, dialing Zac's number as soon as I had cell service.

"Hey, Zac. Is Callie there? It's her mom." I could hear road noise in the background.

"Mom! I'm so glad you called!" Callie exclaimed with great enthusiasm. "Listen. I'm having the *best time ever!* These guys are *so* great. It's like having four big brothers. I feel totally safe with them. And guess what! You're not going to believe this. They invited me to join their roadtrip to Portland, Oregon. Isn't that amazing? They'll just drop me back off in Yellowstone on their way to California."

Sweet Callie has always been somewhat geographically challenged. I consulted Apple Maps in the ensuing silence.

"Portland is twelve hours west of Yellowstone!" I exclaimed incredulously. "Yellowstone is most certainly *not* between Portland and California!"

As a person who allows the fortunes in fortune cookies to shape the trajectory of her life, I'm accustomed to flexibility. But this new turn of events pushed the bounds of my willingness to go with the Universe's flow.

Callie ignored my rebuttal and continued, "I'll be back on Monday. That's only four days from now."

"Five," I corrected her. "It's Wednesday. Monday is five days away."

More silence. "Mom. Please. This is really important to me. We are having the *best* time. I'm happier than I've been since Mia left."

That remark stung a little. I checked with my higher self. Another green light. I was beginning to wonder if the switch to my inner guidance system was frozen on green. The pendulum between fear and faith was clearly swinging toward faith. In truth, I trusted Callie to be a good judge of character. So, somewhat begrudgingly, I agreed to let her join the boys.

"Whew!" Callie exclaimed. "That's really great, because the guys wanted to get an early start this morning and we already made it to Idaho Falls. I would have called earlier, but you didn't have cell service."

Ever since we left Mia in Las Vegas, I'd felt pressure to keep Callie happy. Now that she'd been ferried away by a boisterous group of boys, I felt space to dive into my own healing and focus on long-neglected marketing efforts for Nomaditudes. This time of separation would be as good for me as it was for Callie.

Besides, Gracie and her boyfriend will be here soon. It will be nice to explore Yellowstone with them at a leisurely pace, rather than being tied to Callie's frenetic agenda.

After spending ten days in Eagle deliberating on how to respond to the loss of her Subaru, Gracie was finally able to purchase a new car and continue her westward journey.

With patience and fortitude characteristic of those bound for sainthood, the Conklins not only housed Gracie and her boyfriend, they scoured dealerships between Denver and Glenwood Springs in search of her new vehicle. They even offered to gift her money for a portion of the downpayment.

In honesty, I never knew the final details of the arrangement, whether Karen and Steve paid for part of Gracie's car or not. Gracie avoided answering the question when I asked and I didn't press her for a reply.

There is a fine line between humbling and embarrassing. A healthy ego is humbled and grateful to receive help from a friend. An unhealthy ego is embarrassed. I was embarrassed. How could I ever hope to repay their generosity?

Gracie was incredulous when she arrived in Yellowstone and discovered her sixteen-year-old sister had left with band of teenage boys. "Mom! Are you serious? How could you let her do that?"

Why indeed? Even I was having a hard time explaining it to myself. I certainly couldn't expect Gracie to understand.

Gracie, her boyfriend, and I marveled over the natural wonders of Yellowstone: Old Faithful, exploding pots of mud, the surreal hues of the Grand Prismatic hot spring, and frozen white expanses of thick bubbling waterfalls comprised of crystallized salt. Two short days later, Gracie and her boyfriend were making their way back to western New York, and I was left alone again.

My camp site had a three night maximum stay, so I found another spot on Hebgen that allowed free camping up to sixteen nights. I was sad to leave the idyllic little shoreside camp. But each day that passed without rain was like making it through a round of Russian roulette. One good storm would destroy the road, making my exit entirely impossible. As it was, I was loathe to attempt the road alone. But I had no choice. The trailer bucked over the potholes and the hitch bottomed out in the deeper puddles. I'd disengaged the wiring harness, zip tying it to the trailer to prevent damage.

When I finally made it to the road, a cursory inspection revealed the wheel post on the trailer was bent, but not broken. I breathed a shaky sigh of relief.

I found a new spot on the southern side of Hebgen Lake, one that was a bit more sloped, but still close to the water. This new site provided a dramatic view of the low mountains rising on the far northern shore in the direction of West Yellowstone. Best of all, this new site had cell service!

I was dismayed to discover the trailer's battery was dead, transforming my camper into a glorified tent. I was back to reading by headlamp, buying bottled water rather than using the pop-up's water pump and charging my cell phone in the car.

Free from Callie's frantic pace and the distraction of electronics, my soul breathed a sigh. I settled into blessed peace and solitude on the shores of Hebgen Lake.

As sun set, a full moon rose directly in front of me, shining a path of moonlight across the water that led directly to my door. The tranquil scene calmed my turbulent mind. I felt the cool evening breeze wafting through the screened windows and listened to the twilight sounds of frogs and insects chirping. A night bird twilled, and loons called across the water.

At the edge of the pool of moonlight, a swan emerged, silently crossing the moonbeam and disappearing into darkness on the other side. My eyes filled with tears. I surrendered to feelings of gratitude and wonder.

The next morning, I felt the sunrise. I didn't just watch it, I felt all the emotions that go with sunrise: awe, warmth, hope, magic, power, inspiration, safety. For the second time in twenty-four hours, tears of gratitude dampened my cheeks.

Each day on Hebgen Lake, I woke at daybreak to prepare coffee, meditate, journal, and watch the sun rise over the low-lying hills to the east. Devoid of another voice to fill the empty space, I had extensive conversations with myself, and was surprised and delighted to find my own company highly entertaining.

I came to realize there was nothing wrong with John, me, our marriage, our divorce, or anything that came before or after. Each was part of the is-ness of everything. Events had unfolded exactly as they were meant to unfold in order to fulfill some kind of deal our souls cooked up before we arrived on this earthly plain.

There on the shores of Hebgen Lake, I could finally see that grace is the secret—grace to accept people for who they are, with all their quirks and idiosyncrasies, fears and phobias, addictions and dysfunctionalities...and grace to accept the same in myself.

I allowed this new reality to wrap its roots and tendrils around my bones, transforming me into something wild, somewhat feral, and frequently un-groomed. During daily forays to explore Hebgen Lake by stand up paddle board, I delighted in the hedonistic pleasure of swimming naked, reveling in the musky scent of sun-baked skin mixed with lake water.

On several occasions, I drove to the library in West Yellowstone to get internet for Nomaditudes projects and to communicate with Apple to get Callie's cell phone replaced.

Any effort expended on Nomaditudes yielded a dead end. College employees, who would be difficult to reach during a normal summer, were impossible to contact during Covid's stay-at-home order.

Fortunately, efforts to replace Callie's phone were more productive. Apple agreed to express her new phone to a drop site in West Yellowstone.

As the days leisurely slipped by, the Big Guy and I became besties again. He taught me that productive activities were the ones that made my heart sing. They were the things that elicited those precious, fleeting bursts of gratitude. Productive activities were those that inspired, excited, surprised, and delighted me.

Exploring dirt roads around Yellowstone, I discovered remote rivers, lakes, and hiking paths. The weight of loneliness provided clarity. A vision of my future took shape in my mind's eye.

I wanted to spend time surrounded by family and friends. I wanted immerse myself in nature. I wanted to connect authentically with my higher self and others in a new, more meaningful way. I wanted to travel the world. I wanted to push myself physically, exploring the bounds of what this body is capable of doing. Most of all, I wanted to ease suffering and impact people's lives.

At night, laying in bed with toes curled, I listened to waves gently lapping the shore. The Big Guy whispered, "You are loved. You are blessed. You are perfect exactly as you are. Come play with me!"

CHAPTER 21

While I was happily cocooning on Hebgen Lake, I received sporadic updates from Callie, texting from Zac's phone.

July 30
Callie: This is Callie. I'm alive and safe.
Mom: Hey Callie, would you please call me?

July 31
Mom: Hey Zac, would please have Callie call me when she can?
Zac: Of course. Service is super spotty right now so I'll have her call when we have more than thirty seconds of service. Haha.
Mom (5 hours later): ?

August 2
Mom: Hi Zac, would you please have Callie give me a call?

When Callie called, our conversation went something like this: "Hey Mom! Sorry I didn't call earlier. We had really bad service. I'm having the most *amazing* time! These guys are so much fun and they take really good care of me. They are super sweet. And they're every bit as crazy as I am. Thank you *so* much for letting me come."

Callie's enthusiasm melted my heart. Suddenly, I couldn't remember the words to the tongue-lashing I'd been mentally prepared to deliver.

"I'm so glad you're having a good time, honey. But you've got to put yourself in my shoes. I was good with you joining the boys' roadtrip. But it's not fair to make me wait three days for a phone call."

Silence. Then Callie replied, "I know. You're right. I'm sorry."

"Okay. I'm just glad to know you're doing well. So... how are you getting back here tomorrow?"

"Tomorrow? Mom, what are you talking about?"

"When you left last week, you said the guys are dropping you off on the way to California. You said you'd be back on Monday. Clearly, these guys aren't going to drive twelve hours to get you here. So where are we going to meet?"

"Mom! I never said anything about Monday!"

Silence. "Honey. You. Most. Certainly. Did. Clearly, your plans changed. You can't just expect me to just sit here indefinitely, waiting for you to come back. What is your plan?"

Secretly, I was thoroughly delighted at the prospect of camping on Hebgen Lake indefinitely. The water and warm Montana sunshine was nourishing my soul. I felt myself getting stronger every day. In solitude, I was actively reconnecting with nature in a way I hadn't experienced since my soul quest.

Callie mumbled something vague about catching a flight to Bozeman from St. George, Utah, outside Zion National Park.

"Zion? Seriously? You've got to be kidding me. On what day? I need a date. When am I picking you up in Bozeman?"

More vague mumbling, then Callie said, "Don't worry, Mom. I'm paying for the flight. It's my responsibility."

"I didn't ask who's paying for the flight. I'm asking *when* is the flight?"

"I don't know, Mom, okay?" Callie exclaimed in exasperation. "This is their roadtrip. You can't expect me to ask them to be in a specific place at a specific time."

I knew most parents would be ripping their hair out. But what was the point of arguing when we both wanted more time to do the things we were doing?

"Events are unfolding exactly as they are meant to unfold," the Big Guy reminded me. "Your timing is perfect. Relax into this beautiful space between, this time of not knowing or worrying about the future. Allow this time for both you and Callie to grow and expand."

I sighed. "Okay, baby. Call me when you book your flight. I love you, and I know you are safe and protected." The words sounded naive. But I knew they were true. Little did I know, my faith would be soon be tested.

It was four thirty the next morning when my phone rang. "Mrs. Rounds? This is Officer Muñez from the Monterey Police Department," a woman's voice said. My heart skipped a beat, cobwebs of sleepiness instantly cleared as a single word monopolized my mind.

Callie.

"Are you Callie's mom?" the voice continued.

"Yes," I replied, wildly searching for the voice of the Big Guy. To my great relief, the Big Guy impressed the knowledge that Callie was physically safe.

"Callie isn't hurt," the woman assured me, "but she's gotten herself into a bit of trouble. I'm having some difficulty piecing her story together. She and her friends were caught trespassing at a construction site. They said they thought the building was abandoned. Are you aware of the fact that your daughter is in Monterey?"

"Yes," I lied. "Well, I knew she was in California, but not specifically Monterey." Another lie.

"So Callie says you are in Yellowstone and you don't have a permanent physical address?" Was it my imagination, or did the officer's voice sound accusatory?

A wave of shame washed over me. "That's correct."

"Are you aware of the fact that we are in the middle of a pandemic and the governors of most states have issued a stay-at-home order?"

"I'm staying on a remote lake in Montana," I shot back defensively. "I can't imagine being more socially distanced than I am right now."

"When Callie was brought in for questioning, she wasn't wearing shoes. She said she doesn't have any shoes." As Officer Muñez continued, the accusatory tone took a sarcastic edge. "She also claimed she doesn't have a cell phone because she lost it in Zion National Park. She doesn't know her social security number. And there is no record of a 'Calista Rounds' in the national police database. Is that your daughter's real name?"

"Yes, Callie's real name is Calista. You probably can't find her in a police database because she's never been in trouble. Yes, she lost her cell phone in Zion. And yes, she decided to spend this summer without shoes. But she's got hiking boots for hiking," I finished lamely.

Why did it feel like I was the one in trouble? Then a startling thought occurred to me. *What if this woman is trying to take Callie away from me?*

"Listen," I said with authority. "Callie is a really good kid. She loves to explore. Whether it's climbing mountains or checking out an abandoned building, she wants to discover something new and exciting. The reason she is even allowed to travel alone with other kids her age is because I trust her implicitly."

"Are you aware of the fact that what you are calling 'exploring' is considered trespassing? And that trespassing is illegal?" After a long silence, Officer Muñez continued. "Well, we have a logistical problem. I am only authorized to release Callie into the custody of a parent or legal guardian. From what Callie said, her dad is not an option."

"That's true," I confirmed with a shudder.

"So it sounds like you are going to need to come to Monterey to pick her up."

I put the phone on speaker and checked the distance on Apple Maps. "According to the map, it's a seventeen hour drive. It will probably be eighteen or nineteen hours with stops. It's four thirty now. I should be there by midnight tonight."

My hands were shaking as I got off the phone. By the light of a lantern, I poured water into a pan and lit the stove, preparing to make coffee for the journey. A few minutes later, the phone buzzed again. It was Officer Muñez's number.

"Mom? I'm so sorry, Mom," said a tearful Callie on the other end of the phone.

"Are you okay, baby?"

"Yeah. I hurt my elbow when—"

Callie's voice was cut short and Officer Muñez's came on the line. "We decided that Callie could be released into the custody of one of her travel companions if they are over eighteen years of age and we have a written letter of permission from you."

I got the officer's email address, thanked her, and hung up the phone.

With great relief, I scrawled a handwritten permission letter on the back of a piece of scrap paper, took a picture of it, and sent it to Officer Muñez. It wasn't the over eighteen hour drive I had been dreading most. It was the critical eyes of the police.

I turned off the burner under the simmering pot of water and climbed back into bed, taking deep breaths to calm my trembling body.

My phone rang again. It was Callie, calling from Zac's phone. "I'm really sorry for the hassle, Mom. Just so you know, they weren't releasing me to Zac's custody to be nice. They weren't legally allowed to hold me because I'm a minor. So if you weren't going to get here 'til midnight, they had to release me to child protective services. And if that happened, the arresting officer would have been in big trouble. He tackled me from behind when my hands were up. There's a huge gash on my elbow."

"Oh my gosh, Callie! Why did he tackle you?"

"At first, he just yelled 'stop,' and I thought maybe some homeless guy was chasing me. Then another guy said, 'Stop, Police!' So I stopped and put my hands above my head. But the big guy kept running and tackled me anyway. It's like he wanted to hurt me. He was a new guy and the supervisor got mad at him. But the supervisor told the police officer not to put the fact that he tackled me in the police report. Child protective services would have found out and that cop would have gotten in trouble."

Callie continued, "We didn't know it was a construction site, Mom. It just looked like an abandoned building. You know I would never do graffiti or break anything. We were just looking around. But there must have been a security guy who called the police. I'm really sorry."

"I know, honey. I love you and I'm happy you are safe. *Please* make better choices, okay?"

In life and in parenting, I often choose the bold path over the safe path.

I thought about the times when I chose to act boldly instead of playing it safe. The richest experiences in my life were distinctly countercultural. Society would deem many of these endeavors crazy, unsafe, or even impossible. Acting boldly cultivated playfulness, intuition, self-reliance, and confidence. Those attributes were foundational to my sense of self.

If I hadn't had those formative experiences, testing my own inner strength from an early age, where would I be now? Probably on anti-anxiety medication, antidepressants, or curled around a bottle.

Cultivating boldness, trust, and a deep sense of self provided me with the confidence to embark on a journey across the United States in a pop-up trailer.

That thought sent a shiver down my spine.

Boldness. Callie's path through anxiety and depression will require boldness. I need to show Callie that I will continue to trust her as long as she's tuning into her higher self. She needs to feel empowered to follow her soul when it calls her to make decisions that challenge social norms while not allowing her ego to run the show.

I don't know where inner guidance comes from. But it's either something to be trusted, or it's not. There is no middle ground. I choose trust.

CHAPTER 22

Trusting inner guidance in the wake of Callie's arrest was like passing some kind of cosmic test. I became aware of long-established beliefs I didn't even know I'd held and decided to remap my personal constellation with "boldness" as my new North Star.

Instead of looking to Nomaditudes as a vehicle for external validation, I decided to follow the Big Guy's suggestion to adopt a smaller footprint, one that would provide income for travel, a way for the kids and I to spend winter somewhere warm, and no expectations beyond that.

Callie called a couple days later. "I booked my flight to Bozeman. I'm flying in from Denver late Saturday night," she chirped.

"Denver!" I exclaimed. "I thought you were flying from St. George, Utah!"

"Nah. That was way too expensive. Besides, the guys really like having me around. I bring their energy up. Some of them have been going through some pretty tough stuff. I'm like their therapist now."

It was with no small amount of relief that I finally collected Callie at the airport in Bozeman three days later. Returning to West Yellowstone, we got a message that Callie's new phone had arrived.

Callie was elated. "This is perfect, Mom! Thank you so, so, so much for getting my new phone. Some of the best Instagram spots are in Grand Teton National Park! I can't wait to get those shots. Let's go there right now!"

After collecting Callie's new phone in West Yellowstone, Callie enthusiastically recounted her roadtrip adventures with the boys, fully restoring my faith in inner guidance. As stories from the trip unfolded, Callie kept coming back to one pinnacle experience.

"It was so amazing, Mom. The boys had set up their tent next to a river. I'd seen a cave farther up the side of the mountain, so I went to check it out. As soon as I went into the cave, I felt this rush of energy and knew I needed to spend the night sleeping in the cave. None of the boys would stay with me, so I spent the night sleeping alone in the cave. It was incredible. I felt as safe as I would at home in my own bed. It's like my higher self was right there with me, so I didn't need to be afraid. I felt so guided and protected, like I'd never be scared again."

I knew exactly what she meant. It was the same feeling I'd had on my soul quest in the desert. This roadtrip had been a rite of passage for Callie. It changed her. She seemed stronger and wiser than she had been just ten days earlier.

"What if you'd said no to the roadtrip, Mom?" Callie said with a shudder. "I wouldn't have had the chance to meet my higher self that way."

What is it about the pilgrimage that elicits spiritual transformation? Does everyone have this deep desire to travel, or are Callie and I unique?

I thought about those Israelites, wandering in the desert for forty years. The Big Guy said it wasn't a punishment. It was an opportunity to learn to trust in God's daily guidance and provision.

Wandering is a blessing, not a curse. Building trust is more important than finding a home.

I found myself thinking about those Israelites who finally inhabited the land of Canaan.

As they plowed their fields, pulled their weeds, dug their wells, watered their crops, paid their bills, checked their email, and answered their texts, did they ever miss wandering in the desert? Did they miss the feeling of surrendering to God's grace, as he provided for their daily needs? Did they miss the desert's soft voice at night, whispering in their ears, "You are loved. You are loved. You are loved"?

These are the musings that occupied my thoughts as we traveled south out of Yellowstone and into Grand Teton National Park. The sheer magnitude of wilderness area encompassed within those two national parks is mind boggling. With a brief stop to watch a grizzly near Oxbow Bend, we arrived at Schwabacher Landing in Grand Teton National Park over three hours after departing West Yellowstone.

The parking lot at Schwabacher Landing is an Instagrammer's dream. With a wood split-rail fence, an expansive golden field of grass, and purple-pink mountains on the distant horizon, even the most inept photographer can capture drool-worthy content. I was that inept photographer, and Callie was my subject. A spectacular setting, Callie's high-tech iPhone, and a truly gorgeous subject made up for my inadequacies.

As the sun set, we faced with a dilemma. T. A. Moulton Barn was just ten minutes from Schwabacher Landing. Callie desperately wanted to shoot T. A. Moulton Barn—one of the most famously photographed barns in the world—at sunrise. A quick perusal of travel apps like Hotwire and AirBnb revealed the fact that lodging anywhere in our vicinity was cost-prohibitive. I looked at Callie. "Is Moulton Barn really that important?"

"Yes, Mom. This is one of the big ones," Callie exclaimed. "Especially since I have my new phone! Plus, one of the top hikes on my list is the secret trail to Delta Lake. It's not on the maps, but it's one of the most amazingly beautiful places I've seen. I really want to find it."

"We're three hours from the camper, so we can't go back to Hebgen Lake. We'd need to sleep in the van," I replied. "Are you sure you're up for that?"

"Absolutely!"

Scouring Campendium, Callie found a camping spot at Atherton Creek, half an hour from Moulton Barn. "Sunrise will be at six twenty-three," Callie said. "But we need to get there a little earlier because daybreak is better than sunrise. We should plan to arrive no later than five forty-five."

Another five o'clock wake up. Ouch.

Hungry and tired, we drove into Jackson, WY and splurged on a six dollar Dairy Queen chicken finger value meal for me, a grilled chicken salad for Callie, and a large pecan cluster Blizzard with Health Bar crumbles to share.

By the time we rolled into Atherton Creek at ten o'clock that night, the campground was full. Campendium said it was okay to use the marina parking lot on Lower Slide Lake if Atherton Creek was full.

"No Overnight Parking" signs posted around the marina lot suggested Campendium was misinformed. However, we saw three or four camper vans and even a tent occupying the marina lot. With no alternative option, we decided to risk a midnight eviction.

Due to a prevalence of grizzlies in and around Yellowstone, we never kept food in the pop-up trailer. For that reason, the back end of the minivan functioned as both wardrobe and pantry. A disheveled heap of duffle bags, boxes of food, and piles of clothing filled the space behind the back seat. Rather than folding the back seat down, Callie stretched out as best she could in the upright back seat while I pushed food and gear in the back to one side, curling up in the small space I'd managed to create.

Unbeknownst to us, Atherton Creek is just under seven thousand feet in elevation. Temperatures dropped. Through the night, we scrounged every spare piece of clothing we could find. By the time my alarm went off at five the next morning, we were cold, stiff, and entirely unrested. Callie and I were so miserable that despite the early hour, we were both overjoyed to leave.

Cold air blasted from the minivan's vents as the Honda's engine roared to life in the early morning darkness.

The car's thermometer registered a near frigid outdoor temperature. "Seriously? Thirty-five degrees in August?" I exclaimed. Callie and I cupped our hands over the vents in an attempt to thaw them.

A half hour later, we pulled up to Moulton Barn and parked behind four cars that beat our pre-dawn arrival. Photographers were pouring out of their vehicles, clinging to warm cups of coffee with one hand while adjusting lenses and aperture settings with the other.

"No Drone" signs posted throughout the property extinguished any hope of getting drone footage of the rising sun hitting the famous barn.

"I am so bummed I don't have a real camera!" Callie declared despondently. "We're at one of the most famous photography sites in the world and all I have is my iPhone camera."

"Be glad you've got that!" I exclaimed. "If your phone hadn't arrived, you'd be using my iPhone 7!"

As the sun rose behind us, illuminating the sharp, austere, rock faces and snow-tipped peaks of the Tetons, Moulton Barn veritably glowed. At first, the glow was soft and subtle, the light growing stronger with each passing second. Despite the crowds that had gathered, there was something deeply personal in watching the incomprehensible beauty of the scene as it unfolded, like watching a wooden flower bloom before our eyes.

Moulton Barn has seen a century of sunrises. But this one was ours. Photographers left mere minutes after the sun hit the barn's face. Callie and I stayed. We danced in the sunlight, spinning and playing, reveling in the sheer beauty of the morning. I grabbed my phone and took pictures as Callie ditched her jacket and spun around, her white skirt flaring, arms flung out to the side in an expression of pure joy.

After a quick breakfast in the car, we made our way to the Lupine Meadows. According to Callie's research, the secret trail to Delta Lake could be found just over three miles from the Lupine Meadows trailhead parking lot.

Callie, always the faster hiker, was soon far ahead. She waited for me at the place where the trail to Delta Lake broke off. We soon discovered, the "trail" to Delta Lake was not really a trail at all. Rather, it was a full-on scramble up a mile-long boulder field. At times, I could pick out a path through the boulders, but soon lost it again. The terrain became steep enough to require hand-over-hand climbing. However, the view at the top was worth every drop of sweat.

Delta Lake was pristine. Snaggled spires of rock teeth that looked like a giant alpine grin shot up from a saddle of trees at the head of the lake. The lake itself was a surreal aquamarine blue. Having arrived twenty minutes ahead of me, Callie had already made friends with a group of boys who were daring each other to take a plunge into the lake's icy glacier-fed waters.

Callie serenely stripped off her shirt (yes, she was wearing a swimsuit!), marched past the boys, and cannon-balled into the water. One of the boys followed her lead. Spluttering and laughing, they fast-paddled to shore to warm up on the sun-baked rocks.

Not one to sit still for long, Callie was soon clambering up the mountain with drone in hand to get footage at the far end of the lake. Then she climbed two pine trees to suspended her hammock above a cliff overlooking Delta Lake and produced a collection of images that would bring tears to the eyes of even the most seasoned travel photographer.

After two hours, Callie wanted to spend a little more time at the lake. I was tired and ready to make my descent. On the way down, I encountered not one, but two women who required a wilderness EMS rescue due to sprained ankles in the boulder field. I said a little prayer of thanks for my hiking poles.

Regaining the main trail proved to be problematic. It was impossible to know exactly where the "secret trail to Delta Lake" rejoined the route to Lupine Meadows Trailhead.

I stopped several times and listened carefully. Thankfully, at one point, I heard voices in the woods just above me. I'd overshot the trail by a few hundred feet. Without those voices, I would have kept going down the boulder field into the wrong valley, losing my way in the wilderness beyond.

The voice I'd heard belonged to a couple from Idaho Falls, Idaho. As we hiked together, chatting with a camaraderie so commonly found on hiking trails, I began to wonder if Callie would know where to exit the boulder field. Would she hike down alone or with the boys?

As I stopped for a water break, the boys from the lake marched by en masse. *Hmm…I guess that answers that question.* Suddenly, shadows from the trees seemed menacingly long. It was late in the day. It seemed like it was taking forever to hike down. Did it take this much time on the way up? The climb through the boulder field had been mentally and physically exhausting. I didn't realize an eight mile hike would hurt this much.

I stopped again, a little longer this time. *Where is Callie? She's such a fast hiker. She should have caught up by now.*

I pictured the wide expanse of thick green forest at the base of the boulder field. *If she overshot the trail, how long would it take for her to realize her mistake? Would people still be coming down the trail by the time she figured it out? She doesn't have cell phone service. What if she ends up alone in the dark?* I fought to control the rising panic.

After miles descending steep switchbacks, the trail finally leveled out near the parking lot. Imagine my surprise and relief when I saw Callie and two hiking companions leaning on the car, awaiting my arrival.

"Mom! It took you forever!" Callie exclaimed. "I thought you left before me! I was getting worried about you."

Callie informed me that there was a perfectly good trail alongside the boulder field, which allowed her to descend quickly and safely. With consternation, I realized that I was the one who had gotten lost.

"You shouldn't have gone down through the boulder field," Callie admonished. "Two women sprained their ankles in there!"

Driving back through Yellowstone en route to our campsite, we stopped at a lake to witness one of the most beautiful sunsets I've ever seen. Dead tired, in a blissed-out post-hike exhaustion, we lacked the energy to do anything by stare in wonder at the magnificence of God's extended firework show.

The next morning, it was time to say goodbye to Hebgen Lake. I'd spent half a month camped along her shores. Reminiscing on powerful meditations where I was transported to a different state of consciousness, tears of gratitude welled in my eyes. I thought of the carpet of fish swimming in the water's depths, skinny dipping beneath remote stretches of forest, and watching the swan drift across a moonbeam-bridge right outside my window.

Recalling the ache of loneliness, I discovered a part of me missed the solitude. I was grateful that I'd embraced the aloneness while Callie was gone, though I was truly happier when she was with me.

I was eager to continue the journey west, to savor the rare sweetness of an unscripted adventure with my beautiful teenage daughter. Something told me our biggest challenges were still to come.

CHAPTER 23

We covered most of the distance from Yellowstone to Hungry Horse, Montana in silence. When Callie and I did talk, our conversations were introspective, spiritual, and deeply bonding. I was quietly settling into my new skin after mentally and spiritually molting on the shores of Hebgen Lake. Callie seemed to be going through a transformation of her own.

After Mia's departure, Callie spent even less time on social media. In the days following the roadtrip with the boys, she disconnected almost entirely. It was as if she was cocooning, her bones liquifying in a process of transformation that can only be described as miraculous. A roadtrip that started out as a means of achieving social media recognition had evolved into something earthy, wholistic, and organic.

Callie and I shared a new cohesive energy, a unifying power that had been there all along, but was just now being solidified.

Callie was in charge of finding our next camping spot. She'd become something of an expert in reading between the lines on Campendium reviews. By examining the meager scraps of information Campendium's user's provided and careful scrutinizing photos, she was often able to discern whether or not a prospective camp site's access road was favorable for a minivan pulling a pop-up camper.

Manifesting campsites became a daily exercise in trust, a treasure hunt to discover another little gift of love from the Universe. It wasn't easy, as public campgrounds were full most of the time. Besides, we considered it a moral failure if we had to pay to camp. Packing up the trailer each morning, it was as if we were tossed up into the air, knowing the Universe would catch us again before night fall.

With a combination of National Forest Service maps, Campendium, and another app called iOverlander, Callie often "sensed" her way to spots that felt like they'd been specially designed for us. Each day created deeper trust and a certainty that we were indeed guided, protected, and loved by something greater than ourselves.

Moving through space and time with the sole purpose of discovery, I found the process of exploration was as much internal as it was external. I was redefining what it meant to be "me" outside the context of wife, mother, friend, daughter, business owner, or volunteer. For a very long time, "I" was defined by roles I believed others expected me to fill. Now, I was exhilarated to discover that "I" could be defined to mean anything I wanted it to be!

In endless stretches of road with nothing standing between me and my glorious mind, I kicked off the identities that once clothed me. Their layers now felt stifling, like wearing winter clothing in the middle of July. Relieved of their weight, I felt light, free, and wild.

While I was shedding metaphorical clothing, Callie was ditching the real stuff. "What's the point in wearing bras and underwear?" wise Callie asked. "If we just wear skirts and dresses, we'll hardly need to do any laundry at all!"

As luck would have it, five Patagonia dresses formed the core basis of my wardrobe. In fact, I had already become accustomed to hiking in a dress. What purpose did undergarments really serve anyway?

Still, I hesitated. Ditching bra and panties felt brazen. A woman of my age should act more dignified.

Who the hell am I trying to impress?

And just like that, a thread of social and cultural comportment was loosened, untied, and released.

We pulled into Montana, bound for Glacier National Park. Campendium listed a single spot—a paved parking lot along the Hungry Horse Reservoir—in Hungry Horse. However, Callie found that iOverlander listed multiple free camping sites beside the reservoir.

"Wow! With that many options, I'm sure we'll find something," I replied confidently when Callie showed me the map.

Admittedly, my time on Hebgen had lulled me into a false sense of complacency. I'd almost forgotten how much energy was required to hustle a new place to stay every night. We were coming into the weekend, so I expected free camp sites (especially those close to Glacier National Park) to be busy. But Hungry Horse Reservoir was more than busy. It was packed.

Fellow boondockers are normally fairly friendly, easy-going folk. This was not our experience at the Hungry Horse Reservoir. The campers there were cagey and territorial. Twice, I entered pull-through loops with at least one vacant site and was instructed to "move along." My smile and little wave went unanswered.

We'd lost cell service shortly after turning off Highway 2 in Hungry Horse. Now, half hour down the reservoir, it was getting late. We smelled dinner cooking on nearby campfires. Shade was deepening under the thick pines at water's edge. I came to a fire road on my right, leading away from the reservoir.

"I wonder if we'd have better luck away from the water," I wondered aloud.

"The people here don't seem to be very nice," Callie replied. "It might be good to put some distance between us and the reservoir."

I ventured up the single-track dirt road. Though the road was narrow, it was well maintained. My minivan was able to make the climb with little effort. However, in ten minutes, we hadn't seen a single spot to turn around, much less camp. Another five minutes later, I lost my nerve. It had been a hot summer with no rain. There were rumors of forest fires breaking out across the western part of the United States. I was afraid of getting cut off from the main road if a fire broke out.

"Okay, honey. I'm not comfortable being this far out. We're at least forty-five minutes from cell service if something goes wrong. Help me look for a place to turn around."

A few minutes farther ahead, the road widened just a bit. "Hop out to guide me through this, okay?"

"Mom. There is absolutely no way you are going to be able to turn around here. The road isn't wide enough."

I gave my daughter a mischievous grin. "Don't worry. Your old mom has some tricks up her sleeve." I proceeded to solidly wedge the pop-up trailer and van perpendicular to the road, the van still mostly facing up hill. Trees on both sides prevented us from straightening out, much less making the turn downhill.

"Nice. Now what?" Callie asked.

I hopped out of the car, intending to disconnect the trailer from the van, drive to a place where I could turn the van around, and reconnect the trailer facing back down the mountain.

Feeling cocky about my creative solution, I blocked the wheels, dropped a flat piece of wood under the post of the tongue jack, and disengaged the wiring harness and chains. I was about to crank the coupler off the trailer ball when the crank—which just moments ago had been solidly welded to the trailer's frame—came off in my hand.

I stood there looking back and forth between the crank in my hand and the place where the crank belonged. Like a kid trying to reattached the piece of a broken toy, I kept pressing the crank to the trailer jack, praying it would magically find a way to adhere itself.

The sun had already dipped behind the reservoir. As if on cue, an army of mosquitos launched an attack. "Not. Funny," I said, looking skyward.

I climbed back into the car holding the broken handle. "What's that...Oh my gosh!" Callie exclaimed, recognizing the trailer jack's handle. "Mom! What are we going to do?"

"There is absolutely only one option. We need to keep going up."

As the road got steeper and more rutted, I muttered a fervent little prayer. Thankfully, the road forked a little ways up, providing a frightfully tight but legitimate turn around.

"Yes! Yes! Yes!" Callie and I exclaimed together when both van and trailer were finally angled back down the mountain. Whew! Disaster narrowly averted. Or so we thought.

Returning to the paved road at the edge of the reservoir, I noticed a pull off that had just been vacated. A partially extinguished fire still simmered in the fire pit. "This is it!" I declared. "It's like it was left here just for us!"

We pulled into the wide spot. It was right next to the road, so there would be no peace and privacy. But after our ordeal, we were thankful to simply have a place to spend the night.

"This is great. But how are we going to get the trailer off without the crank handle?" Callie asked.

"I'm glad you asked! Watch and learn, little one." I proceeded to disengaged the wiring harness and chains and release the coupler from the trailer ball. Then I walked around the trailer and cranked down all four stabilizer jacks until they were just touching the ground at four corners around the trailer. Moving to the front stabilizer jacks, I cranked one, then the other, gently lifting the camper off the ball of the minivan's trailer hitch. Just as it released, I realized with horror that I'd forgotten to block the wheels.

The trailer disengaged from the ball and started rolling backwards, crumpling the trailer's stabilizer jacks as the trailer made its slow-motion journey towards the edge of the parking lot and the steep wooded slope that descended to the reservoir below.

"*No! No, no, no, no, no!*" I yelled. I grabbed the front of the trailer and dropped to the ground like an anchor as the trailer's weight threatened to pull my elbows out of their sockets. Callie ran to the back of the trailer. Together, we were able to arrest its progress. Shaking, I ran for a rock and crammed it under the nearest tire.

By this time, it was fully dark. I stood next to the trailer, shaking and crying. "It's okay, Mom. Everything happens for a reason. It's all going to be okay," Callie said. She didn't sound convinced.

The trailer post was sitting on the ground. Pitched forward at an angle, there was no way to sleep in the camper.

With a broken crank handle and no stabilizer jacks, we couldn't get the trailer back on the minivan. And even if we managed to find some way to get the trailer on the minivan, the folded stabilizer jacks would drag on the road, potentially damaging the camper's undercarriage. The trailer was officially stranded.

We slowly walked back to the car, climbed into our seats, and sat in the dark in stunned silence. Finally, the fog of panic cleared and I said, "Here's the plan. We'll lock up the trailer as best we can. The trailer jacks are crumpled so I doubt anyone can move it. I'm going to need to find someone with a truck to lift the front of the trailer high enough that the front jacks won't drag. Maybe I can just remove the back jacks with a socket set. I'll deal with all that in the morning. Right now, we need to find a place to spend the night."

When we got back into an area with cell coverage, an internet search revealed a single motel in Hungry Horse Montana. The motel was clearly several decades past its prime. Pulling into the motel parking lot, I said, "Hey. At least it's going to be cheap!"

"We have one room left. It'll be one hundred and thirty-nine dollars," the woman behind the counter said in a gravely voice.

"For one night?" I exclaimed in disbelief.

She stared back, unwavering.

"You're kidding, right?" I asked. "Are there any other hotels in town?"

"Closest town is Columbia Falls. Their hotels are double the rate of ours and I doubt they'd have vacancy anyway. We would have been sold out too, but I just got a cancellation an hour ago. One thirty-nine. You can take it or leave it."

I grudgingly slapped my credit card on the counter, filled out the paperwork, and returned to Callie, who was patiently waiting for me in the car. I started the car without a word and parked at a spot in front of our motel room door.

"How much was it, Mom?" Callie asked. Keenly aware of my financial concerns, she worried over every expenditure.

"Never mind," I replied.

"No. How much?" she insisted.

"One thirty-nine."

"No way! Mom! That's ridiculous! We can stay in the car. We don't need to rent a room in this dump for one thirty-nine."

I sighed. "I'm exhausted. There is no way I'm spending another night sleeping in the car. First thing tomorrow morning, I'll head to an auto parts store and see if I can get a socket set. With any luck, they might even sell replacement trailer jacks. But for now, we both need a good night's sleep."

I did my best to sound confident. In truth, I was still shaking in my flip flops.

What the hell am I going to do? Maybe I could use the van's car jack to lift the trailer. But I still need to remove the stabilizer jacks before we can tow it. What if the bolts on the trailer jack are rusted shut? I really need to find someone with a truck who can tow the trailer to an auto parts store. I can't afford to pay for another night in this crappy hotel.

The walls in the motel were paper thin. I could clearly hear the dialog on our next door neighbor's television. In the room behind the bed, someone with a smoker's cough hacked for five minutes straight, hocked a loogie the bathroom sink, and belched loudly. Lovely.

I finally got to sleep, but woke with a start in the middle of the night. The thought came to me like a bolt of lightning.

Hungry Horse, Montana. I heard about Hungry Horse when I was a kid. Doesn't Mom have a cousin or an uncle that lives here?

From the deep recesses of my mind, I remembered the name Jimmy. Though it was three in the morning, I texted my mom.

The next morning, I received a reply. By extraordinary coincidence, my mother's cousin, Jimmy, and his wife, Sharon, were indeed two of the six hundred and thirty-four fine residents of Hungry Horse, Montana! My mom sent Sharon's contact information. With any luck, Jimmy—or someone Jimmy knew—had a truck big enough to rescue my stranded camper.

I called the number my mom had given me and an answering machine picked up. It was not voicemail, but one of those honest-to-goodness answering machines, with a beep at the end of the inbound call message.

"Ah…hi, Jimmy and Sharon. You probably don't remember me. I'm Helen's daughter, Christy." With that I launched into a long-winded description of the dire circumstances leading up to this somewhat bizarre call, ending with, "And so if you happened to have a truck…well, that would be a really good thing. Bye!"

Standing in the hotel parking lot, I tried to quell the anxiety that was rising in my chest,

The Big Guy prompted, "Try to see this from your soul's perspective."

I closed my eyes and took a couple deep, calming breaths. A perfectly clear image of a child riding a roller coaster was impressed on my mind. The child's arms were flung wide, hair blowing back in the wind. "Wheee!" the child exclaimed in delight.

"Wheee? Are you fricking kidding me? Wheee?"
Opening my eyes, I saw the housekeeping lady staring at me.
Oops. Guess I said that out loud.

By noon, I still hadn't heard from Jimmy and Sharon. If we were going to avoid another night in an overpriced room with cardboard-thin walls, I was going to need to take matters into my own hands.

A quick stop at two garages in Columbia Falls confirmed what I'd suspected. Nobody was available to spend the afternoon driving to Hungry Horse Reservoir to retrieve my stranded trailer. I found a Napa Auto Parts store and purchased a socket set and WD-40 to loosen the trailer jacks' bolts.

Callie looked at me doubtfully. "Do you really think this is going to work?" she asked.

"What other choice do I have?"

It was a gorgeous, sunny afternoon when we made our way back to Hungry Horse Reservoir. Rounding a corner, our sweet little camper came into view, bringing to mind a forlorn puppy waiting for its family to return. A wash of love came over me. I felt so much gratitude for my little rolling home.

"Let's get to work," I said, hoping a can-do attitude would bolster my confidence. I figured my car jack was most likely in a rear compartment in the trunk.

We emptied half the contents of the back end of the van—which looked like an over-stuffed pantry and messy closet all rolled into one—before checking the owners manual and discovering that my minivan's jack was actually stored in a compartment under the carpet behind the front seats.

I finally extracted the jack, managed to assemble it, and positioned it under the metal frame of the pop-up trailer. Just then, an angel appeared. Granted, he didn't look like the kind of angel you see in books. This angel took the form of a man in his mid-sixties with a disheveled mop of gray hair and several-day-old whiskers. Nevertheless, I could see right through his grizzly disguise. He was indeed an angel.

"Need some help?" the man offered shyly.

"Absolutely!" I exclaimed a little too eagerly. I told him our sad story, ending in my failure to block the trailer's wheels. Feeling like a complete idiot for that rookie move, I tossed around words like "trailer jacks" and "coupler" to mitigate feelings of incompetence.

The man chuckled. "Well it looks like you got yourself into quite a bind. Let's see what we can do about that."

It was somewhat gratifying to see that my roadside angel wasn't much more adept at handling the car jack than I had been. However, after a few awkward twists, he managed to lift the trailer's front wheels off the ground.

"Okay. Why don't you see if you can get your minivan hitched to the trailer. That way we can work on this thing without having to worry about it coming off the car jack."

I did as the angel instructed. Free from the trailer's weight, the pop-up's four stabilizer jacks de-crumpled a bit. "Just a second. I have an idea," I said.

Grabbing the stabilizer jack crank handle, I inserted it into the wheel nut and started turning. To our amazement, the stabilizer jack screeched in protest, then started to retract. Excitedly, I moved to the other side, with the same result. Though the rebar crank shafts on the stabilizer jacks were clearly bent, they were straight enough to allow the rusty jacks to fully retract, thus avoiding the need to remove them with the socket set.

Callie and I jumped up and down with delight. I grabbed the man's hand and pumped it up and down profusely. "Thank you, thank you, thank you, thank you!" I exclaimed, partly to him and partly to God, whose divine providence was clearly responsible for this happy turn of events.

The man declined my offer to compensate him for his help and gave a little wave as he shuffled back to his truck. Callie and I joyously removed the rocks behind the camper's wheels and motored back onto the two-lane road, relieved to finally put Hungry Horse Reservoir in our rearview mirror.

In Kalispell, Montana, I was fortunate to find a trailer repair service that was willing to squeeze us in. In less than half an hour, the crank handle mechanism had been replaced and we were back on the road.

Callie discovered another free camping spot on iOverlander, not far from the entrance of Glacier National Park. According to the National Forest Service website, the Middle Fork of the Flathead River provided camping spots on a pebbled beach at river's edge. No online description could have possibly done justice to the scene that awaited us.

As we crossed the bridge spanning the Flathead River, white water rafting guides were drawing boats out of the water at a river launch site to our right. To our left on the far side of the river, more than a dozen camper vans—ranging from old rusted pickup truck campers to custom-built overland vehicles—were strewn helter-skelter along the river's shoreline. Callie squealed with delight.

Crossing the bridge, I noticed that each of the vehicles on the beach below had high clearance. And none of them was towing a trailer. Coincidence? Possibly. More likely than not, there was a rough road ahead.

Rough doesn't even begin to doesn't begin to describe that road. With potholes that could swallow a Prius for breakfast and have room for a VW Bug for lunch, the road would clearly have been deemed impassible by any sane person. Fortunately, my claim to sanity had been relinquished many miles back.

Callie too was determined. After all, this river-side conflagration of hippies, river rafters, and #vanlife ne'er-do-wells were "her people." There was no turning back. Walking along the van, Callie called out instructions and words of encouragement.

We finally arrived at the beach, and navigated our way down a makeshift pebble road that skirted the tree line. All heads turned to watch our progress. I'd be willing to bet serious money that ours was a the first and only Honda Odyssey minivan (much less one pulling a pop-up trailer) that ever graced that beach's shores. To boot, I was a good two decades older than the oldest person there. Callie, however, was in her glory.

I finally got a call back from my mom's cousin's wife, Sharon. My mom's cousin, Jimmy, had died a few months earlier. But Sharon and I made plans to connect two days hence. Meanwhile, Callie and I decided to go hiking in Glacier National Park the following morning.

Like just about every other day that summer, morning arrived without a cloud in the sky. We left the trailer at river's edge. This proved to be a good decision, as the road to Glacier National Park's Logan's Pass proved to be gut-wrenchingly narrow.

Our hike from Logan's Pass was truly glorious. Wildflowers bloomed effusively in cheerful shades of yellow, violet, and lavender. Periodically, hordes of tourists scurried off the trail, huddling together to photograph wild mountain goats who bucolically munched high alpine grass. Jaw-dropping views awaited us around every bend.

The day hike from Logan's Pass provided two options. We could either do an out-and-back or an eleven and a half mile descent to the Loop parking lot. The shuttles that normally made the return trip to Logan's Pass from the Loop lot weren't running due to Covid, so we settled on a hybrid model. I did an eight mile out-and-back hike from Logan's Pass, then drove down to the Loop to meet Callie, while she made the eleven and a half mile descent.

Callie was considering an additional one point four mile spur from Granite Peak Chalet to Grinnell Glacier, so I knew there would likely be time to kill as I awaited her arrival.

An hour passed after I arrived at the Loop parking lot. Then an hour and a half. Callie is a fast hiker and her route would have been mostly downhill. In comparison, my leisurely eight mile out-and-back to Logan's Pass included a four mile uphill climb.

I was starting to get anxious, and expected her to show up at any moment. But that moment passed, as did the next one and all the moments for another hour. The sun was dipping low in the sky. I knew we still had an hour and a half of daylight, but this was grizzly country. Grizzlies tend to be more active at dusk.

My throat got a kind of choky feeling. I attempted to mitigate the discomfort by chewing on a granola bar. But that only made the problem worse since the granola bar was overly dry to swallow.

Finally, unable to remain in the car, I tried to stave off fear by hiking up the trail to meet Callie. There were noticeably fewer people coming down the trail now.

Why does this keep happening? Why do I keep letting Callie go, then obsess with worry?

"You're doomed to repeat the same lessons, over and over, until you transcend them," the Big Guy replied. "What is the lesson you need to learn?"

Trust.

I willed myself to trust. Engaging in mortal combat with my own fear, I was dismayed to find my fear was winning once again. Another agonizing forty-five minutes passed, as I was certain each hiker rounding the next bend would surely be Callie. But it never was.

I began interrogating passing hikers. "Did you see a sixteen-year-old girl with curly blonde hair hiking alone?" My own words made my stomach churn. How had I agreed to allow her to hike all that distance in bear country by herself?

Finally, I received a couple of perplexing reports. Yes, they had seen a barefoot girl who matched that description hiking alone. *Hmm...barefoot?*

I made an arrow out of rocks, pointing in the direction of the parking lot, then scraped "This Way Callie" into the dirt. Making my way down the trail, I repeated the little message a half dozen times, more for my encouragement than hers. Finally, when I was just twenty minutes from the parking lot and the gloaming hour was neigh, Callie caught up with me. She was, indeed, barefoot.

I fought the urge to scold her as a few tears of relief leaked from the corners of my eyes.

"Mom! You won't believe what happened! I was on the trail to Grinnell Glacier when a mountain goat dropped onto the trail behind me. At first, I thought it was cool, and started taking pictures. But then he charged at me! He was in the middle of the trail and wouldn't let me pass. I was literally trapped on the glacier overlook for over half an hour!"

"Then my hiking boots were hurting," Callie continued, "so I took them off and tied them to my backpack. But it must not have been a very good knot, because the boots came untied. I didn't even know they fell off my pack. I had to hike the last four miles barefoot!"

Just then, a girl came around the corner holding one of Callie's boots. Spying Callie's bare feet, she asked, "Is this yours?"

"*Yes!*" Callie exclaimed, then asked sheepishly, "I don't suppose you saw the other one?"

The girl shook her head. "Sorry."

And so, as we entered Washington—a state with more hiking destinations than any other state on Callie's Instagram hit list—my daughter had absolutely no footwear of any kind.

CHAPTER 24

I'd planned to get new hiking books for Callie in Spokane. But due to Covid, stores weren't allowing customers to try on clothing, and that included shoes. The outdoor store in Spokane didn't allow returns or exchanges either. I wasn't willing to shell out a hundred and thirty dollars or more for hiking boots that potentially wouldn't fit. So we left Spokane without boots, hoping to find another outdoor store en route to Seattle with a more lenient return policy.

It was well after dark in mid-August when we arrived at the Okangon-Watchee Wilderness Area outside Leavenworth, Washington. Due to the late hour, we opted to pay for the last remaining campsite at the National Forest Service campground, as opposed to searching for a free dispersed camping spot on Campendium. Exhausted, we set up camp and dropped off to sleep, preparing for an early morning departure to Colchuck Lake.

Morning arrived and to my great elation, I found a spare pair of tennis shoes while rummaging through the back of the car.

"Look, Callie! I found tennis shoes! You can wear these for the hike!" I exclaimed.

"Those are Mia's. They don't fit me. They give me blisters."

"Well, what the heck are you going to wear on the hike?" I asked in consternation.

"I've been going barefoot all summer, Mom! And I just hiked half the trail from Logan's Pass barefoot."

"Honey. The hike to Colchuck is nine miles round trip. The trail notes say it's a seriously tough climb. It's rated difficult! You can't do this one without shoes."

"Mom!" Callie replied in exasperation. "It's not like we have another option! We're not going to drive all this way and not do the hike. I'll be fine," she insisted.

To appropriate a phrase from the Borg in Star Trek, when it comes to Callie's content creation, "Resistance is futile."

I pouted as we ate bags of stale salad for breakfast. Then we got lost twice en route to the Colchuck Lake trailhead, further souring my mood.

Callie was jubilant, excited at the prospect of spending the entire day shoeless. She took off at the pace of a mountain goat while I maintained marmot speed. The trail's topography beyond the parking lot was relatively flat, winding through thick boreal forests.

Just as I was becoming accustomed to the easy terrain, the trail steepened sharply, an uneven natural staircase of rocks rising in unending switchbacks. Periodically, the rocks gave way to a small flat stretch where Callie's bare feet left prints in the dirt.

The route to Colchuck Lake is heavily trafficked. Several middle-aged men were accompanying a group of around a dozen boys who looked to be in their late teens or early twenties. I speculated that they were part of a church group or were having a Boy Scout reunion.

Leapfrogging up the trail, I often struck up conversations with fellow hikers along the way. Most of the men in the group hiked at a pace similar to mine. The boys were eager to catch up with the elusive barefoot ghost hiker, who had managed to pass by them, unnoticed, at one of the overlooks.

After a few hours of hard hiking, we finally arrived at the hallowed shores of Colchuck Lake. It was truly magnificent. The lake itself is nestled beneath the snowy flanks of three of the highest peaks in Washington: the 7,800 foot Enchantment Mountains to the southeast, 8,842 foot Dragontail Peak due south, and 8,705 foot Colchuck Peak rising above Colchuck Glacier on the southwest end of the lake.

Callie and I reconvened for a swim in the icy, crystalline water of Colchuck Lake. Within minutes, our skin was numb. We turned as we heard someone calling from shore. Callie waved to a guy she had met on the way up. He was a local kid, hiking with his family to celebrate his brother's birthday. He offered to take Callie to a "totally sick cliff jumping spot," and she happily complied.

Emerging from my icy swim, I flopped down on a warm rock and watched Callie and her new friend swim around a distant bend. Breathing in the sunshine and mountain air, I reveled in the unsurpassable beauty of the landscape.

Suddenly, I heard a ruckus behind me, and turned to discover my backpack was being molested by a posse of six or seven chipmunks. They'd already managed to extract an errant bag of trail mix and were doing their level best to gnaw a hole in the bottom before I caught them.

"Shoo!" I swept up the bag of trail mix and my backpack in one stroke, sending chipmunks flying. One little guy, who was still inside the pack, nearly gave me a heart attack as he launched his way to freedom.

Crap. I'll have to be more careful. It would be a long trip down on an empty stomach.

Even at this distance, Aasgard Pass—which separates Dragontail from the Enchantment Mountains—looked foreboding. The pass's impossibly steep ascent climbs two thousand feet in a mere three quarters of a mile. The Washington Trails Association website describes the Aasgard Pass Trail as a "thigh burning, chest-burning, eye-popping endeavor that offers as many extraordinary views as beads of sweat that will fall from your brow."

Not surprisingly, Callie returned from her swim to ask if she could climb Aasgard pass...barefoot. If I was her age with her passion to capture epic drone footage, I would most certainly have wanted to do the same. Besides, the Big Guy said I was doomed to repeat these scenarios until I learned to trust. This was my chance to learn.

We agreed to reconnect at a time that allowed us to return to the parking lot before sunset. With an hour and a half to kill and no cell service, I entertained myself by feeding chipmunks. After all, these chipmunks were already morally ruined. So I tossed tiny peanut chunks to the aggressive little rodent robber barons.

As the rendezvous time approached, I felt a familiar anxiety rising.

Remember? This is supposed to be your chance to demonstrate trust. So just trust! Maybe walking will ease the anxiety.

No longer hungry, I dumped the rest of the peanuts on the ground, which instantly manifested a hoard of ravenous chipmunks, who were joined by noisy bluejays.

Sweeping up my pack, I headed toward the other end of the lake meet Callie.

At the point where my little spur merged with the main trail from the parking lot, I saw an elderly man making his way up the path. Though he was a couple hours behind the rest of his group, I recognized him as one of the men we'd encountered on the ascent.

Leaning against a rock, I watched him slowly and patiently descend a small scree slope, his hiking poles bearing the full burden of his weight. He looked tired. Sweat stained the armpits of his shirt and leaked out from under his wide-brimmed Tilly hiking hat. I indicated a natural seat in the rock where I'd been standing. "Why don't you take a rest?" I offered.

We chatted for twenty minutes. His name was Tom, and he was seventy-two years old. This was his fifth trip up the Colchuck Lake Trail. He planned to climb Aasgard Pass in the morning. Tom was delighted to hear that it was Callie's barefoot prints he'd been following.

"Hah! You've got to love a girl who hikes barefoot!"

Tom entertained me with stories from his trips to Colchuck Lake.

"Five times, I've made this trip," he said, pausing to watch scenes from the past replay in his mind. "Every time, it's different. Every time is an adventure. One time, there were two climbers on Dragontail Peak who fell to their deaths. Search and rescue teams were out there for two weeks, but they were never able to find the bodies."

I smiled at this unlikely tale. Tom was clearly an artful storyteller who approached his craft with passion and enthusiasm, ready to stretch the truth if it added to the tale's entertainment value.

"Another time, a father and son were climbing that face above Aasgard pass. The pass had received heavy snowfall late in the season. The son was climbing the face and his father was belaying from down below. The son had just gotten off a phone call with his mom when a rock slide let loose, burying the father in rocks. The son fell too. They both died."

I gave an involuntary shudder, remembering that my daughter was descending that same pass.

Noticing my reaction, Tom said, "Awww, don't worry. That was early in the season, just after the spring thaw. The ground was more unstable then. Your Callie will be just fine."

Tom told me about a time he and three men were trapped in a mid-summer blizzard atop Aasgard Pass. Caught unawares, they spent hours hunkered down in a shallow rock cave they built with their bare hands, taking turns staving off hypothermia with a single threadbare windbreaker.

Then Tom regaled me with local bigfoot lore. He categorized some of the stories as real sightings and others as suspected sightings. Taking a pause, he looked at the distant shore and said contemplatively, "See that remote rock area over there? There's no trail on that side of the lake. But there are plenty of deer for food. It looks like just the kind of place a bigfoot would live, doesn't it?"

I smiled and replied, "Yeah. It sure does."

"Well, I'd best be heading off to connect with my group," Tom said. "They'll be wondering where I am. Thanks for listening to my stories. It was good practice, 'cause those are the stories I'll be telling around the camp fire tonight!" We said our goodbyes and Tom shuffled off, his hiking poles trailing limply behind him.

Twenty minutes later, Callie appeared around the bend. By my calculation, she was a half hour past our meet-up time. I was about to reproach her for her tardiness, but the look on her face stopped me. She was clearly distressed.

"Mom. Something bad happened. I just went past the camp with the Boy Scout group. A man had a heart attack. I think he's dead."

"Tom," I whispered. I felt his presence and knew it was true.

Just then, a couple panicked members of Tom's group ran up to us. They'd been fishing farther down the lake when another hiker gave them the news. "We were trying to catch fish for dinner, so we haven't made it to the camp site yet. Do you know where our group is camped?"

Callie agreed to show them the way. The two men and l had a hard time keeping pace with the barefoot teen. Arriving at the camp site, we came upon a somber scene. The group was assembled around a large campfire. A sleeping bag, presumably holding Tom's body, rested on the ground beside a large boulder. Even the older men looked like lost little boys. My mothering instinct kicked in.

"Rough day," I said, stepping into the middle of the group. "I know this seems really tough right now. But Tom would want you all to know that he died exactly how he wanted to die, on his own terms. He loved this place. Did you know this was his fifth time hiking up the Colchuck Lake Trail? I can't think of a more perfect ending to his adventurous life. He was an outdoors man. And he took the opportunity to make his exit from this world in the outdoors, just like he always wanted."

The older men nodded.

I told them how I'd met Tom on the trail, and how he'd shared his campfire stories. "Tom used his last breath to tell me these stories, because he knew I'd share them with you."

I recounted Tom's tales, veritably word-for-word, with the same inflection and heart Tom used when telling them. It felt like Tom was speaking through me. A tear of gratitude leaked out of the corner of my eye.

Callie and I left the men as they bid farewell to Tom on the shore of his beloved Colchuck Lake.

A little over an hour later, the forest was darkening as a helicopter flew overhead en route to the group camp. Shortly after, the 'copter made its return trip. "Bye, Tom! Safe journey!" Callie and I yelled, jumping up and down, waving to the helicopter. It disappeared over the horizon, glinting in the last rays of sunlight on Tom's last day on this earth.

"Ooh! Did you feel that?" Callie asked.

"Yes, I did," I replied in response to the surge of warmth and love that washed over me. "Thank you, Tom."

CHAPTER 25

Thoughts of Tom occupied my mind as Callie and I drove through the Mount Baker-Snoqualmie National Forest towards Seattle.

So much of this trip has been an exercise in trust. But it's impossible to deny that bad things happen! Tom died of a heart attack. How will that impact his friends? And his family?

The Big Guy replied, "Trying to see the blessing in someone else's adversity is a fool's game. Their adversity is their own. It does not belong to you, nor should it shape your decisions."

But why do we have to go through adversity in the first place? If God provides for all our daily needs, doesn't that build trust? Why do people need to struggle?

"People become complacent. They take good fortune for granted. Consequently they don't feel blessed. Why do bad things happen? Because you are loved. God's healing and love are offered in precise measure to meet each challenge. Adversity brings you back to question, 'Do you trust?' In answering 'Yes,' you receive God's love. You feel blessed."

What about the times I don't feel blessed? What about the times I just feel frightened, or lonely, or abandoned?

The Big Guy smiled. "That's the real question, isn't it? You don't doubt God's love, or His ability to orchestrate all things for good. You doubt your own worthiness. Each challenge in your life, without exception, is a special gift, chosen especially for you to help you become the person your soul has chosen to embody. Be assured, dear one. Your worth has never been in question. You are worthy."

Inspired by the natural beauty and expansiveness of the Mount Baker-Snoqualmie National Forest, Callie scoured Campendium and iOverlander for a camping spot that would provide easy access to Mount Pilchuck, the first destination on her list of hikes near Seattle.

After several weeks camping on national forest land, we'd been spoiled into thinking that national forests reliably yield free "dispersed" camping options. According to the Bureau of Land Management website:

> "Camping on public lands away from developed recreation facilities is referred to as dispersed camping. Most of the remainder of public lands are open to dispersed camping, as long as it does not conflict with other authorized uses or in areas posted "closed to camping," or in some way adversely affects wildlife species or natural resources."

Unfortunately, forty minutes outside Seattle, the free camping spots we'd come to rely on were hard to come by. Most dispersed camping spots are located along secondary roads and show evidence of previous use. We scoured the roadside, taking any two-track that branched from the main road. But every likely spot was already taken.

I was driving at a snail's place, scanning the woods, when Callie exclaimed "Stop! I think I saw a spot." Sure enough, nearly concealed by brush and overgrowth on either side was a small gravel pull-out. The little driveway widened into a perfectly lovely, flat, camping spot, complete with a big stone fire pit.

There was only one problem: it looked as if this site had very recently been ransacked by a bear. There was garbage strewn all over the ground. Evaluating the scene was a study in campsite forensics.

It had rained, and everything was wet. Someone had clearly left in a hurry, as unopened bottles of ketchup, mustard, mayo, and relish had been abandoned. The garbage looked to be several days old, ripped from white plastic bags laying in shreds. Remnants of packaging from lunch meat, cheese, crackers, and chips had been torn from a damaged cooler laying nearby. I made a mental note to be especially careful not to store any food or garbage in the pop-up camper.

Callie and I set to work cleaning the site, using garbage bags as gloves. Within minutes, we had a beautiful little camp surrounded by massive stately pines. I loved the fact that heavy undergrowth nicely concealed the camper from the road. We were planning to spend the following night in a fire lookout tower atop Mount Pilchuck, and I needed to know our little camper would be safe without us.

We rose early to prepare for the climb to Mount Pilchuck. Despite the fact that I'd owned an outdoor store fully stocked with gear from well-known brands like Patagonia, Osprey, and Big Agnus, I'd somehow failed to take my backpack, my sleeping bag, or a fully functional sleeping pad, as mine had been repaired with a patch. A thirty-nine gallon Hefty Strong Lawn and Leaf trash bag—stuffed with a puffy Honcho Poncho jacket—would serve as my sleeping bag. A duffle bag with shoulder straps served as my backpack.

Callie's situation was equally abysmal. We stopped at REI in Seattle and *finally* got Callie a new pair of hiking boots. But her backpack was nothing more than an Osprey book bag. Callie would be sleeping in her hammock with a sleeping bag that only had insulation on one side, since it was meant to be paired with a sleeping pad.

As per usual, Callie ascended Mt. Pilchuck much faster than me. Though the morning had been sunny when we left the popup trailer nestled in its little roadside roost, a thick morning fog had rolled into the valley below the Mt. Pilchuck parking lot. Ascending through the cloud, I was aware of the fact that we were likely missing the views that made this steep, rocky hike gratifying.

In the fog, I continued my conversation with the Big Guy.

This roadtrip feels like a microcosm of life. The healing, learning, and growth I experience here affects larger cycles, impacting my remaining years on this planet. What lessons do I still need to learn?

"Don't take life, or yourself, too seriously," the Big Guy impressed on my mind. "The love you see in the faces of the people you meet is just your own soul's love being reflected back to you. It's no more complicated than that."

"People like to believe that they have the right to expect more from certain people—like parents, spouses or children. It's not true. Like kids playing at the playground, they come and go in your life. Have a blast playing with the ones who want to play. Be grateful for your time with them."

I thought about Callie and the times I felt anxious.

"What's really causing that anxiousness?" the Big Guy prompted.

Callie is a strong hiker, with excellent backcountry navigational skills, especially when she has her phone. But I worry that she isn't safe.

"So where do you still need to develop trust?"

I need to remember that her inner guidance system is protecting her, just as mine protects me.

Rock slides made it difficult to pick out the trail. After a couple hours of hiking and a few wrong turns, Mt. Pilchuck's austere lookout tower finally came into view. It was perched on a high rock slab, with near vertical walls that seemly provided no access to the tower.

The trail traversed a spine of rock, ending in a jumble of massive boulders strewn at odd angles. It looked like God got tired of building the mountain and just dumped all the extra pieces at the top. The other side of the Mount Pilchuck fire tower was a sheer cliff that dropped a couple hundred feet to the valley below.

People were strolling along a wide porch that surrounded the lookout tower on all sides, so there was clearly a way up. Just under the porch, I spotted a metal ladder screwed right into the rock face. The ladder ended half way down a sharply sloped boulder. A man steadied himself at the base of the ladder, then reached down to pull his wife up. Her foot slipped and she cursed. Though a fall at that particular juncture wouldn't end in death, it would likely yield a sprained ankle or broken leg.

With so many wilderness trails reduced to pedestrian thoroughfares, it was refreshing to discover a high point lookout whose wild ruggedness was largely untamed.

Callie called from the ramparts above me. "Mom! Mom! You've got to see this! It's amazing!"

Ascending the ladder, I crested over the top and inhaled sharply. The view literally took my breath away. The early morning fog had cleared, permitting expansive views for a hundred miles in every direction. Puget Sound stretched out to the west like a massive sleeping giant. To the south lay the ethereal Three Sisters volcanoes, as well as Mount St. Helens and Mount Rainier.

The entire tower was enclosed in windows, which would provide astounding sunset and sunrise views while protecting Callie and I from the elements. Callie had already strung her hammock in a corner to claiming space in the event other hikers were planning to spend the night as well.

A group of college-aged boys reached the summit shortly after we arrived. As we exchanged climbing stories, Callie and I made mental notes for future excursions. The day wore on and visitor traffic thinned.

Wanting to get back to their cars before it got dark, the boys smoked some weed then made their way down the boulder field. About fifteen minutes later, I heard a cry of excruciating pain from the switchbacks below.

"Shit! Oh my god. Oh my god. Argh! Fuck!"

I turned to look at a couple sitting on the rock below me. They sat unmoving, listening attentively. They'd heard it too. "Are you all right?" the man below me called out.

"No," came the answer. "I think my leg is broken."

Within minutes, we heard a flurry of activity on the trail below as hikers gathered. News from an ascending climber confirmed our suspicions. One of the weed-smoking college boys had suffered a broken tibia. He was stabilized, but would require a helicopter airlift.

In surprisingly little time, a helicopter was hovering just off the fire tower's deck, and a wilderness responder was lowered to assist the injured hiker. An updraft from the helicopter's propellers blew our hair into a tangled mess as we watched the EMT work diligently to secure the boy and haul him to safety.

The helicopter flew away, and we assumed the day's excitement was over. But wilderness climbs can pose danger to even the most skilled hiker. More drama lay ahead.

The small handful of hikers who lingered to watch sunset were those who felt confident descending the steep, rocky trail by headlamp.

The lookout tower was nearly vacated, so Callie stretched out her hammock and I laid my inflatable camping mat on the floor. Just as the sun was descending beyond the horizon, two men who looked to be in their early thirties arrived at the threshold of the lookout tower. They were both breathing hard from the strenuous climb.

A minute or two later, one man had regained his breath. But the other was still panting. I noticed sweat beading on his forehead. "Are you okay?" I asked.

The man shook his head. I stepped out onto the porch of the lookout tower where the man's traveling companion was snapping photos of spectacular colors streaming across the sky. "Your buddy doesn't seem to be doing well. You might want to come back in to check on him."

"I'm sure he's okay," the man responded. "He's probably just dehydrated. The guy's ex-military. He can handle a little exertion."

I shrugged and went back inside, followed by another two guys who had just arrived at the lookout tower. When we entered the room, the ex-military guy was still panting heavily.

Within seconds, his eyes glazed over. He dropped to his knees and pitched forward, his elbow and shoulder breaking the fall before his head hit the floor. Shit.

The two men behind me sprang into action. The younger of the two, a bookishly handsome guy in his thirties, dropped to his knees and rolled the ex-military man onto his side. "I'm Kevin. I used to be an EMT," he said.

"I'm Christy," I said. "How can I help?"

"When he comes to, I think he's going to need water."

I found an empty plastic water bottle and poured some of my water into it.

Now cradled in Kevin's arms, the man seemed to be regaining consciousness. He started shaking. I helped Kevin wriggle out of his jacket and wrapped it around the man's shoulders.

"I can't feel my hands," ex-military guy said, alarmed. "And one foot. They're numb."

By this time, ex-military's hiking buddy came inside and was alarmed to find his friend on the floor. "Wow. In honesty, we've only hiked together once before. I had no idea he was actually in trouble," the man muttered to no one in particular. He introduced himself as Ben. And ex-military's name was Mike.

"There's no way in hell I'm going to make it down," Mike said. "I still can't feel one foot and the other one is tingly. I'm going to need a helicopter."

Kevin and I looked at each other. "My phone doesn't have cell service," he announced as he checked his phone. The other two men in the lookout tower shook their heads as well. No service.

Glancing down at my phone, I had one bar, but my battery was at two percent. It was pitch black outside and the temperature was dropping quickly. Despite being wrapped in Kevin's jacket, Mike was shaking on the floor.

Ben knelt down next to Mike. "Hey dude, are you sure we can't just get some fluids in you and hike down? A 'copter rescue is going to cost you a fortune."

I pulled Ben aside. "Forgive me for being overly cautious, but I was on a hike a couple days ago where a man died of a heart attack. Granted, he was a lot older than Mike, but it might make sense to take precautions."

Ben knelt back down beside his friend. "Dude. What do you think? How are you feeling?"

"Not so good," Mike replied. "I don't think my insurance will cover wilderness rescue. And I don't have the money to pay for a 'copter. But I know my body. There is no way I'm going to be able to make it down."

"You can spend the night up here and leave in the morning," Kevin suggested. I stared at him open-mouthed, aghast at the prospect of trying to keep Mike alive through the night if things took a turn for the worse. Temperatures were continuing to drop. We didn't have extra clothing to keep Mike warm. My cell phone battery would soon be dead. Options were limited and our window of opportunity was closing.

I stood up decisively. "Listen. This is no game. Mike, are you going to be able to make it down?" Mike rose to stand, staggered, and dropped back down.

"That would be a clear 'no,'" he replied.

"Okay. Then we're calling for support." I dialed nine one one and was forwarded to the wilderness responder dispatch centre.

"Listen," I told the dispatch operator, "I'm down to one percent battery, and we have a man who needs help." I put Mike on the line.

After a brief conversation, it became apparent that no help would be coming. The helicopter had just arrived at the hospital. Since Mike was conscious and not in immediate danger, the 'copter would not return to the mountain in the dark. The operator recommended Mike take shelter in the lookout tower.

"Shit," I said. I hung my headlamp from Callie's hammock to provide light. We all sat for a few minutes in silence, deliberating this new turn of events.

Kevin put an arm over my shoulder. "I think we could use a beer," he said, procuring bottles from his backpack. He opened the beer and handed one to his hiking companion, one to me, and took a big swig of the third.

"Wow. Beer in glass bottles? Aren't you afraid of broken glass in your backpack? Here I thought you guys were seasoned hikers!"

"We are," Kevin's traveling companion said, introducing himself as Bob. "We belong to a hiking club and hiking with glass bottles is clearly frowned upon. This is our little act of anarchy," he said with a wink. We laughed, grateful for a moment of levity.

Mike was still laying on the floor, talking to Ben. "I seriously can't stay here tonight, dude," Mike said. Mike's face looked ash-white in the wan beam cast by my headlamp. Inky blackness had fully engulfed the lookout tower. The temperature had already dropped fifteen degrees in the wake of the setting sun, and was continuing to drop more by the minute.

Kevin pulled an extra sweater from his pack, as Mike was still wearing his jacket. "We're going to get you down, Mike," Kevin said decisively.

Ben looked at Kevin dubiously.

"I don't know if that's a good idea. That kid broke his leg in broad daylight. And he wasn't physically impaired."

"Yes, but he was mentally impaired," Ken reminded his hiking buddy. "Those boys were smoking weed."

"Still…" Ben hesitated.

"Up," Kevin commanded, extending a hand to Mike. Mike grasped Kevin's hand and was bodily pulled to his feet. He staggered a little, but stayed upright. Using a spare rain jacket, Kevin created a makeshift harness, looping it around Mike's chest and under his armpits. "We'll use this to lower you down the ladder and get you off the rocks. On the trail, I'll walk behind you and arrest your fall if you pass out again."

At this point, Mike and Ben had been in the lookout tower for nearly two hours. I glanced appreciatively at Kevin, thankful that someone was finally taking charge.

Callie and I watched the men struggle to get Mike down the ladder and over the treacherous pile of jagged boulders. Upon gaining solid ground, they were able to make faster progress. Callie and I tracked their headlamps as they slowly switchbacked down the mountain over the next hour, finally disappearing from sight in the expansive forest below.

Suddenly bereft of human drama, the lookout tower was silent. Callie climbed into her hammock, and I did my best to make myself comfortable on the floor.

I'd assumed that deep exhaustion would ensure a good night's sleep. But all night, mice scurried around my head. I put earplugs in my ears to block the maddening sounds of scrabbling. But I awoke abruptly as a mouse ran across my makeshift sleeping bag.

It was impossibly early when I heard voices the next morning. The sky was still dark, barely a shade lighter on the eastern horizon. Someone was stomping on the wood deck outside, fending off the morning cold. I was stiff from a frigid night on the hard wooden floor. In addition to the mice, my air mattress had deflated.

After a few half-hearted blows into the deflated mattress, I gathered my lawn-and-leaf bag around me, re-fluffed the Honcho Poncho (which provided meager insulation), and tried to snatch a last few elusive winks of sleep. Just too damed uncomfortable, I finally got up.

Stepping outside, I realized how much our little shelter had been protecting us from the elements. A biting wind blew my hair sideways. I pulled the poncho's hood over my head and scurried back inside to eat a breakfast of canned sardines and soda crackers. Callie had just ripped open a foil pack containing Indian-style curried lentils. We shared the few remaining ounces of water we had left, having contributed the majority of our water to Mike's rescue mission.

If you've ever watched a sun rise in the mountains, you know the process is tantalizingly slow. Daybreak lasts an hour or more as the horizon shifts in shades from indigo to light blue before any hints of red, orange, or yellow begin to appear. Despite the cold and exhaustion, I felt a happy kind of awe.

Air currents poured over the mountain to the west in what can only be described as a waterfall in the sky. A thin line of clouds formed an aerial river, which cascaded before pooling into the valley below. Rather than being static like most clouds, these clouds were rippling and roiling like turbulent rapids.

Soon, the reds, oranges, and yellows accumulated on the eastern horizon, stretching to meet the waterfall of clouds. Callie's drone went up and quickly sped off in the distance to avoid disrupting the sacred moment we were experiencing. In this way, she was able to document and record the event while savoring it at the same time. Her images from the sunrise on Mt. Pilchuck were surreal.

More beautiful than the sunrise was my daughter's face, filled with awe and delight. There was no trace of sadness in her eyes, no hint of the depression and anxiety that plagued her a few short weeks before. There, perched on the deck of a lookout tower atop a rocky precipice, with a waterfall of orange creamsicle clouds pouring into the valley below…there, she was free. There she was safe. There, I felt like her hero, and she felt like mine.

CHAPTER 26

One of the groups that arrived to watch sunrise at Mt. Pilchuck were three girls Callie's age. Hailing from Seattle's high society, the girls were intrigued by (and somewhat envious of) Callie's itinerant lifestyle. Callie found their lives similarly fascinating as they shared stories of kick-ass hiking adventures and boating in Puget Sound. Within minutes, the girls—now fast friends—were traipsing off en masse to take pictures of the Pilchuck sunrise.

Before descending the mountain, the girls enthusiastically encouraged Callie to call them when we made it back to civilization.

After the drama on Mt. Pilchuck, Callie and I spent a couple relaxing days exploring the North Cascades and stand up paddle boarding on Diablo Lake before heading back to Seattle.

The city came as a shock after spending several weeks in the wilderness. We opted to splurge on a couple nights in a hotel while my Honda Odyssey received the TLC it so heartily deserved. Between appointments to replace the brakes, change the oil, and re-wire the trailer's electrical harness for the third time, we indulged in the decadence of watching television and planned the next stage of our adventure.

It was the end of August, and night time temperatures were already dropping in the high country. Our roadtrip would be drawing to a close in a few short weeks. Christopher would be joining us in Los Angeles to make the return trip across the country, dictating the need to set a firm end date.

Callie chafed at the idea of booking a flight for Christopher. "What if we can't get to the rest of the spots on the list? There are a lot of places in California I still want to see, especially near Yosemite."

"You're the one who decided to spend ten days road-tripping with the boys," I reminded Callie. "There just isn't time to make it to all the places you want to see."

In Seattle, Callie made plans to connect with her new friends from Mt. Pilchuck, who were excited to introduce her to their home town. As the day wore on, Callie's excitement turned to anxiety.

"Mom, we need to find a thrift shop. I literally have nothing to wear."

Watching her rifle through a plastic Walmart bag filled with not-quite-white t-shirts and faded tank tops, I saw her point. "Those girls were really nice. I'm sure they aren't going to judge you for what you wear."

"You don't get it, Mom. These girls are super rich. One of the girls went boating with Bill Gate's daughter this summer. Did you notice they were all wearing Lulu Lemon leggings and tank tops? They had Patagonia jackets and Osprey packs. I look like a homeless person. I'm not asking for Lulu Lemon leggings. I just want to get a pair of leggings that doesn't have holes. In the wilderness, I don't care. But here, I really care. I hate the fact that I care, but I do. I want these girls to like me." A tear leaked out of the corner of her eye. "They're actually really cool."

Remembering the way they supported and encouraged each other at the top of Mount Pilchuck, I had to agree. Though our mother-daughter roadtrip was an incredible experience, I knew how much Callie ached for the companionship for kids her own age. She deeply envied the relationship these three girls had, and I knew she wanted to fit in, even if it was just for a day or two.

"Okay. Let's go thrift shopping," I said.

"Yay, yay, yay!" Callie exclaimed, wiping away tears. "I did a search and there are two great shops in this area!"

We were shocked at the size of the homeless population in Seattle. Tent communities dominated parks, vacant lots, and even took over city sidewalks. Their presence made me feel awkward and uncomfortable. Like in Las Vegas, I thought, *But for the grace of God, there go I.*

Surveying the scene, Callie insisted on using her own money to make care packages for the homeless. She created twenty to thirty paper bags containing all the items you'd think a homeless person would need: non-perishable foods and snacks, toothbrushes, toothpaste, body wipes, etc.

What made Callie's little bags even more precious is the fact that she invested in journals and pens…because life is an adventure. Despite the fact that many Instagram influencers donate to the homeless to as a means to increase their social media following, Callie refused to post anything about her philanthropic endeavors. She just spent the afternoon walking through a tent city, handing out bags and listening to anyone who was willing to share their story.

Watching Callie, it occurred to me that she could have used the money she spent on care packages to buy herself a pair of Lulu Lemon leggings. Instead, she was content with the clean, hole-free, no-name-brand leggings I got from the thrift store that were functional, if not fashionable. A few short months ago, I would have thought nothing of going to the mall to get Callie a new pair of leggings. Now, it seemed irresponsible to buy anything that wasn't second-hand.

As Callie left for the evening, I realized that I longed for backyard bonfires and wine night with the girls. I deeply missed my friends. In that regard, I wasn't all that different from my teenage daughter.

"How was your night?" I asked, as Calle returned to the hotel room after her evening with the girls.

Callie was somewhat reticent. "Good, I guess."

"Did something happen, sweetie?"

"No, it's not that. The girls were nice. They did their best to include me. But their lives are so different from mine. The girl who drove had a sixty thousand dollar sports car. We went to a bougie ice cream shop, where a bowl of ice cream cost twenty dollars. They pulled out their credit cards without batting an eye. But I felt so guilty spending that much money on ice cream!"

"Well, at least was it good ice cream?" I asked.

"The best!" Callie replied. "But honestly, I can't wait to get out of the city. I need to get back to the woods. I need to be sitting in my hammock surrounded by trees. I'm not happy here, Mom."

"Me neither," I replied.

Seattle used to be my favorite city in the United States. Now, just like any other city, Seattle made me claustrophobic. I couldn't wait to escape. The next morning, with no small amount of relief, we hitched the trailer and headed for Olympic National Park, hoping the fresh Pacific air would permeate our skin and cleanse body and soul of city grunge.

Our search for a place to stay on the northern end of the Olympic Peninsula highlights the enigmatic nature of our dance with the divine. For the majority of the afternoon, Callie searched apps and maps during our drive up the Olympic Peninsula en route to Port Angeles. We'd made the strategic error of leaving Seattle on a Friday. The late-summer weekend was incredibly busy, as Seattle's adventure-minded residents flooded national forests, parks, and other public lands.

Dispersed camping spots are available in national forests, but not national parks. The entire region around Port Angeles was a national park. In the course of two hours, Callie called every single campground in the northern part of the Olympic Peninsula. There was nary a campsite to be found.

Earlier in the trip, we learned that some national parks have handicap accessible camp sites that are released for non-handicap use at six o'clock in the evening. These sites are released on a first-come-first-serve basis and are only available in person. Hoping for a miracle, we drove to two prospective campgrounds. But neither had handicap spots to release.

Discouraged, I pulled into a vacant parking lot adjacent to the Clallum County Fairgrounds. As Callie and I tried to decide whether or not the parking lot would be a good place to spend the night, a police car slowly passed behind the trailer and shook his head, "No."

In a last-ditch effort, we drove half an hour to get to a place one Campendium user identified as "a place you could camp along a dirt road." Evening shadows were getting long, and I felt anxiety setting in. It quickly became clear that the road was too narrow and too heavily traveled for setting up a pop-up trailer.

Standing outside the minivan, I was frustrated to the point of tears. "I knew this would happen!" I exclaimed. Even before the words spilled out, I felt guilty for taking my frustration out on Callie. Nevertheless, I was powerless to stop the pointless rant. "You just keep pushing us to move every night. Now we literally have no place to go. I'm exhausted. Every single lot has 'no overnight parking' signs!"

"It's not my fault, Mom. I did my best," Callie replied, deflated. Bearing the brunt of the burden to find our nightly lodging, Callie was just as frustrated and worried as I was. "I'm the one who spent three hours on the phone calling every single campground."

"Right. And there's nothing available. So now what? We're stuck," I snapped.

"It's okay, Mom. Something will come up. Let's just take a deep breath and meditate."

Following Callie's lead, I took a shaky breath and calmed my mind. A few deep breaths later, I listened for the Big Guy.

"Look at the national forest map," the Big Guy instructed.

I argued with the voice in my head: *Callie and I both checked Apple Maps for public land. There's nothing. Besides, we don't even have cell service here.*

"Drive to a place where you have service. Then look at the national forest map for this region," the Big Guy firmly insisted.

With no other option, I told Callie what my inner guidance said. "That's great!" she said enthusiastically. "There must be something we missed!" Buoyed by her confidence, I chuckled at the fact that she placed such complete trust in my inner guidance.

Up the road, when we finally got back into cellular range, I opened the national forest service map on my phone. A tiny dark green spot amid the sea of light green indicated a tiny slice of national forest land inside Olympic National Park. National forests were fair game for boon docking. But it didn't even look like a road led to it. Callie zoomed in on the corresponding area on Apple Maps.

"Look," she exclaimed excitedly. "This might be a fire road!" Sure enough, a tiny squiggly line connected to the main road inside the national park.

"It's worth a shot. At this point, we have nothing to lose."

"Let's visualize the perfect place to spend the night, Mom. It will be quiet and peaceful. Nobody knows about it. We'll have the whole place to ourselves."

Deep in the interior of Olympic National Park, we were following well-maintained national park roads when we finally came to something that didn't fit. It was a sign with a street name that looked like something you would see in a neighborhood subdivision. We turned onto the street and found ourselves in a little neighborhood of A-frame houses that looked like they'd been built in the 1960s or 1970s.

It suddenly made sense. "Maybe this was private land when the government turned this area into a national park!" We drove through the little subdivision in the direction of the tiny line on the map that indicated a fire road. The fire road was wide and well maintained with hard-packed gravel. About half a mile up, it flared out in a wide pull-off that was perfect for our little pop-up trailer.

Consulting the map, I confirmed we were indeed on national forest land. We couldn't believe our luck. "Thank you, Universe!" Callie and I shouted, our voices echoing in the vast empty space of trees and valleys that surrounded our beautiful camping spot.

That night, bathing in the tranquility of an evening chorus provided by frogs, night birds, and the wind in the trees, I gazed at the stars through the screened windows of the pop-up trailer. All the stress, strain, and worry were worth the sensation of blessedness, divine guidance, and relief. Impossible to see at the time, the temporary feeling of despair played a critical role in surrender. All our effort, all or work, did nothing to accomplish the goal of finding a place to spend the night. The answer didn't appear until I gave up and listened to the Big Guy.

A tear of gratitude trickled down my cheek as I drifted off to sleep.

The next morning, we watched sunrise from Hurricane Ridge. Marveling over the beauty of sun-tipped alpine peaks floating above a sea of early morning mist, I wondered how I could ever feel any emotion but gratitude. Much as our daily movement created uncertainty, it also provided the opportunity to receive grace as we witnessed the awe-inspiring wonder of nature's lavish palettes.

Olympic National Park is as famous for its old-growth rainforests as its expansive mountain views. The next point of interest on Callie's itinerary was Hoh Rainforest, which receives as much as fourteen feet of rain each year. Callie directed us to Hoh's National Forest Service campground, which had several empty campsites set amid lush, sacred, primordial forests.

Stepping from the car, I breathed rich, loamy air, warm in the afternoon sun. I couldn't wait to immerse myself in the vibrant, terrestrial energy of Hoh's hoary trees.

Thick carpets of lichen covered every ligneous surface. Callie and I gazed in wonder at huge ferns, massive

Sitka spruce, and western hemlock springing skyward, their lives fueled by the decomposing bodies of moss-laden stumps known as nurse logs. The way these nurse logs nourished and supported the life made me miss my mother and my grandmother, who contributed so much of their life essence to the growth of their children and grandchildren.

Callie and I both hiked barefoot on a hard-packed trail. The rich, black earth felt like silk under my feet. After a mile or two, we tired of the trail's heavy traffic. Checking to be sure no one was watching, we stepped off the trail and darted into the ancient woods.

Dodging one-hundred-year-old cedars, spruce, and firs, we ran barefoot through the forest like the lost boys of Peter Pan. The forest awakened something earthy, wild, and primitive. I felt a deep, sensual longing for the earth, a need engage more deeply with the life energy flowing through trees, roots, lichen, and soil.

Angling towards the Hoh River, Callie found a secluded spot to set her hammock. Delighted at the opportunity to explore the forest alone, I marveled at the moss-shrouded trees towering over me like giant ancestral guardians. Tiny insects and primordial dust glinted with an emerald hue as the slanting rays of morning sun refracted through the forest's verdant canopy.

Feeling the centripetal tug of nature's core, I laid down in the dead leaves, pressed my face against the fragrant loam, and breathed the scent of decay. The ground, teeming with the lives of millions of microbes actively feeding on dead insects and leaves, felt vibrant and alive. New seeds wakened beneath my cheek, and I felt motherly pride for whatever future form those seedlings might take.

Pressing my ear closer to the ground, I heard the earth's heartbeat, and was delighted to discover it was my own. In my mind's eye, I embraced tendrils of encircling roots as they wrapped around my wrists and ankles, drawing me to the earth like a lover.

There, among the trees, I truly felt the meaning of the word "home."

As a teen, I used say that I hated white picket fences —a reference to civility and all its trappings. Now, the thought of houses, with all their doors, walls, and ceilings, made my skin crawl. Like people living on the street, I had become accustomed to the damp, dewy flavor of midnight air. I knew the bone-chilling cold that precedes dawn. I'd become intimate with the scent of grasses and leaves. The woody smell of trees was as familiar to me as the scent of my own body.

In the wild, I wasn't separate from nature. There was wildness inside me that deeply yearned for union with the earth. I struggled to recall a visceral connection we'd once shared with trees, the memory of some raw, primordial sensuality that was deeper, richer, and more intimate than mere contact with human skin.

Hoh Rainforest accelerated a transformation that had been happening in stages throughout our roadtrip journey. The sinews, muscles, and bones of social propriety were decaying—being broken down, composted, and liquified by nature herself. Myelin sheath stretched past my nerve endings and joined the fungal network of mycelium carpeting the forest floor. I could comprehend of the secret language of rocks, trees, moss, and ferns. In awe, I wondered what shape and form this new self was taking.

CHAPTER 27

Callie and I spoke even less than we had before. Words felt superfluous when compared to the connection of shared experience, as Callie was also undergoing transformation. In Hoh Rainforest, she received healing mother-energy far superior to anything I could ever hope to offer. Now, even the pop-up trailer seemed too much a barrier between us and the soil.

Fortunately, we planned to spend the next three nights sleeping in the dirt. The next segment of our trip would take us to three lookout towers surrounding Mount Rainier: Tolmie Peak, High Rock Lookout, and Fremont Lookout. Each tower represented a day's hike. Callie's goal was to hike to each tower to witness sunset, spend the night in the tower, then hike back down after sunrise the next morning. The plan seemed ambitious, even for Callie. It would also require a safe place to park the pop-up trailer.

There were several boondocking options near the little hamlet of Enumclaw, Washington. Callie chose a Campendium spot along Lost Creek. We made camp just as the sun was setting. I marveled at the wide stretch of river that provided an open view of expansive hills, crowned with boreal forests. For what was surely the thousandth time, I whispered a prayer of thanks for the great fortune of witnessing something magnificent.

Early the following morning, we packed our overnight gear into my duffle bag and Callie's Osprey book bag. Our "gear" included the black thirty-nine gallon leaf bag I used as a sleeping bag, my honcho poncho, Callie's hammock, and her sleeping blanket.

We were hoping to get showers before spending the next few nights in lookout towers. The temperature was around fifty degrees, so we were loathe to brave the icy, mountain-fed waters of Lost Creek. There were no truck stops with showers nearby. Enumclaw had a gym, but the gym's showers were closed due to Covid. Callie and I sat in the car, dejected.

Suddenly, Callie brightened. "Hey, Mom!" She exclaimed. "There was a car wash back there. I've always wanted to shower in a car wash!"

I guffawed. "I am *not* showering in a car wash!" Sniffing the dress I'd worn for three days straight, I tried to convince myself that it didn't smell as bad as it did. My resolve wavered. "I probably won't shower in the car wash, but you are welcome to."

The car wash in Enumclaw is right along the busy main thoroughfare, its bays fully visible to passing traffic and pedestrians. So much for privacy! We pulled into a bay, hoping the minivan would block us from public view. We changed into swim suits and dropped quarters into the car wash's coin slot.

In an effort to get this awkwardness over as quickly as possible, I grabbed the wand and turned the dial to pre-soak, thinking that would be safer than high pressure rinse. Pulling the trigger, warm, clean water emitted from the wand, and I aimed the stream at my hair.

Within seconds, it was clear something was going awry. The wand was still spraying water, but something else was coming out too. With horror, I realized, too late, that the pre-soak setting also included chemically pink foam. Moments later, I looked like a giant cone of cotton candy.

Callie, laughing hysterically, grabbed her phone and began videoing.

Suspecting the spot-free rinse might contain wax, I switched the dial to high pressure rinse. Anything had to be better than this oozing pink foam! Aiming the wand at my swimsuit, I pulled the trigger. The impact of the spray caused the wand to kick up, directing its full force at my neck. The water pressure was so fierce, it caused an instant burn on my neck that looked ridiculously similar to a hickey. Callie laughed harder than ever.

"It's not funny!" I exclaimed through fits of giggles, imagining how silly this must look to the pedestrians who were gathering to watch our escapades. "That burn on my neck really hurts!"

On high pressure rinse, I noticed a narrow stream of clean water emitted from the wand, when the trigger wasn't pulled. It was just enough to rinse away the pink foam. I proceeded to suds my hair and skin with shampoo designed for people, not cars.

Benefitting from my mistakes, Callie was able to similarly take a nice, comfortable, car-wash shower while a few curious bystanders continued to watch.

Feeling fresh and clean, Callie and I toweled off, and celebrated our small victory with lunch at Subway. The sandwich tasted decadent after the several days of bagged salads, foil packs of lentils, and canned soup that formed the bulk of our daily diet.

Arriving Tolmie Peak, the first of our three ascents, Callie scampered ahead to explore a mountain lake on the Wonderland Trail. I was excited to witness the awe-inspiring views of Mount Rainier, for which the Wonderland Trail had been named.

After over an hour of hiking, I was starting to think we might have missed a turn. Though the trail wound through beautiful meadows of lavender-colored lupin and skirted Callie's gorgeous azure lake, we had yet to glimpse the nature trails' protagonist: Mount Rainier.

Just beyond the lake, the trail pitched steeply upward. As our climbing began in earnest, I said, "Honey, I think we may have made a wrong turn. According to AllTrails, we should be seeing Mount Rainier. I'm worried this might not be the trail that leads to the lookout tower."

Callie turned around. Looking over my shoulder, she gasped. "Mom. Turn around."

Through lodgepole pines, Rainier loomed like an imposing giant just off our right shoulder. "How the hell did we miss that?" I exclaimed.

Our route had just emerged from a low-lying forest that blanketed the taproots of the great mountain. Having gained a surprising amount of elevation in a short period of time, the great mountain was now visible in all her glory.

Resuming our upward journey, we summited Tolmie Peak less than an hour later. To our dismay, the Tolmie Peak lookout tower was locked up tight as a drum. Peering through the tower's wavy, glass-paned windows, its interior was set up as a diorama, portraying the historical role Washington's fire towers played in mitigating wildfire damage. Callie and I gazed longingly at two comfy-looking sleeping cots in the diorama's display.

A cursory perusal of the surrounding area yielded bad news. The area was posted with signs: "Overnight camping prohibited." Callie and I looked at each other, unsure how to proceed.

A horde of photographers were setting up tripods, laying claim to camera angles that provided the best line of sight for photographing Rainier. "Wow! Are there always so many photographers here for sunset?" I asked a photographer who was in the process of pulling a massive lens from her bag.

"No!" She replied with breathless excitement. "Tonight is the full moon. According to the app on my iPhone, it should be coming up just beyond that rise and follow a trajectory that puts it right off the shoulder of Rainier. So while the sun sets to the right, the moon will rise dead in front of us over Rainier. Skies are clear over the mountain, with just enough westerly clouds to create a burst of color when the sun sets. It's going to be spectacular!" I could hear conversations bubbling amongst the other photographers, echoing the woman's enthusiasm.

"This is going to be amazing, Mom!" Callie declared in a hushed whisper.

"I know! It's too bad we can't spend the night."

"What are you talking about? We didn't just hike all this way to miss sunrise. No way. That's not happening."

A cold wind kicked up dust, sending photographers scrambling to shield delicate camera equipment. "What choice do we have?" I asked. "You saw the signs. No overnight camping. And we certainly can't sleep outside in garbage bags. With this wind, we'll freeze!"

"We can sleep out of the wind at the base of the tower," Callie declared.

"Um...bears?" I replied.

"Then we can sleep up on the deck that goes around the tower. I'm not leaving, Mom. Can you imagine sunrise here? What if it's like Pilchuck! I can't miss that. Besides, you're the one who hates hiking down in the dark. It will take us at least an hour and a half to hike back to the parking lot. And that's after we watch the moon rise."

Callie was right. Recalling the helicopter rescue on Mt. Pilchuck, I wasn't excited at the prospect of making the steep descent in the dark. "Okay," I said grudgingly. "We'll have to sleep on the leeward side of the deck and hope the tower blocks some of this wind."

Ducking into the bushes, we stripped out of our wet hiking clothes and donned every shred of dry clothing we could find. Still, our teeth chattered uncontrollably as we huddled together for warmth, wrapping the garbage bags around us like a blanket.

The temperature continued to drop. Photographers stamped their feet, hands in fingerless gloves wrapped around warm cups of coffee. Gloves. I was jealous. My hands and feet had gone numb hours earlier.

I popped open a can of sardines in olive oil, my go-to meal for the next three nights of fire tower forays. Fish burps aside, I found sardines and crackers provided the optimal weight to satisfaction ratio. Similar to gorp (peanuts, raisins and M&Ms), sardines have a lot of protein and fat. Crackers provide requisite carbs. But my true motivation for packing sardines was that I never had to worry that someone might ask me to share!

That night, listening to the howling wind and too cold to sleep, I thought back to the thirty-six hours John and I spent trapped in a blizzard on Aconcogua. *At least then I'd had a sleeping bag as opposed to a leaf and lawn garbage bag!* I thought woefully.

CHAPTER 28

Callie announced that our second Rainier fire tower would involve a climb to High Rock lookout. Hoping to create professional content for social media platforms, Callie had reached out to Joe Kunesh, a Seattle-based nature photographer she'd found on Instagram. Callie informed Joe that we would be spending the night in a cabin of unknown structural integrity at the top of a cliff. Joe bravely agreed.

We were a half hour late as we pulled into the parking lot for High Rock lookout. Joe approached our car and gave Callie a hug of relief. "Oh good," he exclaimed. "You are a real person. My mom was afraid this was part of a kidnapping scam or something. I was starting to worry." Callie and I found this comical, considering Joe was over six feet tall, weighed more than two hundred pounds, and had a big, bushy, lumberjack beard!

I mused over the fact that Callie and I rarely, if ever, worried that people might intend to do us harm. When I was in my teens and early twenties, I used to worry about being attacked while running. One day, it occurred to me that I was trading my peace of mind for the extremely remote possibility that something bad could happen. If I was going to be attacked, what good would worrying do? And if I went through my life without being attacked, I would have sacrificed countless hours that could have been dedicated to productive thoughts instead of fearful thoughts.

The decision to consciously release fear was one of the most important decisions I ever made. For one thing, I finally recognized that fear is a choice. Choosing to be fearless was much easier than I'd thought. More importantly, from that point forward, my mental activity while exercising was dedicated to solving problems, shifting perspectives, examining relationships, dreaming about the future, and establishing entirely new belief systems.

Though Callie and Joe had just met, they'd instantly developed a comfortable camaraderie, and I could hear them giving each other shit as they scrambled up the trail. It felt good to hang back, take my time, and savor the sunlight slanting through the forest canopy. Squirrels chittered from the trees. I inhaled deeply, drinking in the fresh scent of pine as needles crushed beneath my Chacos. Though the hike was steep, it was only a mile and a half from the parking lot to High Rock lookout tower.

"Tower" is a bit of a misnomer. Unlike the carefully restored, Tolmie Peak lookout tower, High Rock was more reminiscent of the abandoned, ramshackle, fishing cottages that used to dot the shores of Lake Superior near my hometown of Two Harbors, Minnesota. The lookout's white clapboard shell, with its badly chipping paint, teetered at the very top of a precipitous rock outcropping. In the near distance, Mt. Rainier loomed close enough to touch.

We scrambled up a steep rock slab to the tower's entrance, pushed the rusty-hinged door (which was thankfully unlocked), and stepped over the threshold. The open door revealed a single windowless room, dimly lit by sun coming through the cracks in the structure's clapboard siding. Years of graffiti covered dilapidated walls. The room's sole piece of furniture was a church pulpit holding a climbing ledger. Closer examination of the names and dates scrawled in the ledger revealed the fact that it wasn't more than a couple months old.

Callie and Joe tested a few beams, making sure they were strong enough to hold the weight of their hammocks. I spread my thirty-nine gallon lawn and leaf bag on the floor. It was showing stretches from heavy wear. But miraculously, there were no holes.

Other hikers, milling around a narrow deck surrounding the tower, came to explore our dingy hovel. When planning this ascent, we were worried there might be competition for this mountain shelter since it was an easy hike from the parking lot. Whether it was due to Covid or the decrepit condition of the lookout itself, not a single hiker seemed remotely interested in joining us.

Callie and Joe strung hammocks from the rafters. I borrowed Callie's air mattress since mine had a leak and spread the Hefty garbage bag over it. After our experience on Pilchuck, there was no doubt in my mind that this place would be crawling with mice after dark.

Callie and Joe scampered off to take pictures of Rainer, which was now illuminated in the light of the setting sun. I popped open another can of sardines in olive oil. Even this simple meal of fish, crackers, and gorp was satisfying after the afternoon's light hike.

At dusk, as if on cue, the mice arrived en masse. But for the earplugs I'd packed, their incessant scrabbling would have made it impossible to sleep. As it was, a few particularly brave mice intruded on my dreams by running through my hair or over the Hefty garbage bag. Meanwhile, Callie and Joe —safely suspended above the fray in their comfy hammocks —snored happily through the night.

Joe and Callie had a blast at High Rock Lookout. So Joe joined our third and final Rainier tower hike: Fremont Lookout.

I informed the kids that I wouldn't be spending the night atop Fremont. A third night in a Rainier lookout tower would truly call my sanity into question. Don't get me wrong, I love bone-chilling cold and the sound of scrabbling mice as much as the next person. But enough was enough. Bleary-eyed from two nights of marginal sleep, I ascended at my usual leisurely pace as Callie and Joe launched up the Fremont Lookout Trail.

Unlike the other two Rainier hikes, which wound through thick forests, the Fremont Trail was largely open, offering sweeping, majestic views of Mount Rainier. The trail itself was heavily trafficked. At journey's end, we discovered that the Fremont tower was closed to the public like Tolmie Peak's tower. As the tower's balcony offered jaw-dropping views of the mountain beyond, we joined the throng of hikers milling about taking pictures.

In addition to the normal array of tourists gathered to photograph Fremont's spectacular sunset, a crowd of twenty to thirty people had assembled for a surprise birthday celebration. The guest of honor, a woman who was just turning thirty, was due to arrive any minute.

In an attempt to stay warm while waiting for the sun to descend, Callie and Joe began building a stone shelter at the base of the lookout tower using the leeward side of the tower as a windbreak. Birthday guests made jokes about commandeering the structure once it was finished.

After an hour and a half, Callie and Joe's rock enclosure, which was just big enough to fit their sleeping bags, was a fairly impressive structure. The sun was projecting magnificent streaks of color just off Rainier's left shoulder, providing the perfect backdrop for Callie's photo shoot. As the stars came out, Joe featured Callie in some long exposure shots, which required her to stay perfectly still in the frigid night air for extended periods of time.

Stomping and smacking hands together to stave off the cold, we made our way back to the shelter. To our surprise, we found a man standing inside the structure the kids had built, playing bartender with bottles of booze set on the top of the wall. The kids' sleeping bags and sleeping mats had been kicked to the side.

"Excuse me," I said, walking up to the man. "What are you doing?"

"I'm running a bar for the party."

He looked exactly like the type of character who would play the bully in a movie. "These kids just spent the last hour and a half building this shelter. I'm pretty sure you saw that."

"Yeah, they can use it when we're done," he replied arrogantly.

I looked at the bottles of vodka and considered dumping them. Instead, I leveled my gaze, and growled in my best mama bear voice, "No, they are cold. They need their sleeping bags to warm up. And they will be using this shelter right now. Go build your own bar."

"Mom," Callie whispered. "Stop making a scene."

"No, Callie. Your mom's right," Joe whispered. "Who knows how long they'll be here? For all we know, it could be hours before we get to bed."

Rainier's icy breath wafted down my back, setting the hairs on my neck on end. The bartender stared at me, waiting to see if I would back down. I took a step forward, indicating with my thumb that he should take a hike. Thankfully, the guy collected his bottles and left the little enclosure, muttering under his breath.

Callie and Joe gratefully scurried inside to reclaim their space, extended their sleeping pads and sleeping bags, and settled in for the night. I said goodnight to the kids and began my descent down the mountain in the dark.

Though the air was crisp, the wind had died, and the moon was just beginning to crest on the horizon. Following my headlamp's soft yellow beam as it illuminated the trail, I started shaking, not because of the cold, but as a delayed reaction to my encounter with the asshole at the party. I normally avoided conflict like a plague. When I was married, I used to say that John was right in ninety-five percent of our disagreements. But that wasn't true. I simply capitulated ninety-five percent of the time. Though the emotionally-charged exchange at Fremont Lookout left me drained, it felt good to step into my power.

Returning to the Fremont Lookout parking lot near midnight, I still had a forty-five minute drive to the pop-up trailer, which was still parked in the woods beside Lost Creek. After sleeping in or around Rainier's fire towers, the pop-up trailer would feel like luxury accommodations. I couldn't wait!

In the dark, I couldn't find the Lost Creek turn-off and drove past it twice. The long dirt road leading to the river branched a couple times after leaving the main road. As the moon was entirely blocked by tall pines, it was pitch black. Shadows loomed in my headlights, and I realized this was the first night I'd slept alone since my comfy camp on Hebgen Lake.

Somehow, Hebgen felt so much safer. I was edgy as I pulled up to the trailer, and was a little reluctant to get out of the van. Maybe it was all the signs announcing that we were in Bigfoot territory. Maybe it was our proximity to Seattle and its big city problems. Or maybe it was exhaustion from a restless night in the mouse-infested cabin on High Rock lookout.

Danger or no danger? I asked the Big Guy.

"No danger," came the reply.

I gave myself a pep talk.

Silly girl. There's nothing to be afraid of. This site is miles from the road. There are no other cars here. You're totally fine.

Just as I'd almost convinced myself that there was nothing to fear, I noticed the door to the camper stood ajar, and the sense of foreboding returned.

"Hello? Is anybody there?" I called. The thin sound of my voice was swept away by the night wind, making me even more nervous. Retrieving a headlamp from the car, I cautiously entered the camper and searched every inch. It was empty. Standing just inside the pop-up's open door, I cast the headlamp's beam in a wide arch, scanning the woods for anything that might look threatening.

Danger or no danger? I asked the Big Guy again, and again received the reply:

"No danger."

Any fear that is not actionable is irrational. If you can't take action, fear is pointless. Worrying does nothing but create more worry.

Though my mind suspected there was nothing to fear, my heart still needed convincing. Turning off the headlamp, I stepped out of the camper and marched into the blackness. Deep forest shadows were doing their level best to scrub any sign of moonlight from the forest floor. My eyes were slow to adjust, and twice, I tripped over fallen branches.

Fear became a solid thing in the pit of my stomach. Turning around, I saw the outline of my dark, forlorn camper sitting beside the river, dwarfed by towering trees blowing in the wind.

Anxiety grew. The pop-up seemed like such a flimsy shelter, offering little protection from the encroaching wilderness.

After stumbling yet again, I squatted down to pee (just to prove that fear wasn't getting the upper hand), then continued to walk even deeper into the woods, towards the place where it was darkest. Ironically, the more I moved towards fear, the more it retreated. Moments later, the fear was completely gone. I stood alone in the blackness, which suddenly felt silky and welcoming.

Returning to the camper, happy at the prospect of snuggling into a comfy bed, I realized that "brave" was officially a foundational descriptor in this new identity that was forming. The thought made me proud.

CHAPTER 29

The next morning, after collecting Callie at the Fremont Lookout parking lot, we gave Joe a goodbye hug and bid farewell to Mount Rainier, thanking her for her abundant beauty.

From Rainier we travelled through Oregon en route to California. Though Oregon has many laudable attributes, I will likely go my grave identifying Oregon with salmon fish and chips in Astoria and the airplane house outside of Portland.

The funky, eclectic town of Astoria, Oregon was home to Selina's newest hostel. Since Selina had so few properties in North America, I decided that visiting the new Astoria property might solidify relations with Selina.

Callie and I had dinner at a quirky fish house called Hurricane Ron's. The proprietor encouraged me to get the salmon fish and chips. Fried salmon? Wouldn't that be greasy? Little did I know, I as about to partake in a meal whose hedonistic richness would literally make me cry.

Admittedly, after spending two months eating bagged grocery store salads, tins of sardines, and unheated packets of pre-prepared lentils in various Middle Eastern sauces, any restaurant food tasted like heaven. But the sheer decadence of fresh, wild caught salmon, lightly breaded and fried, made my toes curl. Callie and I laughed as tears of sheer pleasure streamed down my face.

After dinner, I called Gracie, who was about to become the very first person to use the Nomaditudes pass with Selina. She planned to spend a month Costa Rica, and her flight would arrive mere days after the country's post-Covid reopening.

I was thrilled. It was one thing to see the Nomaditudes project on paper. But witnessing it come together in real life, with my daughter as the beneficiary, was incredibly rewarding. The prospect of endless travel was suddenly a reality!

My confidence in Gracie's competence knew no bounds. I never worried when my eighteen-year-old daughter announced she wanted to spend a month alone in Costa Rica at the height of the Covid pandemic. It wasn't until we were in the final days leading up to her departure that I started to feel a little anxious.

As I talked to Gracie on the phone, I felt a strong pull to give her my hummingbird necklace. John had given me the hummingbird necklace after my soul quest, as a hummingbird had served as my spirit guide during the soul quest journey. I'd worn the necklace every day for two years.

Parting with the necklace was more difficult than expected. Aside from my wedding ring and a pearl necklace and earrings John had given me when the girls were born, the hummingbird was my most precious piece of jewelry. To me, the necklace represented John's faith in my spiritual journey.

My heart ached as I lovingly wrapped the little hummingbird in a box to mail to Gracie. Tenderly touching the necklace, hoping to imbue it with extra mama energy, I felt John's protective father energy as well and knew the little hummingbird would keep my girl safe. I mailed Gracie's care package from the Astoria post office on my way out of town.

From Astoria, we traveled south to Portland, where Callie found an Instagrammer's dream: A man who lives in an honest-to-goodness Boeing 727…and openly invites strangers to visit his home.

Navigating winding, residential roads on the outskirts of Portland with our pop-up trailer in tow, I was more than a little dubious. First of all, how could someone transport a 727 through this maze of suburban streets? Second of all, how could we be sure this guy would really welcome a couple strangers who wandered up his driveway without any prior communication?

As we arrived at the destination indicated on Apple Maps, a carload of kids slightly older than Callie was pulling up as well. We followed them up a wide, wooded driveway.

"Were we supposed to make reservations or let someone know we're coming?" I asked one of the kids.

"Not that I know," a girl replied. "We've never been here before either."

With the exception of a driveway was a little wider than normal, there was nothing to indicate that we'd actually find a Boeing 727 at the end of the road. But sure enough, there it was, towering over the clearing at the same height as the surrounding lodgepole pines. The airplane home's owner, retired electrical engineer Bruce Campbell, was standing outside as if he had been awaiting our arrival.

"Welcome!" Bruce enthused. "Please, make yourself at home. Do you want to climb on top of the plane?" he jovially asked Callie, indicating an opening at the very back of the aircraft. Bruce deftly scaled the tail section of the fuselage, demonstrating where Callie needed to put her feet to reach an empty engine housing nearly twenty feet off the ground that provided access to the roof of the aircraft.

"Is it okay to fly my drone?" Callie asked.

"Of course!" Bruce exclaimed.

Brimming with excitement, Bruce outlined his plan for converting decommissioned aircrafts to homes. We learned that prior to Covid, Bruce split his time between Japan and Portland. With an infectious warmth infused with an undercurrent of Asian hospitality, Bruce welcomed visitors nearly every day of the year and allowed them to clamber freely over his house.

"I even had a Playboy model do a photoshoot on top of the airplane," he whispered conspiratorially with a mischievous glint in his eye. "And I got photographed naked with the model!"

I choked, blushed, then replied, "Oh. That's nice."

Bruce chuckled at my obvious discomfort. "But the most exciting thing about my airplane home is the concerts," he continued.

"Concerts? I saw some pretty fancy looking lighting in the trees," I replied, happy to be moving off the subject of Playboy models.

"The band performs on the wing of the aircraft. The crowd is fanned out in the woods below. It's incredible. Come on! I'll show you!"

With the agility of a mountain goat, Bruce bounded up a makeshift staircase at the tip of the plane's wing, then extended a hand to help me up. Still holding my hand, he drew me forward onto the airplane's wing. "See! You can bounce on it!"

I broke into a grin and laughed out loud as we tested the flexibility of the 727's wing, bouncing as if we were kids on a trampoline.

Callie looked down from the top of the airplane and waved. Then she struck a modeling pose and positioned her drone for take off. The drone hovered just above the treetops as Callie shot frame after frame of photos. "This is amazing!" she called from above.

When I mentioned that Callie was a singer, Bruce suggested she come back and perform. "I think you'd agree that my aircraft is a most unusual concert venue. She could have a field day on Instagram. And we have a pretty good social media following. Callie could open for one of our more popular bands to get her name out there!"

Bruce walked us back to our car and gave us big hugs. "Thank you for including me in your journey," he said. "Please be sure to visit whenever you are back in the area. I would love to have coffee and hear more about your adventures. And be sure to tell people about airplanehome.com!"

Our surreal Portland adventure continued as we contemplated where we should spend the night. According to Campendium, there was a park near downtown Portland that allowed overnight camping. This seemed a bit suspect, as it was doubtful local residents would allow something like that to fly. But as we pulled down a quiet urban street, there was indeed a park the size of a city block with Vanlife-style vans and small motorhomes parked around its perimeter.

I climbed out of the car to disconnect the trailer. There were kids playing basketball on a court nearby. To my surprise, nobody looked twice as I cranked the pop-up. Once the camper was set in order for the night, Callie and I took a stroll around the block. Signs announced a neighborhood block party would be taking place that night in the far corner of the park. "Everyone Welcome," was printed in block letters at the bottom of the sign. We wandered over to check it out.

Under the street lights, families with young children gathered to dance, share food, and meet the eclectic collection of folks who camped in their neighborhood.

I felt shy and a little abashed. First, Bruce at the airplane home. Now the warm, friendly residents of this little neighborhood. These were people who understood the value of hospitality, inclusiveness, and human connection.

I wondered how it would feel to unshutter the windows of my heart, throw them open wide, and post an "Everyone Welcome" sign.

One time, in Pisac, Peru, I was walking a dirt road to town and encountered a woman sitting on a brick wall over the raging Urubamba River. She was openly sobbing, obviously in deep distress.

I have no idea what possessed me, but I climbed the steps to the place where she was sitting, wrapped my arms around her, and pulled her into an embrace.

She held me, shaking and crying as if her heart was breaking. I felt her tears, wet on my cheek, and kissed her tears away. I leaned back, pressed my lips to her forehead, then drew her back to me again, saying, "You are so precious. You are so loved, sweet one. Don't worry. I'm here. You are safe, you are loved. You are not alone."

After a bit, the woman's sobs subsided. She looked at me and said in heavily accented English, "I know you." It wasn't a question, it was a statement.

"Yes," I replied. "Our hearts know each other. And my heart wants you to know you're loved."

I gave her hand a squeeze and walked away, my body tingling with electricity. The voice of my higher self, my soul, had been speaking through me. Disconnecting from ego, my soul was able to radiate unmitigated love to that woman in her time of need. I'd never experienced anything like it.

Something about that encounter tied directly to my soul quest experience with the Earth Mother. Just as her energy flowed into me during my soul quest, it was her energy flowing through me to meet the needs of this stranger.

I want more of that. I want to offer a mother's love to anyone who needs it.

Remembering how I felt on my first date with John, I wondered, *What if that sense of tectonic plates shifting, creating a new biosphere, was as close to playing God as we get on this earth? If falling in love with a single human being creates a new world, what would happen if I fell deeply in love with all of mankind?*

The shift felt big, as if the cosmos made a subtle course correction.

Wouldn't it be amazing if people were like those delicious little tea cakes we sampled during high tea at the Burj Al Arab in Dubai? Each one surprising, delightful, a treasure waiting to be discovered?

The image made me smile.

CHAPTER 30

The days were getting shorter and nights were getting colder. I booked a mid-September flight so Christopher could meet us in Los Angeles for the return drive across the United States. Feeling pressed for time, Callie and I spent only one night in Mount Hood National Forest before heading south.

We stopped for lunch at Crater Lake National Park in southwest Oregon and overheard chatter of wildfires near Mount Hood. Callie consulted an online fire map and discovered there was a significant fire burning in the camp we'd left just hours earlier.

It had been a particularly dry summer. Fires were springing up at an alarming rate all around the map just to the north of us. Even more disconcerting was the spread of wildfires in California, directly in our path to the south.

We decided top stop at Umpqua Hot Springs before crossing into California. Callie, who'd been a nudist-at-heart since she was a toddler, added Umpqua to her bucket list because it was a renowned gathering place for naked hippies.

Callie found us a free wilderness camp site with the odd name of Lemolo Two Forebay forest camp. This free national forest service wilderness camp was situated at the edge of a beautiful mountain reservoir. There was a time in my not-so-distant past where bath robes, free wine, and caviar in the concierge lounge were my definition of accommodations with "great amenities." Now luxury was defined as pit toilets, picnic tables, and fire rings. By my new standards, Lemolo Two Forebay forest camp was indeed luxury digs.

I decided to hike to the far side of the reservoir and discovered a massive water pipeline. The pipe, partially trenched in a cavernous ditch, was taller than me. I marveled at the staggering volume of water that must be coursing through a pipe of that diameter and followed a trail beside the ditch.

The trail ended at a precipice where the pipeline made a right angle over a cliff and dropped several hundred feet to the valley floor. A massive cylinder rose seventy to eighty feet above me. A ladder ran along the outside of the cylinder. The visual effect was stunning.

A shiver ran up my spine. With sunset less than an hour away, I ran-walked back to the reservoir to rouse Callie from her hammock.

"Callie!" I exclaimed breathlessly. "I have a really, really big surprise for you. You'r going to need your drone."

Without a question, Callie rolled from her hammock and scurried to the van to get her backpack and drone.

"Can you at least give me a clue?" Callie asked as we hustled around the reservoir.

"Nope. You're just going to have to trust me!"

Callie gasped when the pipeline came into view. "Wow! This is amazing! Maybe I can get the drone to track me walking along the pipe!"

"That's not the surprise!" I exclaimed.

"What is it? What is it?" she asked.

Emerging from the woods, Callie gaped up at the cylinder towering above the massive cliff. "You...have *got*...to be kidding me!" She clamored up a stone structure supporting the cylinder and began scaling the ladder. At the top, she launched the drone, capturing footage of a boreal forest, spread out like a carpet for hundreds miles.

The next morning, Callie and I rose early for our foray to Umpqua Hot Springs, which was a mere fifteen minute drive from our camp at Lemolo Two Forebay forest camp. We parked along the road and changed into bathing suits in the car. After traversing a bridge that crossed a river, we hiked the mile-long trail that led to the hot springs.

A half dozen picturesque little pools, bordered by Oregon pine forests, greeted us at the end of the Umpqua Hot Springs trail. Water trickled down the steep hillside, filling pools on lower ledges as the rivulets made their way to the river far below.

As interesting as the pools, rocks, forests, and river were, the human occupants of Umpqua Springs were significantly more fascinating. A few wore swimsuits. Most just wore their birthday suits. Callie and I suppressed giggles as dozens of naked people of all ages, shapes, and sizes unabashedly sang songs and played musical instruments. Though some may have found the nudist festivities off-putting, Callie and I found them utterly endearing.

"Oh, Mom!" Callie exclaimed. "These are my kind of people!"

I feigned shock. But Callie knew it was an act. She and I were both nudists at heart. I followed Callie as she descended the slippery rocks to one of the hot springs. Steam rose from the pool's surface, but it was still a little cool.

"If you want to see a really interesting hot spring, there is one in a cave just at the edge of the river," a man called helpfully from another pool nearby.

I thanked the man as we emerged from the tepid water. Callie and I continued down the muddy ravine, clinging to roots and vines. In some places, we clung to ropes, strategically placed to more safely descend the slippery slope. We finally dropped to a rocky beach at river's edge and made our way downriver to a small group collected at the entrance to a cave.

The small group turned out to be four. They were all male. They were all closer in age to me than to Callie. And they were all naked. One was covered in tattoos. Another had to be close to three hundred pounds.

"Trust," the Big Guy said.

Really? I replied. *Are you fricking kidding me?* This *is the time to trust?*

The Big Guy gave a sage nod of the head.

Callie and I squeezed our way into the cave and lowered ourselves into the shallow water. Warm droplets splashed on our heads from the rocks above. Soothed by the surreal beauty of steam rising from the water, the river beyond, and pristine forests covering the far shore of the river, I relaxed into the warmth of the water.

Callie looked at me inquiringly. I knew what she was asking. We were clearly overdressed. Returning her gaze, I shrugged my shoulders and slipped off my swim suit. She did the same.

Do you want to know something crazy? Naked people have the same, perfectly normal conversations that clothed people have! The thought made me want to giggle. There we were, buck naked, having the same dialog we'd have at a cocktail party or a casual dinner. Who are you? Where are you from? How did you find your way here? After a while, I actually forgot they were naked. More importantly, I forgot *we* were naked!

Callie and I recounted stories from our trip. The men laughed heartily when I told the story about being stranded on a fire road, high in the mountains, after breaking the crank handle on the trailer. I reminisced about Tom and the stories he told right before he died. Callie entertained the group with her adventures that ended in her arrest in California.

"It must be nice to have so much time to travel. What do you do for a living?" one man asked. He looked to be in his early forties.

"I'm a writer. And I'm also working on a student travel project. What about you?" I replied. The man's tan upper body, powerful arms, and strong shoulders made me guess construction.

261

"I used to work in Seattle as a commercial real estate broker. Then I went through a wicked divorce. My ex-wife had primary custody of our two kids, so I only got them on weekends. Unfortunately, I worked most weekends...which was probably a contributing factor in the divorce. After a year, I was burnt out and lonely. So I quit. Started working construction. Now I pick and choose my projects so I can see my kids and travel."

"When your kids are grown, do you think you'll go back to commercial real estate?" I asked.

He chuckled. "Go back to wearing golden handcuffs? No way! I pick jobs that pay well, and spend the rest of my time traveling. I'm in the middle of a ten day motorcycle trip down the Pacific coast. Now that I know what freedom looks like, there's no way I'll ever be tied to a computer screen and cell phone again."

I mused at the many ways my identity had become intertwined with electronics...so much so, that I often felt *guilty* for not spending more time in front of a screen. I vowed to examine the yardstick I'd been using to evaluate my life—to use freedom, instead of productivity, as the measure of a life well-lived.

After a half hour of engaging conversation, I said, "Wow. I'm thirsty. I wish we'd thought to bring water."

"Oh! I know where you can get water," a heavy set man exclaimed. "There's this spring that comes directly out of a rock wall across the river. It's totally safe to drink. And the water tastes amazing. I can take you there."

Callie said, "That would be incredible! I'm super thirsty too." Callie and I donned our swimsuits for the journey across the river. Our hefty tour guide rose from the hot spring pool and opted to make the trip commando.

Though the river was never more than thigh deep, it took effort to navigate the slippery rocks without losing our footing. When we finally made it across, our nude tour guide triumphantly led us to a cliff that indeed had a stream of water, seemingly flowing straight from its rock face.

"Wow! That's incredible!" I exclaimed, pressing my

hands to the wall to lean in for a drink. Looking up, I noticed that the stream did not come directly from the wall at all. It was an optical illusion. The water actually came from a small rivulet, diverted from the main waterfall on the other side of the rock's face. I stepped back, preparing to offer a cautionary warning to Callie, when I saw two Japanese tourists descending the trail.

It was like watching a train wreck in slow motion. The tourists, two men wearing broad-rimmed hiking hats and Osprey packs, had yet to notice us. They were busy staring at a cell phone. Then, the man in the front looked up. He saw sixteen-year-old Callie in her cute little bikini, drinking from a stream of water shooting from the wall. He saw the massive naked guy, lounging casually nearby. He saw me, Mom, gazing nonchalantly at the trees as if this is a scene you see every day here in the grand ol' U.S. of A.

And suddenly, seeing the scene through the Japanese tourist's eyes, I couldn't stifle a chuckle. The chuckle brimmed up to become a snort, then overflowed into a boisterous laugh. I found myself melting into a puddle of hysterics as Callie and the naked guy looked on in wonder.

"What was that all about?" Callie whispered as we walked back across the river.

"Oh nothing. Just you, and the Japanese tourists, and the naked guy...It was all too funny."

"What are you talking about?" Callie exclaimed. "He's not naked...Oh! Oh my god!"

Remember how I said that after a while, I actually forgot the men were naked? Apparently the same thing happened to Callie too!

CHAPTER 31

Wildfires chased us out of Oregon. Though we didn't see the fires themselves, the online fire map blazed orange all around us. Long stretches of highway were eerily devoid of traffic, with the exception of vehicles sporting the words "Fire Safety."

On multiple occasions, we needed to move onto the shoulder to accommodate heavy equipment like bulldozers and tractor plows, used to create fire breaks. Occasionally, the highway passed through an area that smelled heavily of smoke. Burned out stumps and charred ground stretched into the distance. At a gas stop just across the California state line, we heard rumors of road closures ahead and decided to stop for the night.

The Campendium map led us to a decrepit campground right on the ocean. The defunct 1970s era seaside resort was utterly depressing, its ramshackle buildings having been abandoned decades earlier. I pulled up to the reception area, which was predictably closed. A note on the door indicated an after hours phone number that could be used for registration. Nobody answered the phone when I called.

A pickup truck with a topper, the campground's sole occupant, was parked close to the bathroom. I chose a site near the water, disconnected the trailer, and popped up the camper. Desperately in need of a shower, I was dismayed to find the bathrooms were locked. By a stroke of great fortune, a man was a just coming out of the shower and offered his key code.

"The registration office is only open on weekends," he replied in response to my inquiry about registration.

"Then how do I pay for my spot?" I asked.

He shrugged in reply.

It seemed such a shame. The campground location was lovely. Perched above a narrow stretch of pebbled shoreline, clean, salty air wafted in from the ocean. Callie and I unzipped all the camper's canvas and vinyl-covered windows and let the ocean breeze lull us to sleep.

The next morning, we got an early start for Samuel H. Boardman State Park, another spot on Callie's Instagram hit list. The park's steep, rugged coastline featured natural bridges, arches, sea stacks, islands, and beaches. Callie joined other drone pilots, videographers, and photographers who were creating breathtaking images as they perched precariously atop the park's high, exposed stone bridges.

In an effort to attend to Nomaditudes logistics whenever I had cell service, I had scheduled an eleven o'clock Zoom call with two agents from an insurance firm that offered travel insurance for students. Callie and I returned to our campsite mid-morning and were alarmed to see the skies heavy with thick, orange smoke. Knowing it could be another twenty-four hours before I had reliable service again, I was loathe to cancel my Zoom call.

Within the thirty minute span of our phone conversation, the sun was reduced to a red dot in the sky, and a thick, noxious smoke obscured all but a few low lying trees on the forested hillside across from the empty trailer park. Reversing my phone camera, I showed the insurance brokers the scene unfolding in front of me.

"You've got to get out of there, now!" The woman exclaimed in alarm. "Many of those coastal towns only have one road going in and out. You could get cut off!"

Worried by the rapid accumulation of orange smoke, Callie had packed the pop-up trailer while I was on the phone. Within five minutes, the trailer was hitched and we were speeding south, trailing the northern California coastline. Mercifully, we were clear of the heavy smoke within a half hour, though low-lying smog fully blocked the sun.

Callie consulted our list of stops in northern California. "First stop, Fern Canyon. It's one of the places where they filmed Jurassic Park. Supposedly, they have colossal tree ferns that grow as big as forty feet tall! I read one review that said Fern Canyon is located in a state park with super narrow, winding roads. We're going to need to ditch the trailer."

We parked the trailer in an empty pull-off just off the Pacific Coast Highway. This proved to be a very good call, as sections of the road were only a single car wide, requiring us to back up as we encountered oncoming traffic.

The road passed inviting sand dunes beside the Pacific Ocean. But as we were nervous about the prospect of being trapped by encroaching forest fires, we made our way straight to Fern Canyon.

A sign indicated that four wheel drive vehicles were required. But the small parking lot to our left was full. "The road still goes for another mile or two, according to the map," Callie said. "A Honda Odyssey is pretty much a four wheel drive, wouldn't you say?"

"Sure!" I joked. "Plus this isn't just any Honda Odyssey. It's a touring elite! So we've got that going for us, right?"

The road was rife with potholes, but none were worse than others we'd encountered multiple times throughout our journey. Then we arrived at a stream crossing. It had less flow than a river, but significantly more than a creek. The road dropped over an eroded bank, crossed the pebble-bottomed stream, then climbed the other side, soundly validating the recommendation to use a four wheel drive vehicle.

I hesitated. A jeep on the other side of the river was waiting for us to get out of the way. I couldn't see over the lip of the embankment. Callie leaned out the window, surveyed the scene, and declared the river crossing was doable.

As the Jeep's occupants gazed in wonder at the idiocy of the scene unfolding before them, Callie exclaimed "Hit it!" and our little minivan dropped over the eroded bank to river's edge. I punched the accelerator and launched our bucking minivan across the rocky river bottom. Never losing momentum, we careened up the embankment on the far shore and gave a sheepish wave to the man and woman in the Jeep, who were staring incredulously.

Callie and I laughed uproariously. Whether it was Callie's arrest in Santa Monica, swimming with nudists in Oregon, or crossing a river with a 2012 Honda Odyssey minivan, our roadtrip had most certainly taken on a lawless kind of energy.

We arrived at Fern Canyon, which was indeed reminiscent of Jurassic Park. In the throes sheer silliness, Callie started narrating an impromptu TV show she called "Sheriff Callie's Wild West Adventures." In the first episode, Sheriff Callie demonstrates the various contortions you can use to make butt cheeks jiggle when walking in cut off jean shorts. Her second episode included a series of commando roll maneuvers to be used over logs in the event you are being pursued by elk or an errant dinosaur.

Fellow hikers gave wide berth as we streaked through Fern Canyon, or ducked to hide behind moss-covered rocks as if we were running from a dangerous creature. Wet, muddy, and out of breath from the shenanigans, we returned to the car for the second successful river crossing of the day.

Callie fell asleep on the drive back to the road, and continued to sleep as I hitched the pop-up trailer to the van. When we arrived at National Redwood forest, I finally woke her up.

"Hey sweetie," I said softly. "You wanted to show me the redwood forest you explored with the boys during your roadtrip. Do you know where we need to turn?"

Callie sat up, bleary-eyed. A few minutes later, she said sleepily, "Here. I think this is the place where we turned," indicating a paved road on our left. I turned. The road soon turned to dirt and began climbing steeply.

"Wow, honey," I exclaimed. "I'm surprised you thought it was a good idea to take the camper up this road."

"Oh, I was sleeping when the boys and I drove through the redwoods," she replied sheepishly. "I'm not even sure this is the right road."

I looked at her in alarm. "You're kidding, right?"

The dirt road narrowed and took a sharp switch back, the third tight switch back we'd taken thus far. Backing down would be neigh impossible. I shifted my little Honda Odyssey into first gear and the engine strained against the weight of the pop-up trailer. I was thankful that the camper's water tank was nearly empty, lightening the load.

I took three deep breaths, relaxed my face, neck, and shoulders, and calmed my nerves before settling into a quiet meditative state. At the next switchback, the tires spun out, then finally gained traction at the last possible second as we crested a small rise. I accelerated as quickly as I dared on the straightaway in preparation for the next switchback. With no option but to keep climbing, I forced thoughts of the treacherous descent from my mind. Maybe the road would loop, avoiding going back down these steep switchbacks.

Twenty sweat-inducing minutes later, we finally reached the top of the mountain. We hadn't encountered a single car, which was a tremendous blessing, but also somewhat unnerving. We were surprised to encounter a fully paved parking lot a few miles down the road. I got out to stretch cramped muscles, evidence that my attempt at meditation was unsuccessful. A sign at the end of the parking lot indicated a three mile trail through the redwood forest. After the silliness at Fern Canyon, Callie and I decided to walk through the forest separately, giving each other space to experience the reverence these massive trees inspired.

I thought about Gracie and Christopher, and wished with all my heart they could be with me. My arms ached with longing for them. I wanted to nuzzle their cheeks and remind them of how very much I loved them.

An old-growth sequoia beckoned to me, and I pressed my face against the rough, time-worn smile lines creasing her massive trunk. Extending my arms as wide as possible, I pulled the ancient tree to my chest and felt an earthy kind of connection. I whispered a prayer that the love of my embrace would radiate down through her trunk, spreading into her roots, into the soil, and through the earth to my precious children. The power of that mother-love was so radiant, so pervasive, so transformative, I was certain Gracie and Christopher would feel it.

The surge of love made me think back to the way John and I met. In those first few years of marriage, my love for him was utterly consuming. There were nights when I would fall asleep curled against his back with tears of pure joy streaming down my face. I was so grateful to have found my soulmate.

I recalled the sensation of tectonic plates shifting, biospheres forming, as if our love's origin story created a new world. Was that how the experience felt for John? I doubted it. Though John certainly loved me back, my love had been the engine that formed our new world. Being the focus of a love like that would have been like standing in the full force of the sun.

Early in the marriage, we argued bitterly over how much time was appropriate to spend with my parents. I missed them desperately. When the kids were born, three new planets joined my orbit. Did John's world dim when my focus shifted to them?

I slid to the base of the sequoia and sat in soil, permeated with an ageless, earthy wisdom that transcended the impermanence of human toil.

What if people love me less for who I am and more for how I love them?

The thought made me sad.

The Big Guy whispered, "All love is simply a reminder of how you are supposed to love yourself."

It was naive to think that John would love me as deeply as I loved him. More importantly, it was foolish to believe anyone was capable of loving me as much as I was capable of loving myself.

I thought of all the expectations, the pressure I put on myself to be something more, to do something more: the endless struggle to achieve, impress, validate. What if all of it was entirely unnecessary? What if all that suffering, effort, and struggle was simply my messy way of finding my way back to self-love?

I was still lost in thought when Callie and I reconvened at the parking lot.

"Are you okay, Mom?" Callie asked.

"Yeah, I'm just missing Gracie and Christopher." A tear leaked out of the corner of my eye.

"I miss them too," Callie said, giving me a hug.

According to Google maps, the only viable return was the same way we'd come. I was not keen to descend the treacherous gravel switchbacks. Checking the trailer brakes, I dropped the Honda into low gear, hoping the engine would help hold back the weight of the trailer and keep the brakes from overheating. We took our time, and breathed a sigh of relief as the road flattened out at the bottom. It was time to look for a place to spend the night.

We turned off California's iconic Highway 101 to travel inland toward Lake Tahoe. Campendium indicated free overnight camping at Burney Vista Point. We arrived just before sunset. An active fire was burning on the forested hillside opposite the vista's parking lot. Consulting the fire map, we learned that the flames were part of a controlled burn that had been over eighty percent contained for weeks. The smoke at higher elevation made for a magnificent sunset.

The parking lot was empty, with the exception of an old maroon Chevy parked near the lot's entrance. We drove to the far end of the lot. A grassy slope fell away to the west in undulating waves of low-lying bushes and trees. There were beautiful views of Horse Mountain to the south.

It was getting dark, and we were over a half hour from free national forest service campsites in Burnt Ranch. Callie and I were contemplating whether or not this would be a safe place to pop up the trailer. It was certainly private and remote. The burning fire was too far away to be a threat. But I lingered in the car, suddenly overcome with uneasiness. Though there seemed to be no imminent danger and darkness was falling quickly, I couldn't seem to make the commitment to stay.

Just as the last light was fading, I sensed movement behind the trailer.

"Someone is back there!" I exclaimed to Callie in a hushed whisper.

In the passenger sideview mirror, I saw a man ducking low, slinking up the side of the trailer towards Callie's door. He hesitated, slipping between the van and the trailer. I was suddenly terrified he would open the trunk and climb into the van. The hair on the back of my neck stood on end. I clicked the door lock button.

The man heard the lock and stood up. Callie and I watched as he ran his hand through his greasy hair, then started meddling with the front corner of the trailer.

"Oh my gosh!" Callie exclaimed. "Is he putting something on our trailer?"

She rolled her window down a crack. "Callie, what the hell are you doing?" I exclaimed in a hushed whisper. "Don't roll your window down!"

Callie ignored me. "What do you think you're doing?" Callie demanded.

The man stepped away from the car, providing our first clear view. We gasped. He looked just like the creepy bad guy in a medieval movie. Stringy brown hair hung in greasy waves to just below his shoulders. He grinned widely, revealing the blackened teeth of a meth addict. A full-length, threadbare, fur coat looked like something from *Game of Thrones*. He leered at Callie and approached her partially open window. I pulled the car forward and he took a couple running steps, blocking our way to the exit.

"What did you do to our camper?" Callie asked. The man's smile disappeared.

"I didn't touch your fucking camper, you little bitch," he snarled and lunged at the window.

I accelerated quickly, holding my breath that the trailer would clear the man without hitting him. Making a hard right turn onto the grass at the edge of the lot, we raced toward the parking lot entrance. Callie was shaking. In the rearview window, we saw the man running towards the maroon Chevy. I careened onto the road ahead of two cars. We headed toward the town of Willow Creek, which lay ten winding miles ahead. In the event he followed, I was glad to have at least two cars buffer between me and the psycho from the parking lot.

Pulling into the first gas station in Willow Creek, I drove to the pumps at the side farthest from the road and topped off the tank. Moments later, we saw the old maroon Chevy go past, and breathed a sigh of relief.

We pulled back onto the road, but were stopped at the south edge of town. Construction signs narrowed the road to a single lane. A line of traffic was waiting for an automated construction traffic light to turn green.

"Lock the doors," the Big Guy instructed. I complied.

The light turned green. As the line of traffic inched forward, we saw the old maroon Chevy, pulled off on the shoulder. Its driver was leaning against the front hood, peering at vehicles as they passed. I wished with all my heart that we could just disappear. But he spotted us. Locking eyes with Callie, he stood up and moved slowly, with the stealth of a predator, towards the van's passenger side door. An alarming thought went through my head. "Oh my god. What if he has a gun?"

There was a semi truck behind me and a line of cars in front of me. I was trapped on a single lane road. There was absolutely nowhere to go. My heart was beating out of my chest. Even though the light had turned green, traffic moved at a crawl.

In Callie's side view mirror, I saw the man get into his car and merge into the lane a few cars back.

"Faster!" I implored the cement truck directly in front of me. "Faster!" I tried to gauge how many cars were between me and the Chevy, but I couldn't see past the semi. At a curve, I was able to count five cars behind the semi truck in my rearview mirror. Which of them belonged to the psycho meth head?

Danger or no danger? I asked the Big Guy.

"Danger," came the reply.

This fear wasn't irrational. It was warranted, and therefore required a change of plans. Callie and I wouldn't be spending the night alone in a parking lot. Nor would we allow ourselves to be cornered in the woods. Feeling vulnerable and fiercely protective of Callie, I wanted to put as much distance between us and this psychopath as possible.

The narrow, winding road left few options for passing. I hung close to the slow-moving cement truck and capitalized on an opportunity to pass him. The short passing window meant I was the only vehicle with the option to do so.

Clear of the cement truck, I allowed the van to accelerate, gaining momentum as we plummeted down the remote mountain road. We passed signs for National Forest Service campgrounds but kept driving. The man's black leering grin haunted my mind. I thought of the way he stared at Callie like a hungry animal, and my mama bear instinct kicked in.

Shaking and hopped up on adrenaline, we didn't stop until we reached the next major town, which was two hours away. I booked a room at the Red Roof Inn in Redding, California, immensely grateful to have a solid door and deadbolt lock.

As I lay in a real bed that night, struggling to calm my nerves, it occurred to me that this was the first negative experience we'd had with a stranger. In all those miles, never knowing where we would camp from one night to the next, often finding ourselves in deserted parking lots or remote wilderness areas, we had never had a single negative encounter.

Was it luck? Or was it divine protection?
"Silly girl. What do you think?" the Big Guy replied.

CHAPTER 32

We woke to heavy smoke hanging over Redding. Consulting online fire maps, it seemed as if the entire state of California was on fire. Callie was devastated to learn that Yosemite was closed to visitors, as the national park included half a dozen landmarks on her itinerary. Even more troubling was the fact that California's fires were closing many of the national forest campgrounds and wilderness areas that provided our primary source of lodging.

The direness of the situation became clear as we approached Truckee, California on the northern end of Lake Tahoe. After stopping at the south Yuba River for a quick photo shoot and refreshing swim, we continued driving east through Tahoe National Forest in search of a campsite. To our deep dismay, every single national forest campground was closed. The same was true for the campgrounds to the south of Truckee and around Lake Tahoe. The nearest private campground was in Reno, Nevada.

Consulting Campendium, Callie found a highly suspect listing for free camping in a dirt parking area, right in the middle of Truckee. Like many western ski towns, Truckee was once a Mecca for rock climbers and ski bums. But also like many western ski towns, money usurped grunge culture.

Finding free parking—much less a place that allowed free overnight camping—would be like finding a unicorn.

We followed the GPS coordinates to the Campendium location. "This doesn't look right," I said dubiously, gazing at the residential homes across the street from the gravel parking space.

"Only one person stayed here," Callie replied skeptically. "There isn't much information. It just says the spot didn't specify that overnight camping was prohibited, and the police didn't hassle them."

"Does it mention the type of vehicle?" I asked.

"No."

After some deliberation, we accepted the fact that we really didn't have any other option. I dropped the trailer, cranked up the pop-up, and began setting up for the night. Just as we were finishing, a man with the sparse frame and sinuous limbs of a mountain biker stormed out of the bike shop adjacent to the dirt lot. "What the hell do you think you're doing?" He exclaimed angrily.

I dropped back, an inferior dog in the presence of an attacker. "I'm so sorry. I'm guessing this is private property?"

"Sure as hell, it's private property!"

"Oh…I'm so incredibly sorry for my mistake. There's an app called Campendium. It gives the GPS coordinate for this location. I would never in a million years drop a trailer here if I knew it was private property. I'm so sorry for the misunderstanding."

I was secretly hoping that if I stalled long enough, he might have a change of heart and allow me to stay the night. No such luck.

Though the fire was gone from his eyes, he said, "Well, this is private property. So you should pack back up and head on your way."

"Absolutely, sir. I will do that right away. It's just that all of the national forest campgrounds are closed due to forest fires. We checked every one of them. My daughter and I have no idea where to go."

He looked at Callie, standing in the doorway to the trailer. The man's shoulders drooped and his demeanor shifted. "There's a free campsite right where this road dead ends. It's got a picnic table, fire ring, and everything. It's even by the river, and a little farther from the train tracks than you'd be here. I think you'll like it. Nobody knows about it. It's kind of a local's secret."

"Oh my gosh. Thank you, thank you, thank you!" I exclaimed, giving him a hug, which he returned reluctantly. Sure enough, right at the end of the road was a single camping spot, exactly as advertised. I couldn't believe our good fortune. The spot was perfect!

Callie discovered that Tinder was useful for finding hiking partners. Tinder is a dating app that allows people to swipe right or left, depending on whether or not they are interested in opening a dialogue with other people who share the app.

A former US Ski Team racer responded to Callie's query for a hiking buddy. He knew Callie's friend Kaila, the US Ski Team aerialist we had visited in Salt Lake City. Our first day in Truckee, Callie and her new US Ski Team buddy hit it off immediately and headed out for a day of hiking.

Meanwhile, I caught up on emails at a coffee shop in Truckee, bought bagels, and delivered them to the guy at the bike shop who had given us the tip on the camp site.

Returning to the trailer after dinner, I found a police violation warning stuck to the door. Despite the fact that our camping spot had a picnic table, fire ring, and evidence of previous camping activity, the police notice indicated that overnight parking was prohibited. *Grrrr…*

I called Callie with the bad news. Her new hiking buddy offered to let her stay with his family in Tahoe. But I still needed a place to stay. It was late in the day and getting dark. Desperately in need of a shower, I secured a cheap hotel room at a casino an hour away in Reno.

The next morning, I reserved one of the last two spots at a trailer park on the south side of Reno. Most of the campers were long-term residents who spent the season there. It was one of those over-priced parking lots that Callie and I normally scoffed at. The campers were spaced so closely, you could pass toothpaste to your neighbor through the bathroom window. However, this was the only place to be had, and I was damned lucky to get it.

Trailer park folk are an interesting bunch. They are often highly social, inquisitive, and eager to meet new people. But they also tend to respect privacy, providing space when they sense a fellow guest doesn't want to be bothered.

I fell into the reticent category at first, but gradually opened up. In honesty, I was craving adult interaction. Other than a few scattered conversations with my parents, fellow hikers, and naked hot springs hippies, I'd rarely found opportunity for discourse with anyone other than Callie.

Though most of the trailer park's occupants were advanced in years, they were willing to lend a helping hand. I was on my way to get groceries when the minivan dashboard showed a "Critical Error" message. Consulting Google and a YouTube video, I was standing in front of the Honda Odyssey, iPhone in hand, when a man in the camper next to me noticed the hood to my car was open.

"Car problems?" He asked.

"I'm getting a sensor light on the Honda. Looks like I'll need a diagnostics test."

"I've got a diagnostic tool right here!" my new friend exclaimed.

Consulting the screen, the man said it was throwing a PO101 code, which indicated a mass airflow (MAF) issue. Looking it up, he said that in most cases, the fix shouldn't be expensive. But it was important to deal with it, because some of those codes could cause the engine to simply stop working. A mental image of Callie and I standing in the middle of the desert beside a stranded Honda Odyssey sent a shiver down my spine.

Fortunately, there was a Honda dealership in Reno. Unfortunately, it would be two days before they could get me in for a quick diagnostic appointment. It would be weeks before I could get on the repair schedule.

Our biggest time constraint was the fact that Christopher was flying into Los Angeles three days hence to join us for the return trip across the United States. Yosemite was already off the agenda due to fire closures. But I'd been hoping to take Callie into the Inyo Mountain Range to visit the place I'd gone on my soul quest two years earlier.

I thought it would be cool to have a ceremony honoring the end our three month adventure in a place that was considered deeply sacred by indigenous cultures. It was frustrating to be stranded in Reno—which was not the spiritual venue I would have chosen for ceremonial closure to our roadtrip journey.

I called Callie with the bad news. Not surprisingly, she wasn't disappointed at the prospect of spending a few extra days in Tahoe. She was having a great time being entertained by her new US Ski Team buddy. Plus, she had made even more new friends.

Two days later at the Honda dealership, a service technician reset the MAF indicator light. We crossed our fingers that the code was the result of a faulty sensor and not a bigger problem. The delay put us on a tight schedule. Christopher would be arriving in Los Angeles the following day, and we had an eight hour drive ahead of us. Callie said goodbye to her Tahoe friends and I bid farewell to my little trailer park community.

Heading south out of Reno, we hopped on Highway 395 outside Carson City, which passed just to the east of Yosemite. It was heartbreaking to be so close to one of the most famous national parks in North America but unable to explore it.

"What if those beautiful places burn, Mom? What if I never get the chance to see them in my lifetime?" Callie asked.

The thought was sobering.

An hour later, the Honda's engine light came back on. I realized the landscape looked familiar and consulted the map.

"Hey!" I exclaimed. "This is the Inyo National Forest! This is where I had my soul quest."

"Wow," Callie replied. "It's eerie that your engine light came back on, just now."

My soul quest had been one of the most impactful experiences of my life. Surrounded by familiar landscape, the memory of that bizarre adventure sprang to life in my mind's eye.

In early 2018, my friend Dee had given me the book *Soulcraft* by Bill Plotkin. The concept of embarking on a wild, crazy, rendezvous of the soul sounded like a fun way to embrace the journey to elder-hood. Dee and I decided to sign up for a retreat together.

The night I signed up for the course, I began having strange dreams. Normally, I never remembered my dreams. But after enrolling in the soul quest, my nights were filled with images. They streaked through my consciousness like heat lightning, so vibrant that they felt more akin to visions. A frequent visitor was a Black woman who referred to herself as a Pachamama.

From trips to Peru, I'd learned that the people of the Andes revered the Pachamama as an Earth Mother: a warm, loving goddess of fertility. In my dreams, this Pachamama explained that she came from an African lineage that was much older than the Andean tradition, but that my image of the Pachamama was the closest point of reference.

It was hot and humid in the dream where I first met my Pachamama. I was walking barefoot on sun-baked earth towards a ramshackle, clapboard cabin, shaded by two massive oak trees. The door to the cabin stood ajar. Just as I reached to push the door, it opened of its own accord, revealing two rickety wooden steps that descended to a recessed dirt floor.

The cabin was comprised of a single room, dimly lit by a few dingy windows. A dozen Black women in simple cotton muslin house-dresses were scattered around the room. Some sat in chairs, sewing. Others were working together on a quilt, which was fanned out on a large table at the center of the room. The quilt contained the sun, moon, planets, all the stars of the galaxy, and universes beyond our galaxy.

Some of the women looked at me with curiosity. Others seemed wary and apprehensive. Not a word was spoken aloud. But I heard their thoughts as they communicated with the woman who had opened the door to me. "Why is she here? Why did you let her in?" they inquired.

My Pachamama said simply, "Because she needs to see."

In visions over the next several weeks, my Pachamama revealed that she was one of many entities whose collective power is vast—virtually limitless—when viewed from our dimension. They were there at the beginning of time, the life force behind all living things.

The Pachamama are responsible for all shifts in energy as it changes form. From the sprouting of a seed to the birth of a star, the Pachamama play an integral role at their inception. As a collective, they are the formative entity that weaves a patchwork quilt of energy, knitting together universal forces with as little effort as it takes to mend a sock.

My Pachamama explained that they feel great compassion for humans in their suffering, even as they weave tragedy into the fates of man. The Pachamama offer supernatural comfort, especially when a woman loses a child. They are known by many names. Their role is found in the belief systems of nature-based religions, which have been practiced by indigenous communities throughout all of human history.

"Why do I need to know all of this?" I asked my Pachamama.

With deep compassion, she replied, "You will be tested."

One night, a couple weeks after my first dream, I woke from a dead sleep. John was out of town and I was alone in my bedroom. I sat still, listening, wondering what had woken me. The bedroom was much darker than normal, like a shadow filled the room.

Then I heard a voice. It wasn't a dream and it wasn't a voice in my head. The sound didn't come from a single point in the bedroom. Instead, it seemed as if it came from darkness itself. This deep, masculine, commanding voice asked, "What are you not willing to give up for this soul quest?"

I didn't answer. It wasn't that I was scared, shocked, or confused. After many nights of vivid dreams and bizarre encounters with my Pachamama, I wasn't even surprised. It just didn't occur to me to reply.

The voice repeated the question again, more loudly and insistently, "What are you not willing to give up for this soul quest?"

Oh. Maybe this isn't meant to be a rhetorical question…

Then the voice was so loud, I felt the sound waves reverberate through the room, "What are you not willing to give up for this soul quest?"

Without thinking, I blurted out, "*My happiness!*"

There was a whoosh, like the air was sucked out of the room, and with it went the pitch blackness that had been filling it. Ambient light filled my bedroom as moonbeams filtered in through the windows. I shivered. The experience was too visceral to pass off as a dream.

What in the name of all that is holy was that about?

In the past, existential inquiry left me with more questions than answers. Therefore, I'd become perfectly comfortable with unanswered questions. This is part of the reason the visions didn't really bother me.

More importantly, I think I never really took the dreams seriously. After all, they were pretty trippy. My definition of "reality" was more akin to a highly flexible framework, as opposed to a concrete structure. As such, I never felt the need to rationalize or justify the dreams. They just…were.

The day of the soul quest arrived. Dee and I flew from Buffalo to Las Vegas, where we met up with a few other questers for the four hour drive to the Inyo Mountains. Due to a number of detours along the way, our four hour journey became five and a half hours. By the time we arrived at camp, the other members of our soul quest team had already assembled. They were in the midst of introductions.

After introductions, we learned that points of the compass can be assigned attributes, which can then be used to set intentions. I'd brought small items from home, little touchstones that represented each of my family members. Using my family members as guides, I decided to dedicate each of the four days of the quest to a different directional point of the compass.

Callie was my south. She represented childhood and playfulness. Callie wore life lightly, rarely letting circumstances weigh her down. Many of our friends wistfully commented how great it would be to spend just a moment living in Callie's world, where everything was bright, beautiful and filled with magic. My symbol for Callie was a little stone with the words "Let It Go" engraved on it. When she'd given me the stone for Christmas, Callie said, "Whenever you are feeling frustrated, or angry, or sad, just let it go! Because nothing is worth trading for your happiness."

Gracie was my west. She represented the tumultuous teenage years. Gracie was deep, moving water, sometimes flowing in a wide slow-moving river, sometimes raging in anger, sometimes plunging deep into the earth to explore and create subterranean caves and caverns. Gracie was literature, poetry, and expression. She was power and insight and wisdom. Gracie loved all living things. My symbol for Gracie was a little container of honey from the bees she'd raised.

John was my north. He represented adulthood. John was responsibility and protection. He directed our family's path, deciding what business venture would best provide for our family, where we should live, and what new adventures we should pursue. He represented safety and stability. My symbol for John was a green aventurine stone. I chose it because aventurine sounded like "adventuring," which had been the hallmark of our life together.

Christopher was my east. He represented the ethereal spiritual realm. Christopher was my empath. He was highly aware of the emotions of the people around him. But unlike many empaths who feel emotionally overwhelmed by this heightened awareness of energy, he managed to stay in happy, balanced, and free. Everyone loved Christopher because he genuinely cared about people, taking an interest in their lives without carrying the weight of the world on his shoulders. My talisman for Christopher was a shell he'd given me when we were on the beach. The shell was broken on one side, allowing air to flow through it. For me, Christopher's shell symbolized a love as wide and deep as the ocean.

Our group leader was standing in the middle of the circle, recapping the significance of setting intentions, when I heard a new voice in my head. It was similar to the voice of my Pachamama, but much more commanding. I came to refer to this new voice as the Earth Mother. "Get to your knees, child. You're on holy ground."

I pursed my lips, suppressing a smile at the image of dropping to my knees right in the middle of a bunch of people I'd just met. *Hi. My name is Christy. I came here straight from the loony bin. Just ignore me while I get down on my knees in the dirt!*

But the Earth Mother commanded again, "Get to your knees. You are on holy ground." I was surprised to discover that I was fighting a physical urge to drop to the ground, like a hand was pressing down on my shoulder. The impulse was as strong as the urge to sneeze. I quickly excused myself and shuffled towards the outhouse, pretending I needed to use the bathroom.

Skirting around the back of the outhouse, I headed into the desert. Dodging tall clumps of sage brush and cactuses, I was barely out of sight of the campground when the voice came again, "Get to your knees. You are on holy ground." This time, when the Earth Mother said the word "knees," my legs crumpled beneath me, and I was kneeling on the ground, palms planted firmly on the dirt in front of me.

The power hit me in waves, rising up through the earth, riveting my hands to the ground. My hands felt like they were shooting out roots, anchoring me to the earth.

Then wave upon wave of ecstasy coursed through my body as I received a message straight from the soil.

"Whether you had the perfect mother, a terrible mother, or no mother at all is irrelevant. All pale in comparison to the all-encompassing love of the One Mother." The truth of these words permeated every membrane of my body as bliss rolled through me in wave after wave. Tears streamed down my face, and my throat ached from the effort of enduring a power that surpassed anything I'd ever felt.

When it was over, I stood shakily, wondering what in the hell just happened. Returning to the group, Dee looked at me quizzically. Bewildered, I shrugged and whispered, "I think I just had a spiritual orgasm!"

Later that afternoon, we arrived at our wilderness camp, which faced the snow-capped Sierra Nevada mountains. Our trip leader showed us how to use our tarps to create a makeshift shelter. Though some shelters looked better than others, none were sufficient to fend off the late-spring sleet storm that accosted our camp during the night.

I'd set my tarp too high and the wind easily drove rain sideways under it, pelting my sleeping bag. As sleet stung my face in the darkness, I climbed the rock buttress supporting the tarp and yanked ropes free. Back on the ground—extracting my sleeping bag from a puddle—I angrily wriggled back into the soggy sleeping bag, rolled the tarp around me like a burrito, and shivered through the rest of the night, praying for sunrise.

In the early morning light, the rain stopped. I changed into dry clothes.

As our trip leader gathered the bleary-eyed members of our group, each of whom was commiserating over the toils and tribulations he or she had endured in the night, I was once again overcome by a that strange sneeze-like urge to drop to the ground. I abruptly got up and scurried out of sight, found a ring of tall boulders, and fell to my knees.

The sun was cresting over a hill in the distance, and I felt a deep, aching, sensual joy as the sunlight caressed the rain-soaked earth. I felt the sun's touch like the embrace of a lover, caught between a masculine sun and the Earth Mother as they united in the morning light. Again, the feeling of bliss coursed through me, over and over, in waves even stronger than the previous day. Moaning, chest heaving, gasping for air, I was sincerely worried I might have a heart attack.

Tears streamed down my face in gratitude, awe, and wonder at this incredibly profound experience. It was so confusing. What did it mean? What was I supposed to learn from this? Why was it happening to me?

I made my way back to camp. Reluctant to rejoin the group with a tear-streaked face, I hovered near the food tent, where the trip leader's wife and another quest leader were preparing breakfast. Yet again, my knees buckled, and I dropped to the earth. I was profoundly embarrassed.

What in God's name was happening to me? It was weird enough to go through this alone in the desert. Being in the presence of other people while gasping and sobbing in the throes of some kind of euphoric spiritual orgasm was completely mortifying! I just wanted to roll under a sage bush and hide until it was over.

The women preparing breakfast rushed over to make sure I was okay. Seeing my face, the trip leader's wife assured me that everything was fine. This was perfectly normal. In the throes of ecstasy, I looked at the woman, dumbfounded. What about this could possibly be considered normal? "I feel...like I'm having...a spiritual...orgasm!" I panted.

"No, sweetheart," she chuckled as tears filled her eyes. "It's not an orgasm. You're being birthed."

Orgasm? Birthing? What's the difference? This was, by far the most bizarre thing I'd ever experienced.

At this point in the story, I think it important to mention, there were *no* hallucinogens or drugs of any kind involved in this journey. Three days of preparation were followed by a three day "solo" in the desert with only a tarp, sleeping bag, water, and ceremonial items before being finished by three days of integration. This was day two of our nine day retreat.

Over the next two days, I completely fell in love with each member of our group. As the oldest woman attending the retreat, I adopted the role most comfortable to me. I became "Mom:" nurturing, caring, offering a shoulder when someone needed support. Some of the group participants actually started calling me "Mom." It all felt relatively "normal."

Then, during my four day solo, the trippiness continued. The fabric that separated me from other living beings melted away. I could talk to…yes, converse with… plants, birds, rocks, trees, etc. and hear their reply. It was like the Earth Mother's gift of rebirth opened some kind of translation tool that interpreted energy as words.

I spent my four day solo living in a place I called the hummingbird house.

An honest-to-goodness hummingbird showed me around her house, instructing me where and how to enter, where to leave my shoes, where I should sleep, the best place to watch sunrise and sunset, and even where to go to the bathroom.

How the hell am I understanding a hummingbird? I mused.

Each time I did a self-designed ceremony, the hummingbird hovered inches off the end of my nose, bearing witness. Each time I watched a sunrise or sunset, the hummingbird watched with me, hovering just off my right shoulder.

Though I slept alone for three nights under the stars with no tent and no food, alone in the middle of the desert, I was never in the least bit cold, hungry, or scared. I felt deeply protected, and slept as soundly as I would at home in my own bed.

The first morning of my solo, I woke at daybreak.

"Come and greet your day," the Earth Mother said.

"Is it okay if I greet it from inside this nice warm sleeping bag?" I asked.

"Come and greet your day," the Earth Mother repeated gently. "I have made it warm for you."

Sure enough, despite the fact that it was early morning in the mountains, the air wasn't cold.

During my morning bathroom routine, a little mouse popped his head up a couple feet away. He ducked back down, then popped up again, closer this time. Finally, he climbed up on the rock, easily within reach, and sat on his haunches, staring at me as if he was waiting for me to remember something.

Oh! I'm dedicating the first day of my quest to the South! The mouse is the animal symbol of the south! Thank you, little one!

With a happy heart, I remembered that Callie would be my guide today. This was going to be fun! Scanning the horizon, I tried to picture where Callie would go.

She'd climb to the top of the highest hill, of course!

Due east of the Sierra Nevada mountains, the high desert landscape of the Inyo Mountain range was devoid of trees. Rocks shaped like ancient, stone-carved visages dotted the landscape, lending a sacred air to a vast sweeping valley that rose to the mountain top beyond.

It was impossible to gauge the distance. Would the trek to the top of the mountain take two hours or four hours? Since I hadn't eaten since dinner the night before and wouldn't eat again until breakfast three days hence, every calorie mattered.

I set off with a light daypack, an extra layer, and one and a half liters of water. *This is going to be so fun!* I thought, fully energized and excited for the hike. There was no doubt that I was channeling my inner Callie.

As I walked, the Earth Mother told me that much of my quest would be spent collecting fractured pieces of my soul that had been lost at various points in my life. My family members would serve as guides to find these pieces.

My first directive was to climb the mountain. There, I would collect a piece of my soul that was fractured when John pulled me from the mummy's tomb on El Plomo.

Dirt two-track roads crisscrossed up the valley. I did my best to follow them in the direction of the mountain. As one veered off in the wrong direction, I'd set out across the desert in search of another one. After an hour and a half, the valley rose steeply and the roads ended. The top of the mountain still loomed far in the distance. Undeterred, I continued picking my way uphill amidst fields of boulders and cactus-studded earth.

The Earth Mother's presence was with me through the journey, conveying intimacy for each of the rocks, flowers, cactuses, and sage bushes we passed.

The day became cool when intermittent clouds blocked the sun's light. On several occasions, I kicked myself for not brining a rain jacket. The sun was lower in the sky when a wind from the south began to pick up. I had easily been hiking for over five hours, and was just getting to the weather-beaten conifers that crowned the mountain's crest.

Finally, after traversing the final spinal ridge to the summit, I sat down on a log for a much-needed break.

Now what? How does one go about reclaiming a fragmented part of their soul?

I listened for the Earth Mother's voice, but she was silent.

Really? You had a lot to say about rocks and plants! But when it comes to connecting fragments of my soul, I'm on my own?

A cold wind rushed up the sheer face of a cliff. The sun's proximity to the western horizon was making me nervous. After traveling all this distance, it would be challenging enough to find my camp by day. At night, it would be utterly impossible.

I leaned into my intuition, listening harder. There was nothing.

Fine.

I bent down, grabbed the log I'd been sitting on, awkwardly hoisted it over my head...and then realized I had no idea what to say and dropped it again.

I feel like an idiot!

After a moment, I bent down again, grabbed the log, hoisted it over my head, and proclaimed, "I claim the piece of my soul that was lost in the Incan child's tomb on a mountain far away! I thank my family for bearing witness. I thank

Mother Earth below and Father Sky above." With that, I set the log back down, shrugged, and scurry-walked back down the steep slope in a race against the setting sun.

Did I do that right?

How could one know? It could have been my imagination, but I somehow felt fuller, more whole, but lighter at the same time.

The next morning, I was sore. Having returned to camp in the gloaming the night before, I marveled at the miracle that guided me through the desert to arrive back at the hummingbird's house within moments of darkness. The hummingbird was there to greet me upon my return.

My stomach growled. It had been thirty-six hours since its last meal. Not one for fasting, I wasn't really sure what to expect. Though most of my fellow questers were most apprehensive about sleeping alone in the desert, my biggest fear had been going three days without eating. I was surprised to discover that my body only protested at meal times.

Rolling out of a warm sleeping bag in the cold pre-dawn light, I thought about the day ahead. This second day of my solo would be dedicated to the West, and Gracie would be my guide.

I listened for the Earth Mother's guidance. She said this second day, I would be recovering other fragments of my soul.

One was lost when Gracie and I battled over her naps when she was three years old. Giving birth to three babies in four years left me spiritually and physically depleted. In this state of weakness, my spirit wasn't strong enough to do battle, and my soul had been damaged in the fight.

My spirit continued to splinter through ensuing years whenever Gracie and I fought. Tiny fragments of energy, some as fine as a strand of hair, lay strewn across space and time.

I wasn't surprised my soul was fractured with those two events. Both felt devastating at the time. Both surpassed my ability to provide what I felt my daughter needed. Both left me feeling like a failure as a mother.

As I watched the sun rise, I felt Gracie's presence with me. She loved sunrises. The hummingbird hovered just off my shoulder as well.

While making a breakfast of herbal tea, an inquisitive bee hovered over my pillow and sleeping bag, flew in and out of my backpack, and came to rest on the tea bag. Seeing the bee filled me with inexplicable delight.

Dipping the tea bag in Gracie's honey, I set it on the rock and waited. Within minutes, a small swarm of bees were hovering around the honey. Watching them made my soul happy.

It wasn't long before a big black lizard decided to join the party. He would do little push-ups with his front legs, stand perfectly still, then scoot a few steps closer to the bees.

Do lizards eat honey?

The lizard continued to do is funny little dance, closing the gap between him and the honey. With horror, I thought, *Do lizards eat bees?*

One bee broke away from the rest and flew to the place where the lizard was crouching. The bee made a slow, lazy circle around the lizard's head, then landed right in front of him. The lizard pounced, and the bee disappeared.

I gasped. *That bee wanted to be eaten!* The intentionality in the bee's actions was unmistakable. *I wonder if there is a part of us chooses our death. And what if our souls choose the adversity in our life too?*

Instead of feeling sorry for myself and for the situations that caused those fractures in my soul, I began to feel grateful for this exciting treasure hunt to restore them. Those little fractures were blessings in disguise.

Much of the previous day's trek up the mountain had been filled with conversations with the Earth Mother. I suddenly realized that restoring the fragments of my soul had nothing to do with the log-raising ceremony at the end of the day. It was the journey to the top of the mountain that made me whole.

I wanted to make a circle of rocks for the night vigil at the end of the solo.

Would you help me find special rocks? I asked the Earth Mother.

"Each rock is special," the Earth Mother replied.

I know. But please help me find the right rocks to contain the energy during my night vigil.

"There isn't a rock on the planet that wouldn't be able to contain that energy. That's the very function of a rock. It holds energy," The Earth Mother replied. "Some people think that rocks themselves contain a specific energy. That's not the case. There isn't a stone or crystal that can create happiness if a person doesn't already have happiness inside of them. However, certain rocks have the ability to reflect and amplify one energy or another. But the main purpose of rocks is to bear witness. Any rock you choose will be both worthy and honored to bear witness during your night vigil."

While collecting rocks, I saw a beautiful Indian Paintbrush flower in full bloom, and it reminded me of Gracie.

You are so gorgeous! Thank you for sharing your beauty with me.

The Indian Paintbrush asked for a sip of the tea I was holding. I gave her a splash.

The Earth Mother told me that while humans use their five sense to acquire information, nature communicates vibrationally. Does your awareness extend to the mountains beyond this hill? Can you "see" the mountains?

"You would call this desert one ecosystem. To us, it's more like a family. My family extends to those mountains, so yes, I am aware of them. When a plant, tree, or animal in our family is hurt, the entire family feels it. But we don't feel destruction from another ecosystem—or another family—unless it is on a massive scale."

What about the destruction of the rain forest? Is that something you feel?

"Yes. That kind of destruction reverberates through the planet. I also feel forest fires from other ecosystems. And the energy of earthquakes is transferred to us through rocks and soil."

Is nature angry with humans for the destruction we cause when we create farms, or build our roads, houses, and cities?

I sensed the Indian Paintbrush's smile. "In most cases, we are no more angry with humans when they build than we would be with a lion who kills a gazelle. Humans were created to create. In their creative process of building cities and roads, they inadvertently harm nature.

"Similarly, the gazelle harms nature when she tramples and eats the grass. The lion harms nature when he eats the gazelle. It is the way of the world. However, destruction that is heedless and willful has consequences. Such is the destruction of the rain forest. This type of destruction causes a shudder that travels through nature around the world. Just as there would be a consequence to the lion who kills all the gazelles in the herd, there is a consequence for man's unnatural behavior in destroying the rain forest and causing unnecessary death."

I thanked the Indian paintbrush for her wisdom.

Gracie would be so excited to hear about my conversations with the rocks and flowers. These little chats were the perfect way to get in tune with my inner Gracie.

Returning to camp to meditate, I was just nodding off to sleep when a bee hovered in front of me, buzzing in my face. I stood up to follow the bee, grabbing Gracie's jar of honey as I passed it. To my surprise, the bee flew slowly, and I had no trouble following it.

After a ten minute walk into the desert, we arrived at the bee's hive.

Do you have a message for me? Can you tell me how to restore the pieces of my soul that were lost?

The bees didn't reply. I suddenly felt silly talking to a bee. Actually, talking to bees wouldn't be too strange. Expecting a reply? That was crazy.

I sat watching the beehive as it swarmed with activity. Three big black lizards hovered nearby. Not a single bee was consumed. Again, I had the feeling that the bees weren't eaten unless they chose to be eaten. Laying on a flat rock, I fell asleep in the warm afternoon sun.

Some time later, I woke to the sound of the hummingbird's wings whirring above me. She'd come to take me home. I followed her back to the hummingbird house, waiting as she stopped to sip nectar from a few flowers en route.

She told me that the fractured pieces of my soul had been restored by the bees while I slept. There was no need to do anything else.

I took pictures of "Gracie's sunset," as well as the flowers, landscape, and snow-capped Sierra Nevada mountains in the distance.

I also collected two stones to add to my circle of rocks—one with moss growing on it that reminded me of a garden to represent my mom, and another white crystal to represent my dad.

When I awoke on the third and final day of my solo quest in the desert, the wind was blowing from the north. I laughed out loud. The first morning, the wind was blowing from the south. The second morning, it was blowing from the west. Now, on this day dedicated to John, the wind was indeed blowing from the north.

Watching the sun rise, I held John's aventurine stone and welcomed his energy. The hummingbird, who had been hovering nearby, flew away as if to give us privacy.

I felt the weight of John's sadness. There was deep remorse. "I'm sorry," he said. Those words reflected all the apologies that my husband, in his physical form, was never able to make. My arms ached to hold him.

It's okay, Baby. I'm so sorry I wasn't there when you needed me.

Later that afternoon, John's spirit and I sat watching the afternoon sun as it cast shadows on the snow-topped Sierra Nevada mountains in the distance. We were sitting in a place I referred to as the Lanai deck in the hummingbird's house. The hummingbird had again returned to share what seemed to have become her favorite pastime—watching sunrises and sunsets with me.

I felt another wave of emotion coming from John's higher self. He invited the spirit-energy of my parents to join us. There was appreciation and gratitude mixed with regret. John turned to my parents and said, "I'm sorry."

Again, my heart melted. Though the Earth Mother hadn't specifically told me what fragments John would help me recover, I knew they had something to do with those early knock-down drag-out fights when I wanted to spend more time with my parents. On a metaphysical level, his apology was accepted and balance was restored.

I made two lists: "List of Beautiful Things My Parents Have Done For Me" and "Places We've Lived and Visited Since We Were Married." Both were long and impressive. With each line I wrote, I felt the missing pieces of my soul falling back into place.

Before the night vigil, I did a self-designed cleansing ritual with sage and essential oils, and entered the space I'd chosen for my vigil, high on a rock overlooking the expansive valley and snow-tipped mountains beyond.

Though May temperatures dipped into the forties at night, I hadn't been cold through the entire three day solo. But then, I felt an odd chill that wasn't just due to temperature. As the sun dipped low in the sky, I felt apprehension, and wished the hummingbird would come for a visit.

The wind kicked up. Attempting to sing one of the chants our group leader taught us, my voice sounded feeble and empty. I called for the hummingbird, and turned to see something frightening. Just behind my head was a kind of bird or large insect I'd never seen before. It looked like a cross between a wasp and a hummingbird. Its presence felt like a portentous omen. In my mind, my trusted companion had been replaced by something vile and sinister.

As hard as I tried to stay awake, I kept falling asleep that night. I felt guilty for my lack of discipline. How hard can it be to stay awake? With all the beauty, grace, and magic that had been revealed, how could I fail at this simple task? I finally gave up and succumbed sleep, tossing and turning to get comfortable on the rocks.

After waking for the hundredth time, I sensed the faintest hint of light in the direction of the eastern sky. But rather than viewing the prospect of sunrise with joy, I felt a growing sense of dread. As the world around me emerged from darkness, I felt utterly and completely abandoned.

The sensation of abandonment tugged at the fractured pieces of my soul that had been lovingly restored, threatening to rip them away. I felt hopeless and alone. Then came rage.

"You can't have them," I shouted to the wind. "They're mine now!" Like a mother protecting her child, I clung to the newly reunited pieces of my soul, though it seemed as if God himself was trying to take them away.

The rage boiled up inside me, and I directed my anger at each of the sacred rocks that had been tasked with holding the energy of my rock circle. With all my strength, I threw the rocks as far as I could, feeling pain in my own body as they struck the earth.

This roller coaster of emotion from spiritual ecstasy to abandonment and rage was truly terrifying.

I'd gone nuts. That was the only explanation. After all, hadn't I been hearing voices? Talking to rocks and flowers? I'd clearly lost my mind.

As I stood on the high rock, surrounded by barren desert and veritably wrestling with God, the only thing preventing a true psychotic break was the memory of the deep and abiding love I had shared with the Mother. In my darkest hour, I was far from that love. But the memory of it still held power. To dismiss this encounter as insanity would be to discount the truth of that love.

Sobbing, I managed to gather my sleeping bag and stuff it into my backpack, navigate my way through the high desert, and rejoin the group.

We had been instructed to be silent when reentering the camp. Upon congregating in a circle, we were to share a single word or phrase that epitomized our three day solo or the final night vigil.

Every other member of the group stepped forward, faces illuminated by the same love I had received during the first few days of our quest. When it came my turn to step forward, I felt as if every ounce of energy was gone. I barely had the strength or courage to utter the one word pounding a hole in my brain. Finally, in a voice barely above a whisper, I spoke the word "despair" and broke down crying.

Each person in the group held me in turn. I knew their love was there, but I couldn't feel it. Nothing reached me. A thick plexiglass shield separated me from the deeply compassionate people surrounding me. I could see them. I could hear them. But I couldn't feel them.

We spent three days "unpacking" our discoveries. I listened to the profound revelations and insight my new friends and soulmates had experienced while attempting to reframe my own story in a way that would allow me to sleep at night. But I was in shock. What had happened?

Scanning my heart, I couldn't find evidence of a single emotion. Soon after arriving back at camp, the despair disappeared. Like sand draining from a broken hourglass, every other emotion drained away with it. I was a shattered vessel. Nothing made sense.

A chill ran down my spine as I remembered the voice in the darkness, in my bedroom. "What are you not willing to give up for this soul quest?"

"*My happiness!*"

Who am I without my happiness? What will happen to the fun, adventurous mom—the mom who danced in the kitchen, sang dirty rap songs with the kids during soccer carpools, read Harry Potter aloud with each character having its own ridiculous British accent, snuck ducks into a ski resort pond, skinny-dipped, and ran naked down an empty beach with the kids when they were little? Where is the mom who climbed mountains and rode elephants?

The soul quest was so confusing. I didn't feel worthy of the powerful encounter with the Earth Mother at the beginning of the quest. And I certainly didn't feel deserving of the despair at the end of the night vigil. It. Just. Didn't. Make. Sense.

As I drove through the desert beneath the Inyo Mountains during my roadtrip with Callie, it was hard to believe I'd been in that same place just two years earlier. That spiritual encounter felt like a lifetime ago. It it was stupid to think that something as powerful as a soul quest would be all butterflies and sunshine. That's the stuff of fake tarots and pop astrology. Angst, struggle, and hopefully a renewed sense of purpose is the stuff of true spiritual transformation. Just like physical birth, spiritual rebirth is fucking painful. Indigenous people know that. I clearly didn't.

I remembered returning home to Ellicottville after my soul quest. I'd felt for my missing heart the same way an amputee's body feels for its missing limb, trying to mentally reconstruct what those lost emotions felt like. I hugged the kids, willing myself to manufacture love by naming other complimentary emotions: gratitude, warmth, pride, safety. But none of those feelings were accessible either.

In time, I got too busy to play hide and seek with my heart. There was just too damned much work to be done. In addition to placing orders for Patagonia and most of the other footwear and clothing brands in the store, I was the only person who knew how to enter inventory into the store's inventory management system, link the data feed for the online store, or write a blog post.

I went back to playing my role as supporting actor in someone else's play; smiling when I was supposed to smile, laughing when I was supposed to laugh, and acting sad when sadness was required.

One night, I had a dream that our outdoor store was filled with people. There was a festival in town, with music, food, and revelry. It was a bright, sunny day, and the people coming into the shop were laughing.

In my dream, there was a dock, right in the middle of the shop. I was shocked to discover that I was laying dead on the dock, just like the dead man we'd seen lying on the dock on Lake Atitlan in Guatemala. People walked past my body as if wasn't there. John was busy helping customers and the rest of our employees were doing the same.

Then Gracie, Callie, and Christopher walked into the store. They were laughing and carefree, thoroughly enjoying the festivities. Callie carried a red balloon.

Looking down at my lifeless form, I thought, "They'll see me. The kids will notice I'm dead." But they walked past.

I woke up sobbing, gasping for air, frightened by the sharp pain in my chest.

CHAPTER 33

It was hard to believe the roadtrip was ending. Resetting the sensor hadn't fixed the MAF issue. What if the engine simply stopped? I remembered the image of Callie and I, standing stranded in the desert. Mile after mile passed in silence as I alternately worried about the MAF indicator light and ruminated on the soul quest.

After the soul quest, I kept waiting for someone to save me. I wanted John to love me enough to reach through the emptiness, to wake me up, to help me feel something again. But that wasn't fair. No human love could have done that.

What if all the love we ever offer to others is just a reflection of the love we are supposed to feel for ourselves? What if it's like a lock and key...our unique way of loving is exactly the way we need to be loved? No human being is capable of loving us as deeply as we are capable of loving ourselves. And we are incapable of loving anyone else as deeply as they are capable of loving themselves.

Approaching Los Angeles, worry won the battle for mind-share. LA traffic, daunting at any time, was particularly stressful as we rode into the City of Angels with trailer in tow on a wave of weekend traffic.

To make matters worse, the trailer's electric system failed (yet again) and I lost all trailer lights. The only trailer lights that worked were the hazards. The combination of the MAF warning light, malfunctioning trailer lights, and a gut-wrenching journey down memory lane left me exhausted and frazzled by the time we finally pulled into our hotel at Redondo Beach.

After a good night's sleep, we headed to the airport to see Christopher. It had been three months since I'd seen my sweet boy. I was beyond excited. My arms actually ached for him. But there was anxiety mixed with the excitement too. He'd spent the past three months living with his dad. Would Christopher and I still feel the close connection we'd always shared?

I knew Christopher had lost forty pounds since I'd last seen him. Still, it was a shock to see how his physical form had changed. A square jawline replaced chubby boyish cheeks. He was at least two inches taller, and handsome. Though physical change is normal for fifteen-year-old boys, Christopher's three month transformation was dramatic.

Christopher wrapped himself around me as I pulled him into an embrace. Though his physical form was different, he was still my sweet, precious, loving boy.

Callie nearly broke into tears when she saw her little brother. The physical and emotional distance we'd covered made the reunion feel more like a return from years away in foreign lands, rather than a few short months in the western United States. "I love you so much, buddy," Callie said over and over as she hugged Christopher.

The fact that my trailer lights were on the blink necessitated a brief stay in LA to replace trailer's electrical system…for the fourth time.

For some reason, Christopher considered Callie's arrest to be the high point in our roadtrip. He begged for permission to jump off the Santa Monica pier so he could be arrested in Santa Monica like his sister.

Callie, on the other hand, couldn't wait to get away from Los Angeles. After all, it had only been a week since the charges against her were finally dropped. Her goal was to avoid contact with any of the police officers involved in that unfortunate event.

The journey back east was like watching a movie in rewind. From Redondo Beach, we headed back to Los Vegas, which still had the feel of a post-apocalyptic movie.

Callie's most coveted Instagram destination was still on our hit list: a place we referred to as Mars. We knew it was in central Utah, but didn't have the exact location. It truly looked like a scene from another planet. Callie had seen pictures of this place on just two Instagram accounts. When she messaged to see if she could get the GPS coordinates, one person said it would cost her six hundred dollars to get the location. The other hadn't replied.

We stopped at Bryce Canyon so Christopher could visit at least one National Park. Callie and I stood at the edge of the breathtakingly beautiful canyon, each lost in our own sad memories of our last visit. A shiver ran down my spine as a cloud drifted past the sun, temporarily stealing its warmth.

When we got back in the car, Callie's phone pinged. It was a message from her second Instagram contact.

"Mom! You're not going to believe this! I told the girl all about our roadtrip and how my parents recently went through a divorce. She said her parents were divorced too. She's offering to give me the coordinates for free, as long as I solemnly swear not to tell *anyone* where this place is and turn off my phone's geolocation. We're finally going to get the GPS coordinates for Mars!"

"Wow!" Christopher exclaimed. "We get to go to Mars? Is this what you guys did on all your roadtrip adventures?"

"No," Callie said. "Most of the time, we climbed to the top of mountains. Just be glad we can drive to this location!"

The trip to Mars took us to a level of remoteness I never knew existed in the continental United States. We drove for several hours without seeing a town, or even a single car. As the day wore on, the seclusion became a little eerie. What if this Instagrammer picked a random GPS coordinate and sent us into the middle of the Utah desert as a gag? Still, we drove on.

At long last, we made a turn, pulling off the narrow two lane paved road onto a dirt road. The dirt road turned onto another dirt road, which lead to something more akin to a cow path.

"Uh oh," I said. "This doesn't feel right." In pictures, the spot we were looking for looked kind of like the Grand Canyon. We had spent more than an hour driving over flat, featureless desert, with nothing but dry grass as far as the eye could see.

"Just a little farther," Callie intoned. Bumping along the rutted cow path, I dodged a few of the deeper ruts that might rip out the trailer's fourth electrical system.

About a half hour later, the world fell away in a jaw-dropping panorama, reminiscent of footage from a space movie. Ribbon-thin peninsulas jutted out into ravines that dropped several hundred feet to a barren landscape of ridges, rivulets, veins, and valleys in every shade of grey, brown, and pink.

"Oh," we gasped in wonder.

"Let me out, let me out, let me out!" The car had barely rolled to a stop as Callie burst out the door and ran to the brink of the ravine. "Oh. My. Gosh. This the best spot of the entire trip! It's even better than the pink beach in the Great Salt Lake. This is incredible!"

The wind was whipping our hair sideways. Callie punched "confirm" to override the drone's high wind warnings, ("*Mom*! You can't come to a place like this and *not* fly the drone!") and captured some of the most spectacular shots in her Instagram career.

Once, the drone was swept away in a gust of wind and the receiver briefly lost contact with it. Fortunately, it came back online, and Callie was able to guide it homeward.

Another time when she was trying to fly the drone in tight to get still shot, a gust swept it into the cliff. I could see the drone lying on a ledge just below the edge of the cliff. By belly-crawling to the brink, I was just able to reach it.

An hour later, teeth plastered with gritty sand from grinning wildly in a wind storm, we managed to leave the location without loss of life or equipment.

The car seemed eerily quiet after the stress and excitement of flying a fifteen hundred dollar piece of equipment in driving wind.

It felt as if Callie had passed some kind of test. The fact that the final waypoint on her roadtrip hit list was the hardest to find, offered the most dramatic scenery, and required every ounce of her drone-flying skill was almost cinematic. Meeting the challenge with fierce tenacity and sheer guts, Callie passed with flying colors. I was very proud.

Horseshoe Bend, Page, AZ

Bryce Canyon National Park, UT

Fairy Falls, Yellowstone, WY

Schwabacher Landing, Moose, WY

Delta Lake, Grand Teton, WY

T.A. Moulton Barn, Moose, WY

Glacier National Park, WA

Mt. Pilchuck, Snohomish, WA

Mt. Pilchuck, Snohomish, WA

Tolmie Peak, Mt. Rainier, WA

Fremont Lookout, Ashford, WA

Airplane Home, Portland, OR

Umpqua Hot Springs, OR

Samuel H. Boardman State Park, CA

Mars

CHAPTER 34

In the end, many of the fabulous images Callie created during our roadtrip never graced the pages of social media. A series of incidents contributed to the loss of most of the photos and videos she took. The images on the previous pages are some that survived.

In Zion, Callie's professional camera was broken. Then she lost her phone (which wasn't backed up on iCloud). Mia's phone dropped in the river in Pagosa Springs. Callie's data files were corrupted and her computer crashed, likely because the drone files were too large for her decade-old hand-me-down MacBook. Callie created her master video edit using a free trial of a software license, which expired, and she lost nearly a hundred hours of time spent compiling what was to be her final pièce de résistance.

Through a gut-wrenching mental journey, Callie came to realize that this trip was never about seeking approval or validation through social media. It was about coming home to her authentic self. Honing her skills as a drone pilot and learning to use professional photo and video editing software enabled her to become a content creator as well as an Instagram travel influencer. Callie would spend ensuing years traveling the globe, capturing footage worthy of National Geographic.

More importantly, Callie became something bigger, deeper, and more powerful. The free, fun-loving kid—whose Instagram account name of CallieCandy123 epitomized her carefree nature—had become a deeply centered, highly motivated, spirit-driven young lady. Her bold, adventurous spirit grew even bigger, inspiring Callie to follow her dreams to become a free diver, paraglider, and licensed skydiver.

We returned to Bear Creek Lake, the same campground on the western side of Denver where I'd spent the first night in the pop-up camper with Callie and Mia. Instead of worrying over one hundred and five degree daytime heat, I was now more concerned about keeping the kids warm through the night, and bought an extra queen sized comforter at a second hand store.

Callie had lined up a recording session with an EDM artist in Denver. After dropping her off, Christopher and I headed to a coffee shop where I could shift my focus from summer roadtripping to plans for fall and winter.

Gracie was already in Costa Rica. Though I'd received some interest in my Nomaditudes program (mostly from Callie and Gracie's stir-crazy college friends), only Callie's friend, Cyrene, had actually signed up for a month-long stay.

"Fortune favors the bold," I whispered. Cashing in my life insurance policy, I proceeded to spend ten thousand dollars in half an hour.

I booked airline tickets for Christopher, Callie, and I to join Gracie in Costa Rica in mid-October, returning for Christmas in Minnesota mid-December. I sent a proposal to five rental car companies for a two month car rental. Two accepted my offer.

Capitalizing on all-time low vacation rental rates, I secured a one month rental for a three bedroom AirBnb at a beachside resort community twenty minutes up the Pacific coast from Tamarindo. Finally, I purchased one month Nomad passes for Callie, Christopher, Cyrene, and I to spend the second month traveling in Costa Rica.

Clicking the final "Buy Now" button, I felt totally calm and entirely at peace. After two months living off bagged salads and food that was on sale because it passed its expiration date, the thought that I'd just spent ten thousand dollars made me giddy. This was the Universe saying, "Dare-ya!" And I'd just stepped up to the plate, taken the swing, and knocked it out of the park.

"Tag, you're it," I whispered to the Universe. "What have you got for me now?"

The car was quiet as we traveled from Colorado back to Minnesota. Christopher watched movies on his cell phone. Neither Callie and nor I felt the need to fill empty space with conversation. Though we were looking forward to the upcoming trip to Costa Rica, we were both sad that our roadtrip was drawing to a close. Acutely aware that we'd been living in our own little bubble, we were both nervous at the prospect of reintegrating into society.

I wasn't the same person who'd left Ellicottville five months earlier. There had been a fundamental shift. I'd spent most of my life measuring myself by other people's yardsticks, trading my authentic self for empty accolades and achievements.

My soul quest, which had been one of the most truly meaningful experiences of my life, received scant little mind share, and it certainly wasn't a topic I brought up in conversation. I was worried people would think I was crazy. More importantly, I was afraid I might actually *be* crazy.

Then it hit me like a ton of bricks. There's really no difference between believing I'm crazy or believing I'm blessed. They are both just beliefs. But only one of those beliefs is rooted in self-worth.

The Earth Mother's words echoed in my mind, as powerful as the first day I heard them: "Whether you had the perfect mother, a terrible mother, or no mother at all is irrelevant. All pale in comparison to the all-encompassing love of the One Mother."

The words were an honest-to-goodness calling, a clear command to become a human conduit for the Earth Mother's fierce love, a physical embodiment of her playfulness, kindness, and compassion. It wasn't a suggestion or an offer. It was a clear directive.

Accepting the Earth Mother's calling would require me to embrace my authentic self, which included the parts of me that were bold, manic, wildly funny, quirky, passionate, and impetuous. But first, I needed to accept the fact that I was truly worthy of that calling. I needed to own my craziness.

The more I let my crazy out, the more other people felt empowered to do the same. It finally occurred to me that we're all completely nuts. Every blessed one of us. And it's our idiosyncrasies, our most far-fetched beliefs, that make us beautiful. True freedom comes from claiming our wild side and letting it shine. After all, we're all just kids playing on the playground.

How many cases of depression, anxiety, and addiction could be avoided if we stopped manning the battlefield of achievement and just headed to the playground?

I decided that my version of stepping onto the playground would include listening to inner guidance and going wherever it guided me. Over the next year, that decision led me to the top of volcanos in Costa Rica, on a trek to seventeen thousand feet in Peru, to a labyrinth in the Costa Rican jungle on the night of a full moon, and back to my home town of Two Harbors, Minnesota.

On countless occasions, the incalculable beauty, the surreal places, the precious people, and the spiritual epiphanies left me weak in the knees. Over and over, I wondered how any of this could possibly be happening to me.

Callie, Christopher, and I spent the last night of our roadtrip in the Badlands of South Dakota.

Driving a rutted dirt road until we could no longer see lights from the highway, we popped the camper in a wide open field with views of the multi-colored gullies, canyons, and ravines of the badlands in the distance.

Callie found a flat spot and dropped her blanket and pillow outside on the ground. "I'm going to spend this one under the stars if that's okay with you."

Of course it was.

That night, I heard coyotes howling in the near distance, a sound that would have frightened me at the beginning of the trip. Now, it just made me smile. This was our world. The Universe was conspiring on our behalf. Events were transpiring exactly as they were meant to transpire. And my timing was indeed perfect.

My authentic soul came at a price. That price was being exactly and precisely met in the delicious unfolding of this sacred journey...called "life."

EPILOGUE

Where does a story end? When do you finally draw a line in the sands of time and declare, "It is done"? With every moment that passes, every day I spend above ground, I'm less convinced that I am creating this story and more convinced that this story is creating me.

In the fall of 2020 and winter of 2021, the kids and I traveled around Costa Rica and Mexico with students participating in the Nomaditudes program.

If Nomaditudes had become a global brand, this book might find a broader audience. But alas, it was not to be. Selina launched its own Nomad Pass, which quickly eclipsed my Nomaditudes program.

I wasn't as disappointed as one might think. Starting Nomaditudes was yet another attempt at external validation. I was still measuring myself by someone else's measuring stick. If there was anything the road trip taught me, it was that freedom is the brass ring on life's carousel.

During the two years following the road trip, freedom took the form of a succession of "dare-ya's"— playful challenges issued by the Big Guy:

- During the full moon in February 2021, I was inspired to hike alone into the Costa Rican jungle to spend the entire night alone in a labyrinth. It felt ridiculously bold.
- In June 2021, Gracie, Callie, and I ascended to altitudes just under seventeen thousand feet during the forty-three mile Asungate Trek in Peru.
- In March 2022, all three kids and I attempted a midnight summit of a volcano in Costa Rica, and spent several hours clawing our way through the jungle in a torrential downpour. Later that month, Callie and I summited a second Costa Rican volcano.
- I spent the entire month of April 2022 living out of a rental car and sleeping in a hammock on a beach in Santa Teresa, Costa Rica.
- In October 2022, I returned to Peru and spent ten days in ceremony with indigenous Incan priests, with Asungate mountain towering above us. We camped at fifteen thousand feet, where night time temperatures dropped to twenty degrees.

As exhilarating as these shenanigans were, they weren't nearly as profound as the lightyears my soul traversed on its inward journey. Some people are born into this life as old souls. They come to this planet wired for empathy. Others, like me, are new souls. New souls are built for speed, because we have a lot of catching up to do.

We new souls are easy to spot; the winds of insight smack us in the face so hard, you'll often see us picking spiritual bugs out of our teeth. We're also the ones who fall in love with wild abandon. At our best…at our very best…we feel reckless, maniac passion for every tree, animal, and person we meet, weeping tears of gratitude at life's overwhelming beauty.

As *Escape Bound* has expanded outside of the pages of this book to include expeditionary plant-based medicine retreats in Peru, I realize that the story continues to create, and the tale truly has no ending. The legacy of adventure and transformation continues. Maybe some day, the Escape Bound journey might even include...you.

ACKNOWLEDGEMENTS

I want to start by acknowledging the Big Guy. Thank you for the surprising, delightful way you reveal yourself through so many physical and nonphysical faces and forms. With the intimacy of pillow talk whispered between lovers, you fill a space in my soul that is exactly the shape and size of you.

To my parents, Bill and Helen Tranah, I owe a debt of gratitude that could never be repaid in this, or any, lifetime. Not only did you offer physical labor, financial support, and profound wisdom throughout my life, when my year-long traveling ashram finally came to an end, you provided me a home. Thank you for believing in me, even when my life was in shambles. P.S.—I still owe you eight thousand dollars for the pop-up trailer.

My three children, Gracie, Callie, and Christopher Rounds, are my greatest blessing, treasure and source of joy. Each one of you leaves me humbled and in awe. You remind me that "Mother" has always been, and will always be, my highest and best calling.

To John Rounds, I offer thanks for having the strength to pull the plug on our marriage when it needed to be pulled. You always saw the bigger picture. I am forever grateful for a lifetime's worth of happy memories.

Mike Dooley, Esther Hicks, Sara Landon, and Anne Brady-Cronin provided teachings that played a formative role in my post-marriage identity. Their words of wisdom offered a lifeline that got me through the toughest period of my life.

I'm also deeply thankful to my siblings, their spouses and children. Your grace, love, and well-timed jokes provided levity when we needed it most. Thank you Curt, Lisa, Cindy, Dean, Danh, Van, Paige, Tyler, Cullen, Kenzie, Jordan, Jonah, Elijah, Bao, Maddy, Nhi, Loc, Edwin, and Emma. Special thanks to my niece, Linnea Schroeder, for copy editing!

During the writing of this book, there were people who offered support, encouragement, or exactly the right words at exactly the right time. Sometimes, those precious gifts were disguised as criticism. Other times, a conversation contributed to or shifted my perspective.

I offer deep respect and gratitude to Michael Henderson; Kremena Stoyanova; Grant Harrison; Sharnell Valentine; Ella McGuffin; Dale, Lisa, and Mia Litzenberg; Matt Solomon; Ty Simic; Dionne Kress; Darlene Allen; Steve and Karen Conklin; Tim and Karen Conley; Steve and Kate Mairose; Chris, Tammie, Quinten and Kaila Kuhn; Jon and Bridget Foltz; Josh and Jenny Glass; and Tim Austrums.

Finally, I thank you, my reader, for sticking it out to the end. I sincerely hope to meet you face-to-face in this magical, mystical adventure!